The **Second**
Twentieth Century

The **Second** Twentieth Century

How the Information Revolution Shapes Business, States, and Nations

Jean-Jacques Rosa

HOOVER INSTITUTION PRESS
Stanford University   Stanford, California

www.hoover.org

Hoover Institution Press Publication No. 547

Original French edition (*Le second vingtième siècle: Déclin des hiérarchies et avenir des nations*) published by éditions Grasset, Paris, France, 2000

Translated from French by Paul Beecham and Emilie Michel, and revised by the author. Rights for all translated versions of this book are held by Jean-Jacques Rosa.

First printing, American edition, 2006
13   12   11   10   09   08   07   06   9   8   7   6   5   4   3   2   1

Manufactured in the United States of America

The paper used in this publication meets the minimum requirements of the American National Standard for Information Sciences— Permanence of Paper for Printed Library Materials, ANSI Z39.48-1992. ∞

Library of Congress Cataloging-in-Publication Data
Rosa, Jean Jacques.
[Second XXe siècle. English]
The second twentieth century : how the information revolution shapes business, states, and nations / by Jean-Jacques Rosa.
      p.   cm. — (Hoover Institution Press publication ; 547)
   Includes bibliographical references and index.
   ISBN 0-8179-4742-6 (alk. paper)
   1. Economic history—1945–   .   2. Social history—1945–   .
I. Title.   II. Series.
HC59.R63213 2006
303.48′33—dc22   2006007608

CONTENTS

FOREWORD

The wave of democratization at the end of the twentieth century, the fall of the Soviet Union and the nearly total disappearance of communism were all major economic, political and strategic changes of our time, and they all raise the question: why now?

Those changes lead us to ask as well why preceding developments and events occurred as they did. Why did we see what eventually became almost universal rejection of democracy and free markets during the twentieth century? Why should the basic qualities of societies newly-enriched by unprecedented benefits of production and by spectacular progress in social organization be rejected? They were, after all, the consequences of the intellectual and scientific achievements of the Enlightenment and of the Industrial Revolution. In the most advanced countries in 1900 they were uncontested.

Following the First World War nearly every nation discarded the democratic form of government they had prized prior to 1914. They restricted their free and open markets to the benefit of authoritarian, and in some cases totalitarian regimes, and to a greater (and on occasion to a lesser) extent, they endorsed centralized, state-controlled economies. Even Liberal America (in the classic sense of the term) expanded the role of the federal government and federal regulations during the 1930s, while supporting the creation of giant corporations at the same time.

This is the development brilliantly argued by Jean-Jacques Rosa, professor of economics at the Institut d'Etudes Politiques de Paris. It tipped the balance of power toward the "visible hand" of administrative hierarchies, as described by Alfred Chandler, to the detriment of the "invisible hand" of the free market, as described by Adam Smith. This process, so concluded Joseph Alois Schumpeter in a book entitled *Capitalism, Socialism and Democracy* (1942), would result inevitably in the replacement of capitalism by socialism. He may have held out hope that socialism could remain democratic, but facts discredited any such confidence. Socialism, like its right-wing counterpart, fascism, abolished real democracy and suppressed more or less entirely, depending on the country and the time, the mechanism of competitive markets.

On the eve of the Second World War surviving liberal democracies represented a small minority in the world, and even they had begun to embrace more centralized economic practices, which included heavier taxation, thus alarming classic Liberals. Some explained it as a consequence of crises and wars. But following 1945, writes Rosa, the movement seemed to be anchored even more firmly and continued its progress, without slowing, as much in Great Britain, as in the United States and Europe. The author is aware, of course, that the resumption of free trade among western countries was not without its own countervailing effects, but it was a trade, highly regulated as well as subsidized, of far less significance than the questions raised in this volume.

Why, asks Rosa, if democracy is the worst possible system with the exception of all the others (to paraphrase Winston Churchill), was it abandoned by nearly every country in the world between the 1920s and the 1960s? Why did this development take place across the entire political spectrum of the left, the middle, and the right? Why, if state-controlled economies are as inefficient as free market economists contend, did they remain the dominant system for almost three quarters of the twentieth century—until the tide began to turn away from social democracy and interventionism under the leadership of Margaret Thatcher in Great Britain in the 1980s, until Ronald Reagan, on becoming the new president of the United States in 1981, diagnosed the State as the problem and not the solution, and until the dramatic opening of the Berlin Wall in 1989 and the ensuing collapse of communism in the early 1990s?

Intellectuals in general, whose natural predilection is to attach commanding importance to the role of ideas, are prone to assert that "bad ideas" and blind, nationalist passions have been at the root of dramatic "errors" committed by the people and their leaders in their choice of economic and political systems. They thus claim credit for all of the good that resulted from the transformations of the 1980s and 1990s, and consider themselves responsible for the "ideological" victory that forced those changes. They never explain, however, why classical liberalism—the concept of the invisible hand—which was dominant at the end of the nineteenth century, was later repudiated almost everywhere. Where is the explanation of the role played by intellectuals in this transformation?

For some it is tempting to argue that new socialist thinking took intellectuals by surprise in an ideological war for which they were unprepared. But that is far too glib an explanation, unless we ignore that Adam Smith and other classical economists had presented convincing arguments more than a century before against the interventionist and statist practices of the mercantilists and other devotees of Colbert. Indeed, the explanation for the defeat of liberalism, as well as for its recent success, is a challenge to the intellect for which the response is still outstanding.

*   *   *

It is these questions to which Rosa devotes himself in this remarkable book. What are the causes—in general terms, of course, since they affected all nations simultaneously but in varying degrees—of the defeat and subsequent success of liberalism and democracy?

Rosa finds what he calls a "grand cycle" in social organization of the twentieth century. It concerns not only political organization but also the role played by the corporation in the organization of economic production. In this regard he cites the conclusions drawn by Adolf Berle and Gardiner Means in the 1930s which pointed to the expanding scope of corporate concentration (*The Modern Corporation and Private Property*, 1932); in other words, the extraordinary movement toward a hierarchical structure of production that took place in the U.S. in that decade.

As the later recipient of the Nobel Prize in Economic Sciences, Ronald Coase, concluded at the time, one must explain why firms, and especially large firms, exist, and how it is they prosper. One must ask why the production of all goods and services is not decentralized, why diverse components are not supplied independently—for example, by individual craftsmen—and why it is not markets that guide their coordination and assembly? The question is posed because most production processes are centralized from inception under the supervision of managers within a corporate hierarchy. Following Coase's argumentation, the centralized and hierarchal method is more efficient and therefore preferable when transaction costs are high, when the frictions they generate make the usage of markets relatively inefficient. The hierarchy permits reductions in cost by internalizing and limiting the number of transactions. It thus replaces market frictions with management decisions and generates economies in the process.

Rosa relies on this analysis to show what are—and were—the conditions of development of all hierarchies, not only in the corporate setting but also in the realm of public administration, all of which have responded to the same organizational method throughout the twentieth century. For Rosa the essential component of transaction costs is the expense incurred in the acquisition of information, indispensable to any production process. Initially the Industrial Revolution greatly increased production and hence transactions, but the production of information did not grow at the same speed. The relative and increasing lack of information forced the development of hierarchies as the most efficient recourse, as opposed to the imperfections of the marketplace. This was the impetus for the rise of giant corporations and hypertrophied public administration at the beginning of the twentieth century.

The subsequent development of hierarchies, so argues Rosa, exerted a profound influence on social and political organization as well. Adherence to hierarchal authority and control are absolutely necessary for the survival of organizations and are, in a manner of speaking, their fundamental values. Freedom and individual liberty endanger their operation as well as their existence. It follows that the natural and necessary ideology of a society of hierarchical production—corporate, political, or social—is anti-Liberal and anti-individual liberty. It is to this hierarchal organization that the famous "isms" of the beginning of the twentieth century owe their success; namely, those of communism, fascism, corporatism, nationalism, and all the collectivist ideologies.

It is in accordance with this conclusion that the author persuasively explains the democratic and freemarket revolution that we are witnessing today. The transformation in communication technology and the revolution in the transmission, storage and processing of information that occurred in the 1960s and 1970s, and the universal use of computers that followed, abruptly decreased the costs of information sharing. Information is now profuse and accessible to anyone, and is no longer the monopoly of executives of major organizations at the peak of organizational pyramids.

The extraordinary explosion in available quantities of information at the end of the twentieth century revitalized the competitive advantages of the marketplace over the hierarchical system. The grand administrative structures imploded. They were replaced by structures more modest, more specialized and much more numerous, appealing as a consequence to the development among themselves of transactions of increasing importance. The conglomerates that characterized the world of commerce and production until the 1960s, in essence have largely disappeared over the past thirty years, or undergone dramatic transformation.

Large firms have unremittingly "downsized," in the sense that internal communication is now horizontal and no longer deliberately vertical. The number of hierarchical levels in the chain of command—"middle management"—has been reduced, often from twelve or ten to seven or eight. Average corporate size continues to diminish. Governments are increasingly privatizing heretofore public functions and responsibilities. The most heterogeneous among them, from the perspective of culture and population, are fracturing into groups of smaller states, such as the former Soviet Union, Yugoslavia, and Czechoslovakia. Is this in anticipation of what may also occur in China, while in the meantime secessionist and regionalist movements continue to multiply throughout the world? Is it from this moment on that "small is beautiful" because it is more efficient?

Those approaches—or should one say ideological preferences?—which favor hierarchical management, and in particular statist control, have lost the dominant positions they enjoyed in a world of organized concentrations of power. According to this conclusion, ideologies are no longer the ultimate basis of social organization, but the necessary and contemporary expression of organizational requirements. They are no longer absolute nor universally true, without consideration of place and time. To be of value in any given society, and to be widely accepted, concepts of organization must respond to the prevailing and changing requirements of economic efficiency. Those requirements come from the economic dimensions of technology. This explains why the proponents of liberalism were not heard from in the 1930s, '40s, and '50s, and why their listeners and readers became more receptive to those ideas in the '80s and '90s.

Rosa tells us that the contemporary consequences of this transformation are universal. They are the revival of individualism, liber-alism and even anarchism; the fracture and multiplication of nations, the end of authoritarian regimes and of democratic revolutions, the impoverishment of totalitarianism, the disappearance of grand em-pires and of aggressive and expansionist nationalism, the relative ab-sence of conflicts between nations but, also, the increase of civil wars and the proliferation of terrorism. The only counter-example that one may invoke, perhaps, is the European attempt to build a federal and centralized state in the form of the European Union. But it is con-demned to failure, according to Rosa, precisely because it runs counter to the expected organizational efficiencies of the twenty-first century. It is, indeed, a project of the past, of the twentieth century.

The economic, organizational and technical analysis authored by Jean-Jacques Rosa presents a captivating insight into history, politics, and the ideology of corporations and states at the beginning of the new millennium. His analysis sheds more than just light on the ob-jective conditions necessary for the preservation and diffusion of the values of freedom and democracy in modern societies. It captures the fundamental elements of their politics and history; and, therefore, re-calls to life that the future, too, will be made of the force of things.

Dennis L. Bark
Senior Fellow
Hoover Institution
December 2005

INTRODUCTION

Even after its close, and despite the benefit of hindsight, the twentieth century is still wrapped in mystery. It is unique in human history in that it allowed tremendous scientific and technological advances while all economic and demographic curves rose exponentially. Already initiated by the Industrial Revolution a century before, the growth of a new civilization transformed developed societies more than all the changes seen since the invention of agriculture. According to the calculations of J. Bradford de Long and other economists, the average living standard saw little improvement from the first Middle East city-states, 8 to 10,000 years BC, to the late fifteenth century Europe. Then, from a reference level of 100 in the sixteenth century, the standard of living rose to 700 in 1900 and eventually to 6,500 in the year 2000. The world population rose from 425 million in 1500 to 1,625 million in 1900 before reaching almost 6 billion at the start of the third millennium, which almost no one deemed possible only a few decades ago. The average life expectancy kept on rising and infant mortality falling.

But this same century is also among the most contradictory and violent in human history. Worldwide military conflicts succeeded one another while ever more powerful, mind-boggling mass-destruction weapons were invented and put to use. These upheavals were accompanied by political and social revolutions, and by the largest civilian slaughters ever, only matched in numbers by the exceptional rise in population.

These paroxysmal events left observers confused, distraught and often overly pessimistic. It is the *Age of Extremes*, as defined by British historian Eric Hobsbawn, who entitled some of his chapters "The Age of Total War," "The World Revolution," and "Into the Economic Abyss."[1] For A. James Gregor, "humanity had divided according to ideological preferences. Considerable wealth and countless lives were sacrificed during the following conflicts, during the catastrophic wars and the socio-political revolutions of our era. Contrasting sharply with the optimism of the late nineteenth and early twentieth centuries, our era has proved incredibly tormented. . . . The twentieth century is probably the most tumultuous century in human history."[2]

Admittedly, such comparisons can only be subjective and the scale of gravity relative but, similarly, other historians also characterize the past decades as "the century of excess."[3] Undeniably, all observers agree on saying that it was both a time of turmoil, instability, uncertainty and bleakness and a time of spectacular innovations with thrilling prospects. However, it is also true that during the first part of the century political life became so fundamentalist and totalitarian that,

---

1. Michael Joseph, 1994. Hobsbawm's book starts with quotations from artists and intellectuals expressing their feeling about the twentieth century. According to Isaiah Berlin, "This was the worst century in recorded history." René Dumont sees it "only as a century of massacres and wars." Nobel laureate William Golding is quoted in making the following comment, "I can't help thinking that this has been the most violent century in human history." Yehudi Menuhin said, "if I had to sum up the twentieth century, I would say that it raised the greatest hopes ever conceived by humanity, and destroyed all illusions and ideals."

2. A. James Gregor, *The Ideology of Fascism*, The Free Press, 1969, p. 1.

3. Patrice Touchard, Christine Bermond-Bousquet, Patrick Cabanel and Maxime Lefebvre, *Le siècle des excès. Le xxe siècle de 1870 à nos jours*, Presses Universitaires de France, 1992.

as a matter of principle, nothing in human life was considered private anymore. Everything was deemed political.

It was also, on two counts, the century of revolutions. First, because it was marked by a sharp and often violent turnaround from previous trends. As the contemporary French historian François Caron underlined, the word "revolution" acquired this meaning in the 1880s when historians—and especially Arnold Toynbee Sr.—popularized the term "Industrial Revolution" to describe the unprecedented technological acceleration of the late eighteenth century.[4] But, in accordance with its ancient astronomical meaning, this revolution was also, at the end of the period, a loop back to an initial state—in other words, a cycle. And indeed, at the end of the century, the world was restored to its original characteristics of the nineteenth century: liberal capitalism, world markets, individualism and international peace.

At first sight, the contrasting conflicts and innovations, crises and prosperity, massacres and booming demography of the past century seem to defy rational interpretation. The same is true of the temporal incoherence of its history, characterized by the total contradiction in both the ideologies and economic and political systems between the first and second parts of the twentieth century. However, such a contradiction points to an underlying order in the evolution of social systems, rather than pure random chaos.

Indeed, with the benefit of hindsight, a universal cycle of social organization—both economic and political—emerges from the apparent chaos of war, revolutions, economic breakdowns and reconstruction. This great cycle first became discernible after the turning point of the defeat of the Axis powers in 1945, and quite clear since the second Russian revolution of 1989–1991. Thus, during most of its course, the twentieth century was basically a time of universal expan-

---

4. Les deux révolutions industrielles du xxe siècle, Albin Michel, 1997, p. 11. And Arnold Toynbee Sr., *Lectures on the Industrial Revolution*, 1884, although in fact the term "Industrial Revolution" was first used by the French economist Jérôme Adolphe Blanqui (1798–1854) in *Histoire de l'économie politique* (1837, p. 389).

sion for large organizations—both firms and states—and then, during its last third, a time of dismantling and fragmentation for the same giant organizations.

The aim of this book is to provide a rational economic explanation of the great cycle of organization that so profoundly affected and shaped the evolution of human societies during the twentieth century and still does today.

PART ONE

The Organizational Cycle

The Great Cycle stretching from 1900 to the year 2000 divides the period into two successive "twentieth centuries," two unequal sub-periods with opposed but universally shared features.

The first goes from the turn of the century to the mid-1960s and is the continuation of the previous quarter century. It began with intense military and imperialist conflicts between the great powers. Then came the seemingly irresistible rise of authoritarian systems using mass indoctrination of individuals and the merge of recently created giant firms into trusts, konzerns, cartels or zaibatsus.

The second began symbolically in the late 1960s with the student protests in Europe and the U.S. which coincided with the war in Asia and announced the upcoming oil crisis of the 1970s. This "second twentieth century" was characterized by the return of markets and democracy, anti-authority individualism, while private and public hierarchies tended to fall apart.

All the economic, political and social systems were subverted as moral values and ideologies changed back to the dominant beliefs and structures of the nineteenth century. Indeed, up to around 1870, businesses were small organizations with only a few workers and apprentices under the direction of a self-employed craftsman. At that time, the biggest organizations were public administrations. However, the state's role remained limited. Economic and political liberalism reigned supreme, fostering the values of free market, democracy and the right of peoples and individuals to self-determination.

Conversely, the first two-thirds of the twentieth century were the Iron Age, the era of heavy industry, steel, mass production and growing "authoritarian reaction." Even traditional autocracies had never exercised such a degree of despotism and bureaucratic control over the populations. It was the time of giant hierarchies involving hundreds of thousands of people, of command economy and political centralization, of war economy and mass production. Gigantism and mass bureaucracy were the key to competitive advantage, and this had deep social, cultural and political consequences.

This Great Cycle indeed affected all human organizations, bringing about imperialism and centralization during the first period, and states' fragmentation and widespread private and public decentralization during the second.

At first, nation-states relentlessly expanded their ever-stretching borders to form great powers and eventually empires. Initiated in the late nineteenth century, this trend towards the formation of heterogeneous political entities peaked in the early twentieth century with the exponential growth of the French, British, German, American, Belgian—and to a lesser extent Italian and Japanese—empires. The increasing concentration of nation-states around the world seemed irreversible. This trend peaked after World War II with the confrontation of the only two multi-state cartels that were left, under the direction respectively of the United States and the Soviet Union. To many observers, this prefigured the birth of a single world state sometime during the twenty-first century.

And yet, no later than in 1945 did this trend reverse as all the big empires successively broke up into a multitude of new independent and often small-sized states. Their number grew from 74 in 1946 to 192 in 1995 after the breakup of the Soviet Union, and 195 in 2000.

This trend continues in former Yugoslavia and the Balkans, in the Russian-controlled Caucasus, in Africa and Indonesia, while in Europe regionalism and separatism gain new ground. The perspective of a world state is gradually fading away, as the largest and most heterogeneous of them are dismantled and regional, ethnic and linguistic minorities secede. In the overall population of the nation-states, concentration was thus followed with atomization.

This phenomenon impacted not only the state but also all the most cohesive and centralized organizations. The early-century trend towards very big corporations, monopolies, konzerns, trade unions and mass political parties was followed by a phase of intense disintegration of the same large-scale hierarchies. While political entities declared secession and new independent states burgeoned, mammoth industrial and service conglomerates went into decay and break-up in the late '70s—and this continues today. Meanwhile, mass political parties and trade unions experienced a huge exodus of members, which left them notably weakened.

International trade saw the same trend reversal. After having been almost universally rejected during the first sub-period, the market mechanism was remarkably rehabilitated, there again from 1945 on, and gradually regained ground during the following decades. As trade liberalization developed and spread, and largely due to decreasing transportation and communication costs, the world economy entered a new phase of "globalization" in the 1990s.

Apparently, the century was back to where it began with the second globalization taking over from the first, even if still incomplete.

Above all, the late twentieth century was that of human rights and triumphant democracy. While during most of the period individuals had only been considered as part and parcel of vast social communities of class, race, group or nation in the Marxist, racist, corporatist and nationalist doctrines respectively, individualism eventually won out. In democratic individualism, the value of individual life is maximized. The best proof is the recent demand for a zero-risk life and a no-dead war. It seems that nothing is worth a human individual sacrifice anymore.[1]

Undeniably, the past century was, on several counts, a multi-dimensional enigma. It includes as a first component a cycle of the states which affected both their external (or geographical) dimension and their internal dimension measured by the fraction of national income taken by tax or controlled through public property. Second, the enigma is that of the cycle of systems, of nation-states' internal political and economic processes which switched from democracy and market at the beginning of the period to totalitarianism and state control in the middle and back to democracy and market at the end.

Given this double reversal affected all the societies in the world at various degrees, it follows that there must probably be some common determining factors.

During both sub-periods, all societies followed the same evolution. For instance, totalitarianism—the interference of the central state in all the spheres of people's life—has affected at various degrees all the countries of the world and even, up to a point, the few democracies which resisted and fought Nazi Germany, as Hayek clearly underlined in *The Road to Serfdom* in 1944. Even the nations that remained democratic also embarked on a wave of bureaucratization which in its most extreme form resulted in totalitarian serfdom. However, they did not go that far, limiting themselves to a toned down version, that of interventionist, corporatist dirigisme and the growth of the public sector and the welfare state, which aimed nevertheless to control individuals from "from the cradle to the grave"—a laborite slogan that George Orwell's Big Brother would not renounce.

The universal reach of this evolution is more obvious since the dismantling of the Soviet Union, as it is now commonly agreed that nazism and communism were alike in many and essential respects. World War II and the cold war obscured the similarities between these

1. François Ewald, "Des masses à l'individu," *Enjeux*, January 1999.

enemy countries and societies as the belligerents accentuated the differences between them for the sake of the cause. But both sides' internal systems followed a similar path, while their external policies changed simultaneously from nationalism to imperialism, including the most durable imperialism, that of the Soviet Union, which resisted decay during several decades, surviving all others.

No global and coherent explanation has yet been given to the parallel revolutions and world wars that took place during the universal revolution of the Great Cycle. Still considered as the unexpected result of a combination of unusual circumstances and aberrant behaviors, they remain the biggest mystery of the twentieth century and a major intellectual challenge for contemporary social-science theorists.

CHAPTER 1

The Race
for Size,
1870–1960

The first twentieth century initiates a sharp turnaround from all previous trends. Democratization, free trade, relative peace and small-scale wars, the European balance of powers and the Enlightenment's philosophy of progress are supplanted by imperialism and total war, economic protectionism, state control, a radical rejection of the market, and political totalitarianism. The civilization begot by the scientific, economic and cultural revolution of the eighteenth century takes a dramatic leap backwards.

The Great Cycle starts with the size expansion of all organizations, economic as well as political. Gradually, business firms turn into giant corporations—at least compared to what they were before—while states compete with each other to form the largest colonial empire and, internally, control a growing share of their domestic economy.

Centralization, gigantism, bureaucracy and standardization develop simultaneously in corporations, in the state's organization and politics, and in social and cultural matters. Hence the peculiar style which defines the new century: it is the era of hierarchy, command economy, mass meetings and war economy. It is the Iron Age of reactionary autocracy. The large bureaucratic organization wields a competitive advantage over smaller structures and favors authoritarian and centralizing social and cultural doctrines.

This first phase is characterized by a reinforcement of centralization and command power, reduced economic, political and intellectual freedom, and it defines the general tone of this Iron Age. Undeniably, Stalin was well inspired to choose a pseudonym meaning "steel" in Russian.

The industrial and administrative revolution marked the advent of big firms, while states became addicted to imperialism and dirigisme. Taken to extremes, these new organizational structures result in totalitarianism, the ultimate stage of centralization, and bring about the very particular moral atmosphere of the hierarchical society.

THE SECOND INDUSTRIAL REVOLUTION AND THE EMERGENCE OF THE LARGE CORPORATION

At the beginning of the century, the big issue, as suggested by Lenin in *The State and The Revolution*,[1] was to transform the whole society into a single firm and a huge factory. This view is shared in a more limited way by Joseph Schumpeter, a former Finance minister and Austrian economist living in the U.S. According to him, private capitalism inevitably turns into socialism given that big companies are more efficient and innovative, and thus concentration is unavoidable. But are very big firms and centralized states essential to secure prosperity? And is it really possible to centralize a whole society just like a big corporation?

The end of the century vindicates the superiority of decentralization celebrated by Ronald Coase and Friedrich Hayek as well as, recently, the new internauts. But it only occurred after seventy years of centralization during which the hierarchical and centralized organization advocated by Ford, Stalin and Hitler was gradually considered

1. International Publishers, undated, p. 84.

as the solution to the society's problems. This revolution is not only political and Russian. It concerns all countries and organizations.

It results from changes to the structure of the commercial and craft society of the late nineteenth century. According to economist Kenneth E. Boulding, it "was mostly a consequence of communicative advances (telephone, telegraph, typewriter, photocopier) and possibly of a strengthening of the managerial structure. All these changes took place in the 1870s and enabled an enormous expansion of organizations, thus giving birth to giants like General Motors, the U.S. department of defense and the Soviet Union, as well as many institutions which were inconceivable before 1870."[2]

Adam Smith's invisible hand, governing trade between individuals on free markets, was thus replaced by Alfred Chandler's "visible hand,"[3] that is, the centralized and bureaucratic handling of human affairs. This managerial hand governed the big business companies which first appeared in transportation before spreading to all the other sectors. Bureaucracy replaced both the market and the autarkic farming methods of the pre-industrial system.

The real organizational novelty was to apply to these newly-born business and industrial companies the methods that were until then only used by the state and church to manage things and human beings—but not without substantial improvements. This is the administrative innovation that had been foreseen by Auguste Comte and Saint-Simon, and whose contents were later analyzed by Max Weber.

This is a totally new phenomenon. The First Industrial Revolution—usually dated 1780–1860—took place in societies where firms were only small craft undertakings. This revolution was "more than

2. Kenneth E. Boulding, "Economics as a Not Very Biological Science," in Thomas Wiegele (ed.), *Biology and the Social Sciences: An Emerging Revolution*, Westview Press, 1982.

3. Alfred Chandler, *The Visible Hand, The Managerial Revolution in American Business*, Belknap Press, 1977.

industrial"[4] in the sense that it also had repercussions on family, religion and politics.

More than a time of industrial expansion, this was the true birth of factories and companies. Until then, there were hardly more than 1,800 firms or so-called commercial and financial "houses" in Great Britain and production took place at home and mostly in the country.

But it is in fact the second wave of technological breakthroughs, the Second Industrial Revolution, that lays the durable foundations of the twentieth century. Although it is built on the same determinants that gave birth to factories and manufactures, the second revolution radically amplified the new organizational advances. Centralization accelerated, hierarchical structures deepened and the workforce soared, while the managerial staff increased sharply in order to control growing production flows. And as markets expanded rapidly, their own growth simultaneously determined a huge development of private bureaucratic pyramids.

To understand the causes of this transformation, it is necessary to explain why factories supplanted industrial subcontracting, especially as it is the same centralizing factors that transformed with an increased intensity both business firms and public administrations during the Second Industrial Revolution.

The Birth of the Corporation

Before 1750, there was no clear distinction between the company and the family.[5] Since the invention of farming in the Neolithic age, the

---

4. As pointed out by Joel Mokyr in his foreword and his article "Are We Living in the Middle of an Industrial Revolution?" Federal Reserve Bank of Kansas City, *Economic Review*, second quarter, 1997.

5. This date also marks the beginning of the "world frontier" phenomenon: the large expansion of European people gradually caused the extinction of many civilizations on other continents, due to more sophisticated arms, but also to the spreading of infectious diseases to which native people were not immune. William H. McNeill, *The Global Condition, Conquerors, Catastrophes, and Community*, Princeton University Press, 1992.

family cell had remained the basic framework of production in all societies. Companies often consisted of a tradesman who subcontracted work to home workers or to independent craftsmen who worked in their own workshop and sold their products on markets or in small shops. During the first half of the eighteenth century, the production of cotton fabrics was the first major non-farm activity. It was usually organized on a small scale and financed by tradesmen/manufacturers, who subcontracted the spinning and weaving of raw cotton to farmers/workers working at home. The production unit was thus very small and based on family work. Spinning wheels and weaving shuttles provided work for a couple and its children. Some tradesmen had thus thousands of people under them and owned hundreds of weaving looms scattered in the country without directly supervising everyone's work. Besides, the equipment investment per worker remained very low.

Admittedly, there were already large joint-stock companies before the Industrial Revolution. A good example is the companies in charge of overseas trade in the United Kingdom or big pre-industrial firms such as Chatham's naval dockyard or London's Whitbread brewery. Joint-stock companies had already been quite successful in France in Law's time but the great commercial or manufacturing units belonged to the state, like for instance the royal manufactures, the naval dockyards and the big naval trading corporations. Before the mid-nineteenth century, the largest organizations were the first bureaucratic state bodies. In the Caribbean Islands and in America, the great sugar or cotton-growing slave plantations had a rather impressive labor force, which was subjected to an extremely tight control that foreshadowed totalitarian systems.

As Leslie Hannah noted:

> Although there were big-sized firms before the beginning of the industrial revolution, it was the introduction of new mechanical techniques and the application of the steam machine to the industrial process which, from the late 18th century, radically transformed

the nature of the capitalist company and created an economy where factories employing hundreds (and sometimes thousands) of workers became the standard form of production units.[6]

It is only during the Industrial Revolution that all the workers started being concentrated in a same factory, the English "mills" which were referred to as "satanic mills" in the Socialist literature of the time. This new organization of work was made possible by falling transportation costs, economies of scale thanks to the development of centralized energy sources and innovations such as the introduction of gaslight in cities which enabled longer work in winter.

But this revolution was mainly due to the use of new and cheaper energy sources, such as coal and steam power. This changed radically the production process and made transportation much easier with its introduction in the shipping, and especially, the railway industries.

Szostak suggests that the changes in transportation techniques and means, especially in Great Britain, during the decades that preceded the First Industrial Revolution were the decisive causal factor.[7] At the time, various legal initiatives were undertaken to create shipping corporations, lease the construction of toll roads and build or renovate canals. At the dawn of the Industrial Revolution, Great Britain—already favored by its geographical advantage—had the best waterway and road network in the world. It followed that transportation became cheaper and quicker for goods and passengers and the domestic market became more united as it was given a new national dimension.[8]

The growing markets generated by this transport revolution in turn led to an organizational revolution. Indeed, the substantial in-

6. *The Rise of the Corporate Economy*, Methuen, 1976, p. 8.
7. "The Organization of Work: The Emergence of the Factory Revisited," *Journal of Economic Behavior and Organization*, 11, 1989, pp. 343–358.
8. Quoting several specialists, Szostak noticed a few elements of interest. For instance, from 130 hours in 1660, the travel time for the journey from Manchester to London fell to 60 hours in 1760 and only 25 in 1785. Following the digging of new canals and rivers (especially the Bridgewater Canal), the price of coal fell by half in the late eighteenth century in Manchester and Birmingham.

crease of the trade of goods and commodities soon determined major changes. To solve the control and organizational crises caused by these suddenly amplified flows, administrative centralization was undertaken. This very ancient technique, first used in ancient Egypt and Mesopotamia during the agricultural revolution in the beginning of structured societies, proved a much better way to deal with mass production than geographically dispersed subcontracting.

Factories reduced substantially transportation needs as they avoided the first stage in the production process, which consisted of fetching the goods at the subcontractor's workshop before delivering them to the client. Instead of spending his time on the road as a traveling salesman, the company head could focus on organizing production and supervising its employees with the help of permanent executives. As a consequence, productivity and the work pace increased, while cheating and petty theft decreased. Stocks of commodities and goods could now be reduced, while costly machines and tools could be used almost continuously, thus improving depreciation and allowing an increase in investment. Employees could get about more easily. They came from farther away and ate for cheaper at lunchtime as food transportation costs decreased.

It is in the cotton-oriented textile industry that the old workshops were first transformed into modern, highly-mechanized, capital intensive factories and firms. With several innovations in the cotton production processes, and later on the use of steam machines, it became crucial to control more tightly the workers and centralize production. This was the only way to benefit fully from the economies of scale resulting from the use of modern equipment and steam engines.[9]

As soon as 1784, Sir Robert Peel's Bury-based calico company employed 7,000 people. However, the average textile firm used to employ a few hundred only. Indeed, in 1822, textile companies in Manchester were composed of 100 to 200 workers with a capital of 50 to

9. Leslie Hannah, op. cit., p. 9.

90 pounds per employee, that is 5,000 to 18,000 pounds per firm. But in the 1830s this amount rose to 80,000 pounds, reflecting the sharp increase in the capital intensity of the new fabrics.

However, faced with the consumption boom, companies first multiplied instead of increasing their size as the efficient size of each firm was probably strictly limited. The integration of production within factories eventually started in the 1820s and 1830s, but factories were still rather small-sized.

Although the centralization of production units early in the nineteenth century was an organizational revolution, we must keep in mind that the number of employees per company was still much lower than nowadays. The "Representative Firm" mentioned by Alfred Marshall, whose celebrated *Principles of Economics* was the reference text in economics at the beginning of the twentieth century, was still closer to what we would now call a small- or medium-sized company.

But industrial concentration accelerated sharply during the second half of the nineteenth century and paved the way for the radical changes of the first twentieth century.

Mass Production, Distribution and Consumption

While firms were born in Great Britain during the 1780–1860 Industrial Revolution, the large modern corporation first appeared in the United States during the Second Industrial Revolution, the era of mass production, distribution and consumption. According to Alfred Chandler's reference study, the advent of big firms took place in the U.S. during the 1840–1920 period, when the existing farm economy was replaced by a mostly urban and industrial economy.

Factory production only really took off when coal became available in large quantities in the mid-1830s, as the United States lagged behind Great Britain from this point of view.[10] With the availability

---

10. The only exception was the textile industry which had been a precursor as the equipment and production were concentrated in a single place: the fabric or the

of coal and steam power, the whole production process changed. It became possible to use new machines, develop the steel industry and build railways. This created a need not only for rails, wheels, mechanical parts but also glass, leather work and rubber. Thanks to cheap energy and heating and new fast, high-capacity transportation means, factories spread in the 1840s and 1850s.

In the mid-1840s, the price of coal fell from 10 to 3 dollars a ton. The railway network spread to all eastern states. Transit and travel became 3 to 10 times faster within a decade, while for centuries the speed of transportation had depended on draft animals' walking pace. Steam-powered railways supplanted river and sea transportation and this increased even more the volumes transported, as railways could be used all year long unlike canals which were impassable in winter and in times of flood.

Coping with Faster Production Flows

Factories' turnovers rose substantially as the harnessing of energy also enabled the industry to mass produce at unprecedented rates. And this mass production could be distributed to a great number of remote markets through the railway network. The industrial process's overall speed increased significantly.

The organization of the production process and the architecture of the capitalist system were transformed by the acceleration of production flows. This is the central insight of Chandler, who viewed this mutation as the origin of the "administrative revolution," which drove the most industrialized countries into the first twentieth century, some three decades before 1900. This analysis was taken up and completed by James Beniger in a remarkable review of what he calls the "control revolution."[11]

---

factory like in Great Britain. At that time, manufacturing activity was mainly rural and seasonal. Workers were recruited when necessary among the people of the local farms and were paid either in kind or with money.

11. James R. Beniger, *The Control Revolution*, Harvard University Press, 1986.

Since the beginning of human history, the speed of transportation of material goods had always depended on draft animals' walking pace or on wind speed. But suddenly, within a few decades, these standards became obsolete as everything accelerated. Production increased substantially in the factories and was sent across the world from one continent to another. For the first time ever, production flows almost exceeded the human capacity of control. This is why in the mid-nineteenth century some companies were faced with a control crisis which then spread to the whole U.S. material economy during the following decades.

At that time, the society lacked the technical and organizational means to manage flows that big and quick. These required constant, abundant and very precise information. Such a degree of coordination had never been seen before, except maybe during the Napoleonic Wars, after the French Revolution of 1789 which had resorted to mass conscription and tremendous execution speed in military matters. As specialists often underline, war is basically a question of logistics and this is exactly the kind of problem the big firms of the New Industrial Revolution suddenly had to tackle.

The Control Crisis and the Resurgence of Bureaucracy

The control crisis first materialized in the form of big railway safety problems. Then, it spread to the distribution of goods through the new and complex transportation and warehouse network, and eventually to the production process itself as speed often caused technical accidents and administrative backlogs.

Logically, the first response to this crisis was to develop new information systems, given information is always necessary to transform energy and materials into products. But more importantly, the answer came from the development of bureaucracy, which had been invented at the dawn of our civilization precisely to control and coordinate the agricultural production boom three to four millennia BC.

As the control crisis spread through the material economy from the 1840s to the 1880s, it inspired a continuing stream of innovations that enhanced information processing, administrative methods and communications. [. . .] These permanent innovations in transportation, production, distribution and mass marketing reached their height in the 1870s and 1880s; on the eve of the new century, the crisis had been substantially resolved."[12]

These modernized bureaucratic methods allowed producers to deal with mass markets, the major economic breakthrough that resulted from the first two industrial revolutions. And this bureaucratic solution to the control problem which overwhelmed not only the United States but also Great Britain, France and Germany came to dominate all the evolutions of the first twentieth century.

World War II would bring in a bundle of non-bureaucratic (if not anti-bureaucratic) new control techniques but we will detail them later on. For the time being (in the late nineteenth century), the large bureaucratic firm is still the best way to control mass production. According to many historians, these new management methods were born from war, and notably during World War I. But in fact, they date essentially from the mid-nineteenth century and were first intended for managing U.S. railways, which played a major role during the industrial revolution.

This example is very instructive in terms of the solutions found. On the first high-speed single-track two-way railroads, traffic management was necessary but difficult in the absence of control techniques, centralized communications, telegraphs, standardized procedures, coded signals, precise timetables, and synchronized chronometers aboard the trains. Serious accidents were frequent and generally resulted from head-on collisions between two trains on a single line. Obviously, the best solution to avoid those organizational and communication problems was centralized planning. In other words, all the traffic had to be managed by a single company.

12. Ibid., p. 220.

The Springfield, Massachusetts-based Western Railroad Corporation decided to reorganize its bureaucracy, planning, data processing and communications. As Alfred Chandler pointed out, this was the first time ever that a U.S. company took the time to draw precisely its organizational structure as a single systemized chain of command represented by organizational charts.[13]

All the necessary bureaucratic procedures were then defined: prefixed rules, distribution of tasks and responsibilities, work planning, systematic information collection and hierarchical reporting, control with feedback, use of the telegraph to announce the traffic expected and timetable changes, employees in uniforms mentioning their exact position, organizational charts, coded signals, and collection of normalized statistics.

These were the elements of the rational administrative control theory that Frederick Taylor and others called "Scientific Management" in the 1890s. Chandler then renamed it the "managerial revolution," but in fact James Burnham was the first to use this term in the title of his book published in 1941.

This was not the only industrial sector that was affected by the acceleration of production flows. As distribution speed had improved, companies were tempted to increase the rate of production. For example, in the 1890s, a single blast furnace could produce 1,000 tons per week instead of only 60 in the late 1860s. Obviously, this required some synchronization and coordination of many operations and the production rate had to be adapted to the capacity and frequency of the railroad freight.

For all the production processes composed of a great number of successive stages, it became necessary to integrate them vertically within a single firm to achieve centralized coordination. This method was applied to sewing machines in the 1850s, repeating guns in the

---

13. Chandler, op. cit., p. 97, quoting Stephen Salsbury's monograph, *The State, the Investor, and the Railroad: The Boston and Albany, 1825–1867*, Harvard University Press, 1967, p. 187.

1860s, typewriters in the 1870s, electric motors in the 1880s, and eventually the first U.S. cars in the 1890s.

Similarly, in the agricultural distribution sector, vertical integration was undertaken and organized markets developed to simplify the transportation of farm produces from the hundreds of thousands of producers to the thousands of stores. This resulted in the introduction of new forms of organization, wholesalers, department stores and concepts such as marketing, advertising and trademarks.

All in all, it seems that mass production and mass distribution were inexorably leading to an administrative revolution.

The Administrative Revolution

Middle managers were given the responsibility for the coordination of these rapidly-growing production flows and this required the development of more accurate accounting methods. Bureaucratic control is performed by an army of executive supervisors who never work on the actual production but manage, measure and coordinate the production and behavior of the field workers, who really make finished products out of raw materials. Such an administrative and hierarchical superstructure governs the production-process employees. This business administration is the precise reflection of the state administrations set by the European monarchies during the seventeenth and eighteenth centuries, but with much more modern technical capacities.

This revolution was accompanied by an impressive number of innovations—many of which are now common use: the mass production of mail envelopes (1839), precise organizational charts and the first business school (1842), the first shorthand magazine (1848), the hierarchical data collection and processing system in railway companies (1853), the use of blotting paper instead of sand to mop up damp ink (1856), the first distinction between workers and executives in companies according to the line-and-staff concept (1857), the first telegraph ticker that gave prices in continuous time in a brokerage firm (1867), the first patented typewriter (1868), the first automatic filing system for hospital patients (1874), the first modern offices with forms, filing cabinets, telephone books and telephones (1880s), the first collegiate business school (Wharton in 1881), the first accounting firm (1883), the first patented dictating machine (1885), the first business calculator with a keyboard (Comptometer in 1887) and the first card tabulator (the Hollerith system in 1889).[14]

It is against this background of continuous innovation in administrative techniques that Frederick Winslow Taylor started working for Midvale Steel, where he was about to rationalize the ordering system and establish standard times for each element of specialized workers' work. There, he developed his original concept of "scientific management" which not only improved the processing of material flows by using standardized spare parts and coordinating operations, but also formalized human behaviors in order to integrate the whole company into a unified product transformation process.

As he points out tellingly in *Principles of Scientific Management* (1911), "In the past the man has been first; in the future the system must be first." And this is a brief but striking description of the principle that ruled the organization of totalitarian systems for whole societies a few years later.

This move continued in the early twentieth century when Henry Ford built the Highland Park Plant in 1913 to produce the Model T. This marked the beginning of the moving assembly line, which was inspired by the continuous flows in oil refineries. The idea is to make the car assembly process as smooth as possible in order to maximize productivity and avoid dead times and pressure surges that prevent liquids from flowing in pipes. He thus took to their extremes these new concepts, the spare part technique and the idea of standardizing products and work.

14. Beniger, op. cit., pp. 282–283.

Other industries had already adopted these principles looking for greater productivity through the mechanization of all work-stages, as for example Gustavus Swift's meat-packing and -cutting line in Chicago in the 1880s.

In turn, the generalization of factory mass production led to a wave of technical innovations that improved the automation of the production control process during the first decades of the century, just like the development of manufactures during the first Industrial Revolution had resulted in the invention of new and costly machines that modern "mills" could easily amortize.

The control of these rapidly-growing flows was thus achieved by the centralization of several production activities under a common authority, that is the integration of these various processes into a single big organization. As we will see in the second part of the book, coupled with the latest technological advances, centralized organization was a good way to collect and concentrate the costly information necessary to control fast-increasing flows and make the best of it—which was impossible with existing decentralized procedures. It also enabled amortization of the data collection and processing costs resulting from indivisible and costly investments over a large number of units produced and sold.

And it is the economies provided by this centralized administrative process that contributed to the success of ever-larger companies. As administrative management capacity improved, private and public administrations grew bigger.

A New Capacity to Manage Large Organizations

The production of the information necessary to the control of the rapidly-growing flows resulted in the vertical integration of the successive stages of the production process, starting with the extraction of raw materials and ending with the retail sale of finished products, but also in the geographical integration of the factories producing the same goods for regional clienteles, and consequently, in a general increase in companies' size.

Hence the strong growth of production units during the second half of the century from 1860 to 1890. Over that period, companies became multi-unit business enterprises both to deal with the market expansion generated by transportation innovations and to increase the vertical integration of all the production-process stages, from the extraction of raw materials to marketing and distribution. With these developments, end-of-the-century firms gained a much bigger dimension.

The traditional enterprise was a single unit belonging to an individual or a small number of owners operating out of a single office their trade, factory, bank or transportation business. These enterprises had only one economic purpose and dealt in a single product line or service within a single geographic area. Thus, before the birth of the modern firm, the activities of these single unit enterprises were coordinated and monitored directly by the market reactions.[15]

The business head, which was often the only owner, directed and supervised by himself a small number of workers, journeymen or apprentices with little administrative support and, consequently, no work supervisors. Only a few of these companies employed directors with responsibilities similar to those of middle managers in modern firms. But there was no stratified administration where top executives supervised the work of middle executives who in turn superintended field workers.[16]

In contrast, the modern business enterprise is managed by a vast hierarchy of salaried executives and generally composed of several production units geographically spread. Each is specialized in a particular field and produces a wide range of goods and services. As they are commonly owned, the trade between them is internalized and they

---

15. *Chandler*, op. cit., p. 3.
16. Ibid., p. 3.

are not subjected to market and price mechanism. Decision-making and control are performed by the owner's salaried executives. Such an administrative structure of middle and top executives had never been seen before.

Bureaucracies: Public and Private

On the eve of World War I, modern firms had become the dominant institutions in many sectors of the U.S. economy. By the mid-century, they employed hundreds to thousands of middle-management and top executives to supervise the work of tens to hundreds of production units with up to several hundred thousands workers. Such a quick and major institutional change achieved in so short a period had no historical precedent.

This is in deep contrast with the early nineteenth century organizational methods on both the political and economic fronts. As late as the 1830s, for example, the Bank of the United States, then the nation's largest and most complex institution with twenty-two branch offices and profits fifty times those of the largest mercantile house, was managed by just three people: Nicholas Biddle and two assistants.[17] And President Andrew Jackson and 665 other civilians ran all three branches of the federal government in Washington.

At the end of the period, bureaucracy had spread to all human activities, but it had a bad reputation as several perceptive observers underlined. As early as 1837, John Stuart Mill wrote, for example, of a "vast network of administrative tyranny . . . that system of bureaucracy, which leaves no free agent in all France, except the man at Paris who pulls the wires."[18] And Thomas Carlyle, in his *Latter-Day Pam-*

17. Fritz Redlich, 1951, *The Molding of American Banking, Men and Ideas*, pp. 113–124, quoted by Beniger.
18. R. W. Burchfield (ed.), *A supplement to the Oxford English Dictionary*, Oxford University Press, 1972, p. 391, quoted by Beniger.

phlets, published in 1850, complained of "the Continental nuisance called 'Bureaucracy.'"

But it is Max Weber who first theorized bureaucracy in *Economy and Society* (1922), defining its main characteristics as follows: dehumanization of the information processed ("cases" and "files"); formalized and predefined rules to make decisions, answer questions and solve problems; well-defined tasks and duties; high division of labor; hierarchical authority system and separated decision-making and communication functions. The stability of the system was purportedly reinforced by the practice of regular promotion based upon seniority.

The mechanism is mainly based on the possibility to "rationalize" work, a term by which Weber meant the reduction of the volume of information processed by removing or ignoring the data that are not absolutely necessary to manage the process. Never mind if the executives or workers like sport or art. What really matters is their experience, position in the hierarchy, how quickly they process files and the number of mistakes they make for each hundred files processed.

When applied to people, bureaucratic mechanization explains the widespread use of administrative forms, which reduce people to a handful of precise characteristics: civil status, occupation, curriculum and a few others depending on the organization's needs. This depersonalizing approach neglects everything that is original, particular, specific, indescribable or unclassifiable. But when people are not reduced to mere standardized objects, big human groups become almost uncontrollable with the existing knowledge and technologies.

The same organizational concerns and principles of the Ford and General Motors factories, the Napoleonic army, and the Swift meatpacking company in Chicago were then adopted by the mass parties (Nazis and Communists) in the '30s and the state bureaucracies managing industrial sectors, general education or the whole national production. The problems had not changed and neither had the few remedies.

However, these global organizational changes were only noticed much later with the usual lag between perception and understanding and the evolving realities which accompanies every transformation or revolution. Economists continued to analyze production almost only in terms of markets and prices, considering the business enterprise as if it was a single isolated person or a craftsman without taking into account its internal organization and administrative methods for resource allocation. Strangely, the business enterprise as an organization was not mentioned in economics textbooks and was thus nonexistent in theory.

And yet, there were many proofs of the new role of both large-scale bureaucracies and centralized and hierarchical organizations. Once again, the railway industry was at the origin of the first major professional executive body. The 1880s and 1890s saw the construction of integrated systems in transport companies, with a cartelization between companies and the support of professional consultants, managers, investors and speculators.

In 1891, the Pennsylvania Railroad employed 110,000 people against only 39,492 in the U.S. army. Even the United States Postal Service, the largest civil service organization at the time, only employed 95,440 people. Two years later, federal tax receipts amounted to $385 million, while the Pennsylvania Railroad only made $135 million of revenue, but its stock market capitalization of $842 million was to be compared with a federal debt of $155 million.

On the contrary, in Europe, the army and civil services were much bigger employers than private companies. It followed that most managers and administrators came from the public sector, while in the United States they originated from private railway companies. Similarly, transportation and communication infrastructures were financed by the state in Europe and by private investors in the United States.

But, in both cases, companies' race for expansion and production bureaucratization was to take another step forward just before the end of the century.

Mergers and Acquisitions: The Era of Trusts

On the eve of the twentieth century, existing activities entered a phase of obsolescence because of technological advances and heavy investment in new and fast-growing industries. Then appeared phenomena that we would now describe as "macro-economic" but were tellingly called "general overproduction crises" at the time. These were the first major economic crises that were not due to undersupply following bad harvests (classical agricultural crises) but to demand crises resulting from either overproduction or a discrepancy between supply and demand.

Overcapacity became evident in several sectors during the first Great Recession (or Depression) of 1873–1896, when newly-born companies faced natural selection after a period of rapid and uncontrolled growth. As unfortunately the euphoria could not last forever, some companies had to exit, which led to an increasing concentration in a same sector, that is horizontally this time.

The Second Industrial Revolution was distinguished by a shift to more capital-intensive production, rapid growth in productivity and living standards, the formation of large corporate hierarchies, the progressive accumulation of overcapacity, and eventually, closure of facilities.

Although attempts were made to eliminate overcapacity through the creation of trade associations and cartels, not until the 1890s' mergers and acquisitions boom was the problem substantially resolved.[19] The production capacities of merged companies were reduced substantially through internal restructuring and the liquidation of unprofitable companies. During the decade from 1895 to 1904,

19. See Alfred Chandler, "The emergence of managerial capitalism," Harvard Business School Case n. 9-384-081, revised by Thomas J. McCraw, 1992, quoted by Michael Jensen, "The Modern Industrial Revolution, Exit, and the Failure of Internal Control Systems," *Journal of Finance*, July 1993.

more than 1,800 manufacturing firms merged into 157 consolidated corporations.[20]

This movement was partly due to the Great Recession of 1873–1896.[21] As Naomi Lamoreaux underlined, mergers seemed the best way to deal with the ongoing recession. The solvent demand for goods dropped because of falling wages and income, while production capacities increased continuously, which explains the general decline in prices. They were now generally below costs, especially as the reduction in the volumes that companies could produce and distribute on the market resulted in higher unit costs. Business enterprises could no longer benefit from economies of scale. With such small quantities, it became harder to amortize fixed costs.

As the market contracted, companies could only find new customers by engaging in a price war against their competitors and thus worsening deflation. The only solution for a firm was to acquire the clientele of one or several competitors to be able again to amortize its own fixed costs with larger sales volumes. In other words, it was necessary to acquire rival companies. As these operations took place in industries where the number of firms had not risen because of the crisis, they resulted in fewer independent enterprises and widespread concentration.

The increase of the average size of firms was sped up by the late century formation of the first trusts and monopolies, during the great merger wave of 1890–1914. The purpose of these mergers was also to reduce overcapacity by correcting the prior flood of new products, markets and industries.

The 1880s mergers resulted in the formation of big trusts in the oil, whiskey, sugar, lead, cordage and tobacco industries. This movement accelerated from 1890 to the 1920s despite the passage of the

20. Jensen, op. cit., p. 835, quoting among others Naomi Lamoreaux, *The Great Merger Movement in American Business, 1895–1904*, Cambridge University Press, 1985, p. 100.
21. Described notably by Touchard and al.

1890 Sherman Antitrust Act. And the development of electricity and heating distribution systems in the 1920s represented the biggest breakthrough of large organizations since the introduction of railroads in the late nineteenth century.

The layoffs and other social consequences of the expansion of big firms and merger movement explain the existing political turmoil—the protests against the "Robber Barons" and large-scale capitalism—and the efforts to deprive businessmen of the chance to gain political power. Hence, the antitrust laws and the typical U.S. restriction of banks' role in industry.

On the contrary, there were no such concerns in Europe where state bureaucracies were numerous and big private companies still rare. Big trusts were less of a threat given they generally had much less influence than on the other side of the Atlantic. And when they did, they usually cooperated with large state bureaucracies in the same "clubby" atmosphere of connivance that would characterize corporatist systems later on.

Finally, the modern companies, born in the early nineteenth century during the First Industrial Revolution, turned into industrial giants during the Second Industrial Revolution of the late nineteenth century and their role was not analyzed in economic literature before the 1930s, in particular in the work of Berle and Means, Schumpeter, Galbraith and Chandler.[22] All these authors have stressed central role of size and the general trend towards expansion in these big organizations. A crucial factor that mainstream economists did not recognize precisely because business concentration had become so common and omnipresent in the twentieth century, but also because they focused on the price mechanism in perfectly competitive markets.

22. Adolf A. Berle and Gardiner C. Means, *The Modern Corporation and Private Property*, McMillan, 1932, Joseph A. Schumpeter, *Capitalism, Socialism and Democracy*, Harper and Row, 1942, but also Edward H. Chamberlin, *The Theory of Monopolistic Competition*, Harvard University Press, 1932, Joan Robinson, *The Economics of Imperfect Competition*, McMillan, 1933 and more especially Ronald Coase, *The Nature of the Firm*, Economica, 1937, and Alfred Chandler, *The Visible Hand*, op.cit.

The development of the industrial giants was made possible by the use and significant improvement of the administrative techniques previously used by states only.

Yet, at the time, states were also moving towards gigantism. It was the Age of Imperialism, described by Lenin in *Imperialism: The Highest Stage of Capitalism*, and it lasted until the end of World War II. But, contrary to what Lenin upheld, political imperialism does not result of an economic need for new markets. All social organizations, whether public or private, simultaneously tended towards gigantism from the late nineteenth century to the second half—or rather the last third—of the twentieth century. World War I was not caused by un-bridled capitalism but rather by the rise and expansion of state struc-tures.

IMPERIALISM AND STATISM

During this first twentieth century, the discreet state of the nineteenth century became imperialist outside the country and dirigiste within. Admittedly, there had already been large states or empires in the past. Their population was smaller in absolute terms than that of the twen-tieth century empires because the world population itself was much lower before the Industrial Revolution. Yet, a few empires like the Roman or Chinese empires gathered a very large proportion of the world population at their time.

Imperialism reemerged worldwide at the end of the nineteenth century, sustained this time by the extraordinary technical advances of the two industrial revolutions which were much greater than those that had promoted navigation and military conquest in the sixteenth century.

The External Growth of States: Imperialism

While the first wave of imperialism had resulted in the creation of trading posts and fortified towns and various kinds of pillage rather than direct colonization or permanent administration of large countries by the Europeans (except in South America, where the Spanish empire could exploit militarily and pillage vast mineral resources, as the populations were very small), the second wave of colonization saw a new occupational mode by large foreign civilian populations developing new economic activity and benefiting not only from advanced military techniques but also from more efficient agricultural and industrial production techniques and improved methods of administrative management and communication.

The former remotely controlled colonies were quite independent thanks to the long distance and the difficult communication. The home country had little control over the colony. On the contrary, twentieth century colonies were directly connected to their home countries by rapid air transports, by the telegraph, the phone and the radio.

With economic and administrative advances, European nations now expanded into world empires through migration of their population rather than only by pillage and the creation of trading posts. It is that new capacity of wealth creation and the centralized management of the "home country" that enabled such an intense outward expansion of European nations.

This imperialism, the outward expansion of states, was also accompanied by intense inward expansion, a proof of their improved efficiency in the management of people and things. Within the initial geographical dimension of the nation-state, the proportion of the national product managed by the state increased constantly. The state itself became a huge firm whose dimensions competed again with those of large expanding businesses. In the twentieth century, the state regained its status of largest organization in the country which it had almost lost during the expansion of the late nineteenth century giant businesses. The new century was marked by an omnipresent reminder of the state's new big dimensions and was a time of statism, dirigisme and public centralized planning.

E. J. Hobsbawm entitled his book devoted to that period *The Age of Empire, 1875–1914*.[23] Admittedly, that move was not totally new for the states: we mentioned above the Portuguese and Spanish empires set up in the sixteenth century. But in the nineteenth century, they became generally widespread and European occupation intensified. The great powers shared out the world and successfully managed their colonies, now partly inhabited by their own citizens who controlled and supervised local economic activities with their own administrative methods. The states succeeded in managing larger populations. At their apex in 1939, European empires' population reached respectively 485 million inhabitants for the United Kingdom (including 388 million in India), 71 million for France, 70 for the Netherlands, 14 for Italy, and 10 for both Belgium and Portugal.

Touchard et al. canned the 1870–1939 period as "the colonial era": "In 1870, Europe was caught in expansionist fever." As Jules Ferry stated in 1890: "From 1815 to 1850, Europe was unadventurous and stayed at home. Today, we annex entire continents."

The Western conquest ended in 1890 in the United States, simultaneously with the Eastern conquest in Russia and the sharing out of Africa and Asia between Europeans. While colonization had been criticized until 1914 in France (the press in particular condemned it until 1890), it gradually gave way to expansionary nationalism. From 1870 to 1939, Europeans drew a new map of the world.

The second international wave of colonization largely outstripped the first, which had begun with the rise of the states in the mid-fifteenth century and reached its climax in the mid-seventeenth century. Albert Bergesen and Ronald Schoenberg drew a telling chart presenting the total number of colonies from 1415 to the late '60s.[24] After a double peak between 1640 and 1700, the rate plummeted during the whole eighteenth century and most of the nineteenth century,

23. See Weinfeld and Nicholson, 1987.
24. "Long Waves of Colonial Expansion and Contraction, 1415–1969," in Albert Bergesen (ed.), *Studies of the Modern World-System*, Academic Press, 1980.

despite brief spells of colonization, and eventually surged to the high of the 1930s, between the lows of 1880 and 1945. The late nineteenth and the first half of the twentieth century were the most intense periods of colonization in modern times. And indeed, by 1900, there remained only forty-six independent states in the world, all the other countries being under various forms of external control.

Those two waves of colonialism correspond precisely, and quite logically, to periods of restricted international trade. At that time, trade concentrated within the empires and involved mainly the home countries and their colonies. Conversely, free trade re-emerged at times of low colonization, which coincided with the disappearance of mercantilist regulations and state-controlled trade. It was the case in the early nineteenth century after the Napoleonic wars and until 1870. It is also true of the current globalization period, started in the wake of the decolonization wave after World War II.

Wars also tended to coincide with these great waves of concentration of the population of nations: they were particularly frequent when the first colonial wave was at its height, from the second half of the seventeenth century to 1820. Then, a long period of peace accompanies the first decolonization and free trade period from 1820 until the end of the century. And we know what conflagrations accompanied the intense colonization of the twentieth century.

This is no mere coincidence. As states extend their control areas, risks of inter-state conflicts increase. In the colonizing race for the conquest of the world, the rivalry between nation-states (soon to become European empires) were exacerbated. The outward expansion of states reached its limits as the world was not infinite. Now expansion was inevitably carried out to the detriment of another state or empire. In game-theory terms, the outward expansion became a zero-sum game, as a state could only profit from another state's loss. International territorial conflicts thus became much more bitter.

And the correlation with free trade can also be explained easily. International trade was either indiscriminate or preferential, that is with all willing partners or only with the colonies being controlled within some kind of imperial "common market." The larger the empire, the greater the variety of resources available within that vast internal common market and the smaller the need to trade with third-party countries. The home country interest groups could thus impose mercantilism and abandon free trade more easily, and at a lower cost. Conversely, each time colonization faded the home countries only had access to their small and less-diversified domestic market, and they found renewed interest in trading with other partners: free trade was better accepted, when more necessary. The economic needs of a country determine its policy.

Disrupting international non-imperial trade, World War I strengthened the British and French empires. The relationship between home countries and colonies intensified during the inter-war period. The Great Depression of the 1930s was used as a pretext to return to mercantilism and imperial preference.

Indeed, the trend towards the concentration of the overall population of independent nations has been continuous since the last quarter of the nineteenth century despite the collapse and disintegration of the Central Empires following World War I. The gradual concentration of this "nation-states industry" resulted in the formation of two cartels of states after World War II and the suppression of the Axis nations as independent players. Both cartels fought a final duel, known as the East-West "duopoly" of the Cold War—this term being exaggerated given that a full political integration of both superpowers and all their respective allies, whether colonies or protectorates, had never been seriously considered. A cartel is not a fully integrated single firm. Thus a dual cartel is not exactly a duopoly.

The Internal Growth of States: Statism, Dirigisme and Corporatism

States' growth was not only external and geographical. Their dimension also increased within their frontiers through higher tax receipts and the provision of a wide range of new services, new political interventions, regulation of private trade or production of goods and services in place of private firms. Technically, most of these goods and services were still private as they could be manufactured and sold by private businesses. But the state's new economic and administrative capacities enabled it to supplant smaller-sized business companies, just like small- and medium-sized private businesses had been replaced by large trusts or giant companies. These new large-scale management capacities explain why twentieth-century states developed a new range of redistribution activities and intervened as a manufacturer or regulator in all economic and social activities.

In other words, the state's greater involvement in the social and economic life of its country parallels its outward expansion. It is thus unlikely that the increased internal role of the state results solely from the independent development of dirigiste, corporatist or socialist ideologies. If such was the case, it would also imply that the doctrines of dirigisme, socialism and corporatism tend to advocate imperialism and colonialism. Indeed this is what we observe but there is no theoretical rationale for this relation, and initially the socialist ideology opposed nationalism and imperialism.

On the contrary, the organizational approach easily explains that if the state's efficient dimension increases significantly, this has both international (increased colonialism and imperialism) and domestic consequences (the state, as a growing organization, uses a larger proportion of the country's resources: it employs more civil servants and increases its production of public services). Internal and external growth can be pursued simultaneously if there is enough available geographic free space at the frontier or they become substitutes when one of the two expansion modes (international or national) becomes impossible because of specific barriers.

And logically, if public organizations' dimension increases, so should private organizations', that is firms. This is exactly what all the ideologies of the first twentieth century advocated despite all their other differences: as dirigisme was thought to be more efficient to control large-sized than small-sized enterprises, it favored big "national champions" over small- and medium-sized companies. Corporatism organizes the collusion of big private firms gathered together in professional cartels, with the state being one of the country's biggest firms. Finally, socialism simply favors the nationalization of private enterprises to integrate them into the vast capitalist monopoly that the state is.

These different ideologies share the belief in the virtue of large-scale organizations. This belief is in all likelihood the common basis of their various ideologies, while it is unlikely that they developed under the influence of independent determinants leading by happenstance to the same preference for large bureaucracies.

CULTURE AND THE MORAL ATMOSPHERE OF HIERARCHICAL SOCIETIES

Since the beginning of the twentieth century, large hierarchies had existed in all developed societies and spread to the others through colonialism. As these societies' organizational structure changed, the relations between the individuals that composed them also evolved and these new social institutions gave birth to a new culture.

The surprising and yet unexplained evolutions observed during the twentieth century (for instance, the burgeoning of ideologies and totalitarian regimes) resulted in fact from universal organizational transformations.

Each type of organization calls for specific behaviors, specific relations between the individuals that constitute its culture. It is almost sure that the culture of Ancient Egypt would not have met the needs nor adapted itself to the environment of the Amazonian tribal societies, the Inuit of the Arctic or the sixteenth century French society, and vice-versa. The type of organization depends on the technique used and different techniques call for different cultures. This is especially true when it comes to information transmission modes. For instance, mail, literature, cinema, telephone and television determine different cultures. The same is true of horses, sailboats, cars or supersonic jets. A society's culture depends on its social organization.

To be effective, the triumphant bureaucracy of the first twentieth century needed an appropriate culture that it gradually generated: impersonal file processing, forms, formalized procedures, hierarchical relations. These features are incomprehensible to New Guinean aborigines or to Amazonian Yanomamo tribes not because they are intellectually unable to grasp the complexity of these methods but because these methods have no social function in their lives.

The main peculiarity of the bureaucratic culture lies in the atomization of individuals by the hierarchy to isolate them from their fellows and thus impose on them an almost exclusive vertical relation with their superiors. Once they are thus deprived from all personal relations and left with no other social institution to relate to other than the hierarchy which employs them, this culture must also create rules for structuring their private life. Totalizing ideologies thus supplant horizontal social relations, introducing subordination and supervision in all the aspects of individuals' lives, whether private or political, both aspects that gradually merge.

Those specificities contribute to depersonalizing individuals so much that they can be treated in a hardly human (or humanist) way and even in an inhuman way. As they are merely a number lost in an anonymous crowd, the psychological cost to the bureaucrats of inflicting inhuman or criminal treatments on standardized and dehumanized individuals are significantly lowered.

The bureaucratic culture of the first twentieth century thus accounts for the state's criminality and explains why mass murders and crimes against humanity were so common at the time.

From Organization to Culture

The individuals and organizations which compose a society must comply with broadly accepted rules of behavior, institutions without which living among large human groups would be impossible. The bouts of anarchy seen here and there obviously show that, in such conditions, all human activities become difficult and often impossible, so that order—even in its most oppressive form—is often preferred to anarchy because it allows a prosperity which would otherwise be impossible, as Mancur Olson underlines. Undoubtedly, this is one of the reasons behind the stability of autocratic regimes, which look unbearable to the fortunate people living in civilized democratic countries but which the people concerned most probably prefer to the other typically anarchic alternatives.[25]

Thus, almost no human society is totally deprived of institutions, especially the most informal, custom and tradition.

The institutions which we tend to consider as "things" (organizational charts, jobs or buildings) are in fact only sets of rules defining the acceptable terms of interaction between individuals belonging to the same group.

In the contemporary world, these rules are most often written, but they can also be customary, written in the people's memory and transmitted through precedents.

Private and public contracts, the internal rules and regulations of companies, universities or administrations, states' political constitutions, the Geneva Convention relative to the Treatment of POWs are all institutions. Business and labor law institutions define the relations within and between companies. Civil law institutions define the relations within families, among others. Political institutions define the relations between the individuals and the various interest groups within the state organization. Thus, a constitution defines all the po-

---

25. This view is developed by Gordon Tullock in *Autocracy*, Kluwer, 1987.

litical rules and how power should be exercised, be it democratic or dictatorial, presidential or parliamentary.

It is only by convenience that the Constitutional Council and the European Court of Justice are referred to as institutions while they are only bodies in charge of enforcing institutions. Like other economists such as Douglass North, we distinguish the institutions (the rules of behavior) from the bodies which implement them or which they are ruled by.[26]

Institutions and customs are part of a society's culture. And customs can be considered as non-written institutions conveyed through precedents and enforced by the exclusion of any individual who does not comply with the usually codified behaviors from the group, partially or totally.

The notion of culture is often exclusively understood from an educational and literary point of view because our modern civilization has been dominated by written texts. But to a larger extent, it represents all the knowledge acquired that enables the members of a society to communicate, notably by developing the common tastes and judgments (preferences and values) that will then frame and determine individual behaviors. There are thus classical music, pop, scientific, political, literary or movie cultures which represent as many open social groups that individuals can freely join or support.

But there are also business cultures each encompassing predefined rules and behaviors, specific knowledge, past experiences and a savoir-faire peculiar to a given production organization. They play an essential role in promoting and accelerating communications which is absolutely necessary for good teamwork.

Thus, organizational advances are accompanied by cultural transformations, a phenomenon which is particularly obvious in the busi-

26. "Institutions are the rules of the game in a society, or, more formally, the humanly devised constraints that shape human interactions" quoted from Douglas North in *Institutions, Institutional Change and Economic Performance*, Cambridge University Press, 1990, p.3.

ness world at times of mergers and acquisitions. When transformations are broad and affect all the organizations of a society, it is understandable that they can alter its whole culture.

The common evolution undergone by all organizations in the first twentieth century, a move towards a large size that was accompanied by the development of the hierarchical superstructures necessary to manage them, changed the usual or "dominant" type of organization—dominant in a purely statistical sense, which means the most commonly observed. Large hierarchies soon dominated modern societies and replaced smaller structures as well as non-exclusively vertical interpersonal relationships.

And large hierarchies gave a new twist to human relationships and the moral and intellectual conceptions which limit and govern them, making them quite different from those seen in poorly hierarchized societies or those suitable to the good functioning of markets.

Indeed, the hierarchical relation—the essence of hierarchy—consists in the subordination of most of the organization's members to the decisions and directives of only a few, their immediate and higher level superiors, and so on until the company head who stands alone at the top of the pyramid. This implies that subordinates voluntarily submit to the executives and leaders, who in turn control them through monitoring and coercion measures so that they follow faithfully the orders and directives given by the company head.

As a result, there are two diametrically opposite cultures: the market culture which relies on individuals' initiative and diversity and on the non-exclusive bilateral relationships from equal to equal, and the hierarchical culture which requires standardized individuals who submit to the leader's will as part of asymmetric and exclusive bilateral relationships.

Endogenous Cultures

Most studies on culture work on the assumption that the ideas and other representations of culture are arbitrary: "there's no point arguing about taste" *(De gustibus non disputandum est)*. The members of a society would thus be collectively responsible for their overall culture, whose characteristics would be both discretionary (that is, inexplicable) and transmissible, thus forming the "people's spirit." Although the latter concept is mostly discredited nowadays, it still influences a number of pseudo-sophisticated analyses.

Wondering about the lasting differences between culinary cultures, Paul Krugman puts forward the hypothesis that French traditions stem from the astounding variety and quality of local products. It would explain why France's gastronomic taste is by no means comparable to that of quickly urbanizing England which suffered from relative poor food supply during the Industrial Revolution.[27] The existing transportation and refrigeration techniques did not allow to supply the crowded big cities with high-quality fresh products. And so ordinary people, and even the middle classes, were forced into a cuisine based on canned goods, preserved meats and root vegetables that did not need refrigeration (as potatoes for instance). According to Krugman, urban Britons got so used to eating low-quality food that they could no longer tell the difference. When better products became available, the taste inherited from several centuries of bad food persisted. Only very slowly did their taste improve and come closer to the French taste. Gastronomic culture is thus endogenous.

In the economic literature, Schumpeter is among the very few who does not consider culture as an arbitrary assumption. In *Capitalism, Socialism and Democracy*, he explains that the "civilization of capitalism" declined because of the very nature of that system, and more precisely the gradual bureaucratization of big firms where individualist

27. Paul Krugman, "Supply, Demand, and English Food," *Fortune*, July 20, 1998.

entrepreneurs were replaced with private bureaucrats, thus undermining the social foundations upon which the system was based.

This is one of the most telling examples of an endogenous conception of culture. It is the production methods and social structures that generate a certain culture, which meets best their specific needs and "reflects" the material conditions of the society. We recognize here the materialist theory of general political and cultural superstructures developed by Marx.

But the confrontation of the two modern organizational modes used by Marx and Schumpeter—capitalism and socialism—does not really explain the cultural differences observed between the first and the second twentieth century. As underlined by Niskanen, the culture of a very large U.S. firm such as Ford or General Motors is not fundamentally different from that of the Department of Defense or the State Department, which itself is not very different from that of the Ministry of Industry or the Planning Ministry in a Communist country.

In fact, if capitalism is defined as the intensive use of capital equipment (especially machines) and the conversion (the "capitalization") of the future revenues of an investment to their current value, then Schumpeter does not predict the demise of capitalism when he mentions the bureaucratization of very large firms and the disappearance of individualist entrepreneurs. What he really describes is the decline of individualist entrepreneurs and how they were supplanted by large hierarchies and how, as a consequence, the market culture was replaced by the bureaucratic culture. In other words, what Schumpeter explains is the decline of one kind of capitalism, or how market capitalism was replaced by "hierarchical capitalism."[28]

As this transformation was merely due to the almost unavoidable changes in mentality that it generates, capitalism as such did not dis-

28. This expression is notably used by John H. Dunning in *Governments, Globalization, and International Business*, Oxford University Press, 1997.

appear. What occurred in the twentieth century was rather the convergence of a hierarchical capitalism towards an also bureaucratic socialism because of the universal organizational mutations which led to the replacement of market mechanisms by large hierarchies. And, as a consequence, the market civilization was supplanted by the hierarchical civilization.

Depending on whether markets or hierarchies are the prevailing mode of organization and coordination of production and exchanges within a society, one of the two cultures will have a predominant impact on the individual behaviors it will shape, and which will eventually influence more or less all the aspects of social life other than working relations. Thus, the market and hierarchical cultures spread from work to all the other aspects of social life. This will determine, through the unity of individual behavior, the overall culture of the society.

The invention of the factory is a telling example of the radical social and cultural changes that organizational transformations can generate. Originally, farmers and craftsmen worked part-time in rural societies attached to well-established old traditions, but with the First and Second Industrial Revolutions, they moved to large cities where traditions were often non-existent and were yet to be established. These periods also saw the establishment of a very strict discipline, especially regarding the timing of work inside factories and firms. As a result, individuals' freedom to manage their work and organize their personal time was substantially reduced. There was great reluctance to comply with these new constraints.

Obviously, the way work is organized depends on the size of the organization and the society's degree of concentration: work is not carried out the same way in a ten-person workshop as in a ten-thousand-person firm. The regrouping of a large number of individuals favors their anonymity. In such conditions, it is easier to be a "free-rider" (that is to refuse to pay a fee for a service), cheat or even commit crimes since culprits are difficult to identify and thus to pun-

ish. As the probability for a cheater to be caught and punished decreases with the number of people gathered together, the gain expected from such a behavior increases proportionately. That is why
these kinds of behavior are more common in great cities than in small
villages where everybody is acquainted with one another, and also in
large firms rather than in craft workshops where everybody knows
exactly what his neighbor does.

A fundamental problem in large-scale organizations is thus to supervise the productive performance of each of their members. But
their big dimension also affects the degree of cooperation or collusion
between the organizations. As we will underline later on, this explains
the characteristics of the organizational culture and the moral atmosphere in hierarchical societies.

CHAPTER 2

The Political Consequences of Hierarchy

Since its development in the mid-nineteenth century, bureaucratization has repeatedly been criticized for its dehumanizing nature. According to the critics, there is indeed a bureaucratic culture unsuitable to individuals, a point of view developed by William H. Whyte in *The Organization Man* in the 1950s.

Bureaucratization has deep intellectual, political and human consequences. Some have tried to define a specific "*homo hierarchicus*" whose behavior would be radically different from that of an individual living in another environment. But making such an assumption is unnecessary. A man's fundamental behavior can remain the same even if the changes in the incentives and constraints generated by his environment influence profoundly his actions and decisions. The choice behavior itself can remain unchanged but lead to different decisions under different conditions. The constraints limiting individual choices and the results of constrained choices are changing, rather than basic behavior.

This distinction is essential because the belief that human nature can vary according to the circumstances and the environment prevents any systematic and rigorous description of behavior and thus deprives human sciences from stable foundations. If the slightest exogenous shock can change the nature of man, there can be no human science. Besides, according to modern biology and the evolutionary theory, human nature has been largely determined by its biology under selective environmental pressures for hundreds of thousand years and can only change in the very long run after several thousand or ten thousands of generations.[1] Only environmental conditions, positive or negative incentives, and cultural factors can change significantly during a man's life or over a few generations. In other words, constraints vary but not the deep motives of the decision.

This is what happened with the administrative revolution, which disrupted profoundly the social environment as its specific culture contributed to destroy the individual.

THE SPIRIT OF BUREAUCRACY

Indeed, the hierarchical organization relies both on individuals' atomization (they are torn from their traditional environment) and standardization (the impersonal and standardized bureaucratic approach reduces each individual to a file number and tries to make him interchangeable with others).

First, the hierarchical organization isolates individuals from "horizontal" relations, relations with their peers at the same level in the hierarchy, to better integrate them in a vertical one-to-one relation with their superiors. But it also prunes their unique dimensions, their personal characteristics, to standardize them and make them easier to monitor and to control.

Such are the unavoidable methods, facilitating the functioning of bureaucracies and hierarchies, that were discovered and explained by the theoreticians and practitioners of the scientific organization of

1. Edward O. Wilson, *On Human Nature*, Harvard University Press, 1978, and John Maynard Smith and Eörs Szathmáry, *The Origins of Life, From the Birth of Life to the Origin of Language*, Oxford University Press, 1999.

work when large-scale private administrations emerged in the early century.

In the wake of the Second Industrial Revolution, Taylor, Fayol (who was the first to use explicitly the term "administrative revolution"), and Ford developed the scientific management of work, its fragmentation, simplification and mechanization, thus opening the era of big firms and bureaucratic managers, whose consequences on the U.S. economy of the '20s and '30s were described by Berle and Means. Being based on the standardization of individuals, that is the depersonalization of human relations within the hierarchy, bureaucratic rationality resulted in line production whether industrial or administrative that increases productivity through the simplification of tasks and mechanization. This was in total contrast with pre-industrial farm work, where everyone was free to organize work except for a few collective tasks which required a few common rules.

In richer and more densely populated societies, the value of time grew as it corresponded to hourly pays and wages, which, according to the very definition of enrichment, rose with economic development. As a consequence, it became more interesting for both companies and workers to further economize time through an extreme specialization and a standardization of every gesture as a way to increase productivity and wealth.

Then, as giant firms became better established after Word War I, people became gradually aware of the decisive role and power of the executives heading large organizations, more commonly known as "managers." These new organizational structures had deep social consequences, and not only within firms. Indeed, they could also challenge the actual democracy and lead to corporatism, a possibility that was described by authors such as Pareto and Manoïlesco.[2]

This was neither the liberal capitalism of the mid-nineteenth cen-

2. Mihaïl Manoïlesco, *The Century of Corporatism: The Doctrine of Total and Pure Capitalism*, Alcan, 1938. J. K. Galbraith's comments on this issue in *American Capitalism* and *The New Industrial State* came much later.

tury nor socialism, but rather a system of large firms which concentrated capital and labor, characterized by private but dispersed control, and where managers were quite independent from the shareholders. It was a system of intense private bureaucratization which generated its own culture based on the constructivist bureaucrat rather than the individualistic entrepreneur.

That bureaucratic culture was to be found both in private bureaucracies and public hierarchies, and relied on the atomization of individuals, the development and diffusion of ideologies and the standardization of individuals.

THE ATOMIZATION OF INDIVIDUALS

The specific problem of hierarchies that sets them apart from the exchange mechanism of markets is not to choose what good or service to produce, its quality or its price, or even which innovation to promote. In a market, an individual entrepreneur must also face these issues and make the corresponding decisions. Instead, the peculiar hierarchical problem is to have individuals cooperate and work together, although they do not make decisions by themselves and only achieve targets set by others.

As the productive performance of each individual merges within the work of the whole group of employees and is thus difficult to precisely identify and quantify, neither the intensity of the individual's work nor the consequences of his actions can directly affect his wage and living standard. Thus, the representatives of the hierarchies' interests must ensure that the orders expressed at the top of the pyramid are properly executed and that each member of the organization does his best to advance the group's interest.

The unique problem that the hierarchy is faced with is not to define its strategy (all the decision makers have to cope with this issue) but rather to specify clearly the tasks of each member. Those tasks have to be included into a pre-thought general plan without which non-coordinated individual activities would lead to chaos. The hierarchy also has to control that each employee carries out his task properly.

It follows that the bureaucratic culture must necessarily be characterized by a plan which applies to everyone, a commonly shared view, where the community and the decisions are taken at the top prime. Instead of being creative, individual initiatives can prove particularly dangerous for the overall coordination and productivity of the organization. It can only be accepted if it has been submitted to the top of the pyramid and approved, then included in the general plan and finally returned to the basis as a new directive.

The cultural specificity of hierarchy is thus the general recourse to the "prêt à penser" or "ready to think" (central or directed thought) and the reign of conformity. It is vital that individuals comply with the instructions coming from the top of the organization. The choices and decisions of a single individual—supposedly the best informed and most competent—are thus conveyed to the rest of the organization and implemented by up to several thousands of people. Decision makers are only a few while order-takers are countless.

To obtain such a result, the field workers must first accept these rules and second be in a position that makes it easier to receive the information coming from the top and no other. The interferences and noises coming from other sources must be muted. Ideally, field workers should have only one source of information: the leader. In that view, they must be isolated from all the other possible influences. Putting them in a closed workplace under the permanent control of their superiors, with a fixed position and fixed hours, is one of the prerequisites to monopolize the downward information flow to that extent.

Horizontal exchanges between colleagues or with third parties outside the organization must also be avoided. Any relation with other individuals must thus be limited or even forbidden at least during working hours and at the workplace. This target is supposed to be met through the simplification of the tasks and their fragmentation into small individual jobs making the control of workers by supervisors easier, because simple tasks are easier to control than complex tasks. Besides, a fragmented, well-defined and isolated task implies simpler relations with neighbors and colleagues.

In an interesting article about productivity and organization, Albert Breton and Ronald Wintrobe tried to associate these relationships between the individuals within the hierarchy with the notion of "trust capital" which builds up between various people—for instance, the level of honesty between superiors and subordinates or subordinates of the same rank.[3]

Trust is indeed the positive alternative to supervision. Both methods are substitutable and there are three ways to make sure that the directives coming from the top are implemented: mutual trust between superiors and subordinates, close supervision and a mix of these two options.

But most interesting in this article is that the authors underline the necessity of vertical trust-subordination relations and the rather negative impact on productivity of the horizontal relations between subordinates. Indeed, horizontal relations somehow compete with vertical relations for information transmission. They interfere with the messages and directives from the top. They can result in misinformation and disturb decision-making at various levels of the hierarchy, as they compete or contradict the directives coming from the top. They also favor collusion between colleagues of the same rank to resist the orders coming from higher levels, or to distort the directives before transmitting them to lower levels.

Thus, during the Russian revolution, the slogan "all power to the Soviets" was revolutionary as it advocated that groups of field workers at the basis of the pyramid should take concerted decisions instead of

3. Albert Breton and Ronald Wintrobe, "Organizational Structure and Productivity," *American Economic Review*, June 1986.

the top which was then deprived of its power. This phenomenon proved short-lived as it was replaced by the extreme hierarchization of Leninism and then Stalinism. But it clearly shows the incompatibility between the hierarchical organization and the introduction of strong horizontal communication and trust relations. To be efficient, the hierarchy must establish a vertical monopoly of information and lock up individuals in an exclusive one-to-one relationship with their immediate superior, who thus handles several one-to-one relationships with his subordinates. And indeed, his ability to manage a more or less significant number of bilateral relations will determine the number of his subordinates at every level of the organization. Then, the number of subordinates under the control of one superior determines the maximum size of the organization, if the maximum number of hierarchical levels that can be introduced without undergoing too heavy losses of control is known.[4]

This suppression of horizontal relations and enforcement of a vertical information monopoly, when pushed to the extreme, defines the position of soldiers in mass armies, prisoners in penal institutions or slaves working in the vast sugar plantations which prefigured in the sixteenth and seventeenth centuries the almost military organization of the nineteenth-century factories. Taken to its extremes and generalized to a whole society, this situation of vertical monopoly of hierarchical relationships leads to totalitarianism, a system where individuals are totally controlled by their immediate superiors in all the aspects of life and not only at work. All the activities previously considered as "private" become public in the totalitarian framework.

In the case of slavery—an ancient form of totalitarianism—the personal and family life of the slave was no longer private. It did not belong to him anymore as the owner was the sole decision maker. His "personal utility function"—as economists say—is supplanted by that

---

4. This issue was formalized and analyzed by Oliver Williamson in "Hierarchical Control and Optimum Firm Size," *Journal of Political Economy*, April 1967

of his owner. The same is true of the soldier, the prisoner or the people living in totalitarian countries. This has been illustrated in China during the cultural revolution: the individuals' everyday life was totally subjected to the directives coming from the top and people were kept under constant collective watch. Even the term "cultural revolution," which sounded like an exaggerated exotic curiosity, had been perfectly chosen as it was indeed the culture of the whole Chinese society that was at stake.

Similarly, in terms of political systems, the Communists adopted the concept of a single party, thus reducing significantly the number of existing political organizations compared with a democratic system. Communism builds a whole society around a single giant pyramid.

Consequently, behavioral rules change: a much different morphology implies a different physiology. When there is only one economic decision-making pole in the country, the exchanges between the production units are governed by the authorities through administrative decisions and rules. But when there are several independent decision-making poles, exchanges are ruled by market mechanisms. The same is true in politics: a democracy with several parties develops arbitrages between the interests of these various organizations by confronting offer and demand within the Parliaments, whereas the single party settles the conflicts and oppositions using internal hierarchical procedures.

But once the individuals are atomized and virtually reduced to mere vertical relationships within their professional hierarchies, it is necessary to do the same with their private or political actions outside work. And this can be done through ideologies. In highly-centralized societies, their role is to provide all the members of the society with a common view of both its structure and all the aspects of their lives even outside work. That ideology is the same for everyone and constitutes the general conception of life, a practical philosophy. It reinforces the atomization by standardizing the individuals, a method which has the great advantage of making them interchangeable and thus easier to handle for a bureaucracy that necessarily defines standardized tasks. Besides, standardization (and the interchangeability which results from it) leaves individuals powerless against the hierarchy, as they are easier to replace. Both voice and exit thus become ineffective. The society is then composed of a large number of similar individuals, forming a mass.

MASSIFICATION AND THE TOTALITARIAN IDEOLOGY

The first twentieth century is often described as the time of integrated systems of thought. It has been dominated by the vogue for totalizing interpretations of societies. Why has it been the era of "ism" philosophies or, in other words, ideologies?

That puzzling propensity is yet unexplained. It seemed to be an intellectual deviance, which then had to be corrected in view of the traumatic experiences that the implementation of these ideologies is supposed to have generated. But, in fact, the reason of this vogue is rather to be found in the usefulness of the ideologies for the management of large hierarchies. It is due to the bureaucracy's need for a single thought. Breton and Wintrobe's "vertical loyalty" and the sentiment of belonging to an organization are only tentative ideologies. They usually underline the opposition between "us" and "them," between "insiders" and "outsiders," to develop team spirit in sports and business, or nationalism[5] at the level of the country. In other words, the sociopolitical ideologies were the "business cultures" of the national societies with great ambitions of conquest.

Thus, ideologies were not the cause of the major societal transformations that took place during the twentieth century, but their necessary instrument. They spread because they were useful in the organizational and political contexts of the time. They were not arbitrary or simply false. They were instrumental. In short, they were

5. Russell Hardin, *One for All: The Logic of Group Conflict*, Princeton University Press, 1995.

endogenous and not exogenous regarding the world of production and material organization.

It is not ideas that create the world: it is the observation of the world that generates mental representations, inner images, ideas. The best proof of that is the time lag between the facts and the moment the idea is found, and also the persistent influence of ideas outdated by the evolution of social realities, as many authors like Keynes (most famously) but also Beniger underlined.[6]

Loyalty and trust, which Breton and Wintrobe believe to be crucial to hierarchical organization, can help to increase the hierarchy's productivity. They can be reinforced by the diffusion of an ideology, a common organizational thought, a kind of broadly-accepted personal software which prompts the individuals to adopt the same "values" (the same subjective preferences), make the same choices and take the same decisions—those the most in line with the directives coming from the top.

The ideologies, which include all the social moral codes—starting with religions[7]—are the mass doctrines that are used to control the individuals, adjust their reactions to those defined at the top and especially gain the trust of bureaucratic employees. They are necessary to the good functioning of centralized structures because they reduce individual deviances from the directives given by the top, even when the individuals are not kept under close watch, given each individual adjust his own preferences to the priorities set by its leader. At each stage of the hierarchy, there is an inevitable percentage of loss in the content of the top-management messages and directives because of misunderstanding, distortion by parasitic noises and interference or ill-will and sabotage, but it is minimized when ideologies have a strong hold on people. A well-indoctrinated individual who shares—inter-

6. See the introduction of *The Control Revolution*, op. cit.
7. This is how the first highly hierarchical societies turned theocratic and invented an hierarchy of deities.

nalizes—the ideology of his organization is even able to trace back the initial content of an incomplete instruction.

Applied to the whole society and politics, supervision and ideological indoctrination—which requires "loyalty" to superiors in private bureaucracies, that is, complete subordination to the top management's will and orders—can easily degenerate into totalitarianism, which is an absolute respect for hierarchical superiors and the disappearance of any protest and individualism. From then on, the Führer, the Duce, the Caudillo, the Father of People, the Great Helmsman or the Leader Maximo are always right.

Insofar as the individuals share the "values" of the ideology and do not consider looking for their own values, they align their "utility function" with that of the other members of the collective and their leaders. This partially reduces the divergences between the aims of the superiors and subordinates, and the risk of deviant behavior.

The ideologies, which are key to the organizational culture, usefully complement the written institutions such as rules, laws and constitutions. Being easier to understand, more general and internalized, they have a clear advantage over explicit rules in unexpected situations, as the latter are not meant for them. They enable individual field workers to imagine what the top directives would have been when they lack them and accept them more easily so that they will follow them more faithfully under normal circumstances.

Ideologies are an informal complement to culture, which takes over on laws and rules where they cease to exist. They are also used to justify the established order and alter the behaviors of the individuals who become part of that order. They are instilled in them to integrate them more fully into the organization. For an effective, plain, rapid and effortless assimilation, ideologies must be simple (up to the caricature). And they must emphasize the opposition between the members of the organization and the others.

The psychological consequences of that indoctrination are reflected in all societal behavior, and especially in politics. Individualistic values encouraging initiatives, information and communication are replaced by collective values which give priority to organized social entities, conformism and eventually depersonalization. Masses are not just a large number of persons, they are a large number of all similar units.

This explains crowd reactions. A crowd is a mass: a group of standardized and anonymous individuals bound by no structure of social relations, no institution, but only by the belief in the same ideology, the pursuit of some immediate interest, by a submission to a strong view, a passion or a charismatic leader, in other terms, a common smallest denominator. The relations between those depersonalized individuals and their leader are mainly vertical. There is no need to refer to complex psychological reactions in the vein of writings such as Le Bon's *Crowd Psychology* to explain these moves. A simple economic calculation of the costs and advantages of petty and serious crime in conditions of relative anonymity is just enough.[8]

The massification and depersonalization of individuals not only account for the isolated crimes within the crowd but also the methods of state mass murder that characterized the twentieth century.

THE ECONOMICS OF POLITICAL MURDER

The standardization of individuals resulting from their atomization and the diffusion of the ideologies on which they depend gives birth to a mass society. Its government shows great ability to handle very large numbers and significant flows, just like big businesses after the administrative revolution. But that ability to manipulate is also accompanied by an impressively stronger hold on individuals. It becomes possible for a single hierarchy, which has developed the massification of the society enough, to eliminate the opponents of the regime or simply the non-conformists, there again in mass propor-

---

8. Gordon Tullock, *The Social Dilemma: The Economics of War and Revolution,* University Publications, 1974.

tions. This is the case of mass murder and state crime, which will give birth to a notion specific to the twentieth century: crimes against humanity—mostly mass crimes.

On the political scale of a whole society, totalitarianism is the expression of generalized and extreme vertical control—the key to entirely centralized societies. But hierarchization is not limited to the imprisonment of individuals into a monopolistic vertical relationship. It also relies on the standardization, the "normalization," of individuals—each aligning itself on the behavior defined by the center—which changes any organization member into a more easily controllable and interchangeable object. Thus, that member can be replaced at any time, and he is deprived of any power within the organization. Being immediately replaceable, individuals have no other choice than to obey orders.

In highly-centralized societies, the Fordist and Taylorist methods are applied to the whole social hierarchy organized by the state. Bureaucratization determines the "massification" of individuals. Indeed, bureaucracy must treat all the individuals equally without taking into account their particular characteristics—their personality. People become "files" or "numbers" (social security, schools, prisons, camps) behind which their personality vanishes. That makes the handling of those files and the anonymous decisions concerning those persons easier.

That broad depersonalization also makes it simpler to make decisions that are harmful and dangerous for the individuals. It leads to the trivialization and bureaucratization of murder. It is easier to carry out mass executions of depersonalized individuals than to murder individuals one after the other, physically and face to face. If the individuals are numerous and all similar, all substitutable, large-scale physical elimination becomes possible without any difficulty and without disrupting the productive process. The hierarchical organization and the massification of the individuals make state crime possible, especially as the productivity of the administration reduces the organizational and moral costs of these collective executions. This is the key to the technological barbarism of the first twentieth century.

Indeed, that organization first diminishes the intrinsic value of individuals since they can be replaced at any time by other very similar individuals, all the personal characteristics having been ironed out or made identical by the bureaucratic mechanism. At the same time, it is in the interest of the society and its leaders to eliminate all the individuals and groups, who in their non-conformity to the dominant standards, actively or passively spoil the hierarchical transmission of orders. Non-conformity is the main obstacle to effective hierarchical organizations.

Furthermore, this new administrative efficiency enables isolating the deviant individuals that are more accurately identified thanks to the totalitarian information capacity of the hierarchy and also the deviant groups, which the administration can handle as a single element—thanks to the increased productivity of its rational methods— in a mass-production process.

Finally, the individuals within the organization who are responsible for the isolation of the deviants or opponents, and often for the decision to eliminate them physically, can do so with few moral scruples thanks to the depersonalized relationship with the victims resulting from both the standardization of the individuals and the impersonal file processing. Besides, the decision process is fragmented into several stages, often dealt with by different bureaucrats. One of them writes a name on the list of suspects, another one transfers that name onto the list of state enemies. A third decides to put them under arrest. A fourth person decides to deport them. And a lot of people take part in the process which ends in murder. Fragmented decision making dilutes responsibilities. And this in turn reduces the impact, the psychological "reality" and the subjective pain of the decision to murder people.

Murdering somebody by moving a file from one pile to another certainly does not affect someone the same way as murdering somebody face to face with one's own hands. And for those who actually have to kill somebody physically, the ideology, the dedication to general interest, to the state or its leader, acts as a tranquilizer, if not a stimulant.

Conversely, in their article about the bureaucracy of murder, Breton and Wintrobe support the view that the managers at every level of that process are directly responsible, given they make everything possible to submit to their superiors more efficient extermination methods.[9] But that argument is not incompatible with a feeling of lesser pain or guilt due to the very nature of the hierarchical process, much to the contrary.

A similar mechanism—but much less elaborated and bureaucratic given the more rudimentary context—was used as a basis for the policy of constant dehumanization of slaves that ancient and traditional societies generally carried out, especially in Africa. It was simply maintained and reintroduced with the modern expansion of the large plantations ruled by slave owners just before the Industrial Revolution. These were in themselves totalitarian societies, whose functioning bore a striking resemblance with the Russian Gulag, although the slaves were treated better than Solzhenitsyn's companions: the "zeks." The reason behind that is simple: the slaves had been bought by their owner and thus had a market value. Consequently, they had to be kept in good conditions to produce, whereas the zeks could be exploited until death without any yield considerations since they had no purchase price and thus no value in the state-owner's mind.[10] Unlike the owners of "tradable" slaves, the Nazi or Communist state even viewed the value of their prisoners as negative: they hinder—really or supposedly—the good functioning of the hierarchy. This explains why they were more harshly treated than tradable slaves.

9. Albert Breton and Ronald Wintrobe, "The Bureaucracy of Murder Revisited," *Journal of Political Economy*, 1986.

10. For analyses of the way slaves were treated depending on the circumstances and the kind of organizations in which they worked, see Ira Berlin, *Many Thousands Gone*, Belknap, Harvard University Press, 1998.

The dehumanization of slaves, like that of the members of total-itarian societies, is a way to control individuals. It aims at reducing the personal targets, desires and ambitions of average individuals to replace them more easily by those of their leaders. Thus, the personal utility function—in other words, the personality—must be weakened to force individuals to give in to their hierarchical superiors' decisions. The terms used are also very telling: in prisons or in the army, the idea is to "crush the minds," like one tames animals, to subject them to the will of their owners. The domestication of animals, the fruit of the prehistoric experience of man, consists in subordinating them to the aims of the humans to take advantage of their labor force or nutritional resources.

It is then easier to mass murder depersonalized and dehumanized individuals, often explicitly and systematically compared to animals, than to kill fellow humans. This is the reason why slaves have never been viewed as men but as cattle and depersonalized accordingly. It was thus easier to exploit them and treat them like animals, paying no attention to their aspirations but only to the preferences and in-terests of their owners. This also explains why the victims of the Nazi extermination policy were officially considered as "sub-humans."

The methods used for the World War II genocide were not in-novative. They were those of the Chicago slaughterhouses mentioned earlier to explain the progress of the Second Industrial Revolution which gave birth to the large-scale organizations of the late nineteenth century. In a way, the phenomena of mass murder and state crime do characterize the modern civilization as several authors have begun to underline.[11] The genocides look closely related to the mechanisms of bureaucratic dehumanization.

11. Especially R.J. Rummel, *Lethal Politics: Soviet Genocide and Mass Murder since 1917*; *China's Bloody Century: Genocide and Mass Murder since 1900*; and *Democide: Nazi Genocide and Mass Murder*, Transaction Publishers, 1990, 1991, and 1992. See also the recent book by Lionel B. Steiman, *Paths to Genocide: Anti-Semitism in Western History*, Macmillan, 1998, and Zygmunt Bauman's *Modernity and the Holocaust*, Cor-

The mechanisms of these extreme crime cases can be understood since it appears that they only take to its extremes the logic of subordination, that is the individuals' renunciation of their own targets and their (in)voluntary submission to the aims, decisions and choices of their hierarchical superiors.

In most contemporary societies, subordinates do voluntarily forsake their utility function, but this consent is limited both in time and scope by the labor contracts they sign. The delegation of the freedom to choose and self-govern to the superior is consented and partial.

But, in many situations, the renunciation of personal liberties and of the personal utility function can go further, although it has been freely consented. For instance, this was the case with the voluntary servitude of the Europeans that emigrated to the United States in the seventeenth and eighteenth centuries. As they could not afford to pay the journey across the Atlantic to the New World, they accepted to sell themselves as slaves for a few years to the "buyer" who would finance the trip.

And it is mostly because these temporary slaves were too few and sometimes did not fulfil their commitments that a large number of unwilling African slaves were imported to the American continent for the highly-profitable cotton and sugar plantations. At that time, the vast plantations were the largest integrated production organizations and they already implemented the labor fragmentation and standardization methods that were to become widespread in Europe with the Industrial Revolution.

But the extent of the inhuman treatment depends mostly on the size of the organization. To avoid the risk of a drift towards nonconformity and the loss of information and efficiency that increases proportionally to the population studied, the mass organization, the mass hierarchization, needs to resort to increasingly harsh sanctions.

---

nell University Press, 1989, which explicitly develops the argument that mass murders theare intrinsically linked to the very nature of twentieth-century society.

This can go as far as murder and even mass murder in the largest state hierarchies because of the monopoly of violence.

Far from being an inexplicable aberration due to a fit of madness at the apogee of the Western civilization, mass murders and crimes against humanity now appear as the immoral but logical consequences of the centralized organization of ever-growing masses.

THE VALUE OF INDIVIDUALS AND THE COST OF STATE MURDER

A typical example of the theory of the irrationality or the absurdity of state murder, absurdity which is an extreme form of error, is the current explanation of state slaughters of the past century, and more especially those of Nazi Germany and Russian communism.[12] The idea that it was pure madness mainly results from the moral revulsion caused by those slaughters and genocides. It is the same reaction that prompts us to ascribe most of the individual criminal acts to psychological abnormality or lunacy.

Like individual crimes, state crimes are often described as a sudden fit of madness, an aberration or an abnormal behavior with no rational justification. In view of that conclusion, observers then look for the causes of this fit of madness in the ideas, intentions, motives, perverted preferences of the murderers, errors, illusions or cowardly acts of those who let them commit their crimes. The aim is to identify the perversions of the human mind—in this case, the harmful ideologies—that are at the origin of these crimes and to prevent their resurgence through morals, persuasion or constraint.

Even if one believes that this approach may be effective, it does not explain the variations of criminality in space and time, especially as the proportion of abnormal or inhuman individuals in a given population can probably be considered as constant.

Since the pathbreaking analysis of Gary Becker, criminality and

12. Stéphane Courtois et al., *The Black Book of Communism: Crimes, Terror, Repression*, Harvard University Press, 1999.

delinquency theories have evolved by relying on another hypothesis that many empirical works then confirmed: the motivations of delinquents (or even criminals) can differ more or less from those of other individuals, with for instance low moral standards or absolutely no respect for other people's lives. But, despite that, their deviant behaviors are not necessarily mad or irrational. They opt for crime mostly because it is more profitable than respecting the laws and the other people. Their level of delinquency will thus be affected by the society's positive and negative incentives. For a given degree of abnormality in the population, a high arrest rate and severe sanctions will reduce criminal activity. On the contrary, inefficient police forces and a lax justice system will encourage delinquency and criminality. Similarly, the opportunities of making profits that potential criminals are faced with will drive them either toward criminality if the legal structure is very weak or dissuade them from crime if it strengthens—for instance, in the event of an economic recovery and increased opportunities of lucrative legal jobs.

That does not necessarily imply that the society is responsible. Criminals are. But their actions depend on the risk/reward of legal and illegal activities that is determined by the society. For instance, this is true of drug traffic: that activity is so profitable that the risk of an arrest and a sentence is minimized and the traffic develops despite the numerous "wars on drugs" periodically launched by the governments.

In that light, is the barbarism of the twentieth century an aberration, an inexplicable "fit of madness"? Or, on the contrary, is it intrinsically linked to the original characteristics of the contemporary civilization? That assumption was first made by Lionel B. Steiman.[13] Could barbarism be the (partial) consequence of the incentives generated by the modern organization of our technological and bureaucratic society? Obviously, to carry out mass slaughters, mass bureaucracy is needed.

13. *Paths to Genocide: Anti-Semitism in Western History*, Macmillan, 1998.

Whatever their nature, the procedures of political selection cannot prevent an abnormal person from reaching the top of the state. But, obviously, when that leader governs a totalitarian country and has huge power as was the case with Hitler, his destruction capacity becomes terrifying. That capacity would have been much more reduced in a democratic society, where the power is shared and decisions are decentralized.

What distinguishes the modern state from the previous political organizations is the extraordinary concentration of the political, economic and legal authority within the hands of a sole leader. The sentence "I am the state," which is commonly credited to Louis XIV, perfectly summed up that situation. However, the state has much more power now than in the seventeenth century, as it did not yet rely on the social concepts of nation and nationalism invented in the nineteenth century. But it was already bureaucratic and centralized, looking for the rational and anonymous efficiency that Max Weber described later on.

The state is equally rational and efficient when it applies its resources to war and mass murder. Concentration camps were invented by Great Britain during the Boer War in the late nineteenth century. The Nazi state only took to its extremes the bureaucracy of modern war, against a fraction of civilians, arbitrarily selected according to the beliefs—whatever they were—of the few persons that had seized the centralized power. Large-scale murders had already been committed by the German state much before the systematic deportation of Jews and Gypsies living in the occupied countries: it had been used against the Communists and Socialists, against Hitler's rivals within the party, against homosexuals and other "social misfits."[14]

Violence against the troops of the totalitarian state must not be underestimated either. Thus, several tens of thousands of German soldiers of the Wehrmacht were executed during the war. That process

14. Steiman, op. cit., p. 23.

is not peculiar to the German army: French soldiers had been shot as a warning during World War I following the mutinies of 1915, and the diffusion of the film *Path of Glory* describing that episode was long forbidden by public authorities.

So, why were there not more revolts in Germany, Russia or China? Although those totalitarian regimes were more efficient from economic and foreign security standpoints than other imperialist organizations that were even more dangerous for local populations, the terror that these regimes exerted on their population and opponents must not be forgotten.[15] It required exceptional courage—which is by definition very rare—to risk the death penalty, deportation and torture by taking position against a totalitarian machinery which isolated and persecuted its opponents and which, above all, seemed to be the solution of the future that would remain indefinitely, as people believed it would be the case with the totalitarian regimes, in the 1930s.

In fact, resistances only developed where they benefited from outside support and where a future defeat of the totalitarian regime could at least be considered a real possibility.

But as Germany was not the only country to pursue that bureaucracy of murder, it is also necessary to explain the mass slaughters that were not motivated by anti-Semitic or anti-Communist hatred. Thus, from the start of the 1930s, Stalin had exterminated, through systematic starvation, millions of Ukrainians while he set up the Gulag system. In that case, there was no aberrant hatred against the Ukrainians as such and the idea was rather to use a convenient tool of mass bureaucracy to get rid of the regime's opponents. Here, the cause was the search for maximal power and not a particular ideologically based hatred of a social group.

And the extermination of entire ethnic groups was not totally new at the time as the slaughter of the Armenians by the Turks during

---

15. To be convinced of that greater danger, just study how the German army treated the Russian population during World War II and vice versa.

World War I shows. It was thus a characteristic of that period which could differ according to the organizational structures of each society and was more or less marked, but nevertheless widespread, as the events in China, Kampuchea, North Korea and eventually in Rwanda (among others) proved later on. Even democracies were not free of political crimes, as Erich Weede underlined, evoking the importance of "death by government" during the century.[16]

Besides the fact that it concentrates the power within the hands of a few men that can turn out to be abnormal or dangerous once they have reached the top, centralizing bureaucracy also allows slaughters, because it mechanizes, automates and depersonalizes the treatment of individuals, who are reduced to mere abstract cases. This is where its productivity comes from. But this also explains the strange "banality of evil" in these mass slaughters. It does not fundamentally differ from the murder of civilians by military forces during modern wars: the anonymity, the distance between the killer and its victims, the resulting depersonalization of the latter, make their elimination possible. Moreover, that murder is justified by hierarchical authorities to which everyone is subjected in the various aspects of life. The goal is thus legitimated, the psychological cost of the action is minimized and all the conditions are met to maximize criminality so that "everything is possible" as David Rousset wrote about the Nazi slaughters.[17]

That long digression about one of the most enigmatic and dramatic aspects of the century shows that mass murders cannot simply be justified by error, illusion, aberration or collective madness, and illustrates how incomplete this explanation is. Whatever the point of view, the choices made during the past century were not inexplicable aberrations or errors that could have been avoided with persuasion

16. "Death by government" studied by Rummel, quoted by Erich Weede, *Economic Development, Social Order, and World Politics*, Lynne Rieder, 1996, p.18.
17. "Normal men do not know that everything is possible," quoted by Hannah Arendt, *The Origins of Totalitarianism*, Harvest Books, 1973.

and ideological opposition. It resulted from the extremely deep conditions governing human choices, conditions that could not be altered easily and with very significant impact.

These underlying organizational forces determined the fate of nations, the choice of the economic and political systems and the cultural and human dimensions of the civilization, which in turn defined the outlook of the twentieth century.

We must not try to find—as we often do—the cause and responsibility for this century's troubles in the ideologies, since they are largely endogenous and merely fulfill the functioning needs of the dominant organizations. Totalitarian ideologies are nothing but the caricatured reflection of the centralizing organizations' implacable efforts to dominate ever-growing groups of human beings.

Yet, the traditional interpretation of fascist, communist or even corporatist totalitarianism mainly concentrates on individual psychological or psychoanalytic motives or even on the interests of some social groups.

In his book *Interpretations of Fascism*, A. James Gregor gave his four main interpretations of totalitarianism, which merely consisted of explaining the choice of political systems as a consequence of the widespread and indisputable success of totalitarian ideologies.[18] They all come down either to the Freudian explanation—individuals' psychological imbalances and aspirations find an outlet in politics—or to the Marxist explanation—meeting class interests. But why have those aspirations and frames of mind, which had undoubtedly always existed, gained a new significance during the first half of the century, and why have those caricatured conceptions lost their power in the more recent period? There are two answers to these questions: either the theory of error and learning, according to which the people were lured into wrong ideas and then rejected them when their consequences became obvious, or the theory of exceptional circumstances

18. Transaction Publishers, 1997.

(for example, the Depression and the world wars resulting from various kinds of imperialisms). But communism spread long before the Great Depression. And although the previous one (1873–1896) was profound and global, it did not lead to the same political consequences. Besides, the rise in imperialism in itself requires an explanation that the psychological and Marxist interpretations have failed to provide so far. We will show, on the contrary, that the economic analysis of the organization accounts quite well for state expansion which generates first nationalism and then imperialism.

But the totalitarian ideology is above all the instrument that hierarchized bureaucracies, benefiting from a very vast monopoly encompassing whole societies, needed. In a decentralized society, individual frustrations and group interests still exist, but they are no longer expressed through a totalitarian ideology simply because there is no social demand, no productive necessity, for a mass doctrine. Much to the contrary, organizational needs favor individualism, initiative and difference.

The level of competition or monopoly depends on the organization's structure and dynamics, and determines the ideology, that is the general conception of the way the society at large must be organized: a society of independent farmers is unlikely to adopt an ideology advocating collectivization.

The social values chosen and defended in a given society are more or less those which are useful to that particular society and which facilitate its functioning. Otherwise, they would be fanciful, utopian, and would not be adopted by a majority of individuals.

A highly hierarchical society cannot accept much liberty of action and thought. A society of serfdom or slavery cannot advocate a universal vision of dignity and of the inalienable rights of all human beings or else it must give a restrictive and discriminatory definition of human belonging.

Conversely, in an extremely decentralized society, each person must make his own judgments and take decisions autonomously. This is only compatible with a conviction of individual competence and dignity. Philosophical and moral conceptions will thus have to change according to the places and periods to meet the needs of social organization. After all, this is pure common sense if we think that morals mainly aim at setting and enforcing rules to make the life in society possible.

Each transformation in the organizational systems of private productions or public administrations thus change human relationships, that is the culture and "moral atmosphere" of the society. Thus, totalitarianism is the political and social expression of the complete monopolization, of the full centralization of the systems organizing political and economic hierarchical concentration. It represents the most extreme version of dictatorship, that of the single social monopoly.

The race for monopoly itself generates exacerbated conflicts at all levels. When the size of the existing organizations increase, there is only room left for a small number of them, and sometimes just for one. Each must fight for survival with all its might and means. This is what makes interest and ideology conflicts so destructive in these particular circumstances, and leads to the use of the most barbarous methods. In the race for dimension that leads to monopoly, it is no longer a question of making marginal corrections to the frontiers but rather to suppress all the opponents. Unlike during the limited wars of the eighteenth century, the opponent's defeat is no longer enough and its death must come in the end.

If centralization can continue efficiently without any limits, only one society, one organization, one ideology will survive. Most unfortuitously, this reminds us of the Hitlerian slogan of "one people, one empire, one leader." This is simply the pathological ideal of total centralization, of the absolute organizational monopoly.

In more normal conditions, where societies, systems and business firms are faced with "atomistic" competition, where the dimension of each agent is too small to affect the overall social equilibrium, each does its best and works for his own interests without being directly affected by his neighbors' behaviors. Competitors are anonymous and there is room for newcomers. It is important to defend one's business but there is room for everybody, or almost.

But this is no longer the case when being a large organization is a growing decisive advantage. The number of participants must diminish. There is only room left for a decreasing number of firms or states. The aim is no longer to meet the needs of a reduced clientele but to eliminate the neighbor without disappearing. The initial competition between independent actors thus changed into a competition of interactive destruction. Competition within a field has been replaced by competition for the field.

The organizational culture and its ideological expression inevitably reflect the necessary transformation of goals and behaviors. The organization determines the culture and ideology, but not the contrary as claimed by the intellectuals who overestimate the role of the products they manufacture and market, that is the ideas.

This is how the great reversal of the end of the twentieth century was to occur with the decentralizing revolution which reduced the dimension of all the organizations and re-introduced atomistic competition: with this reversal, we drift away from the hierarchical order that was condemned in books such as Bradbury's *Fahrenheit 451*, Orwell's *1984*, and Huxley's *Brave New World*. It also revived the anarchist movements, the trend of "small is beautiful" and the autonomist, independentist and secessionist movements within the nations.

The second twentieth century began with the return of individualism and markets, more especially the political market. In other words, democracy.

CHAPTER 3

The Decentralizing Revolution, 1968–1989

Totalitarianism and centralization reached their apogee during World War II (1939–1945), but the tide turned with the German and Japanese defeats. As empires dismantled, the number of independent states increased and international trade recovered at the instigation of the United States and the GATT. Economic growth picked up worldwide, at least in the countries where industry was already quite developed before 1929. Gradually, as the state and regulatory bodies weakened, domestic markets gained more freedom and the number of democracies increased worldwide.

Undeniably, during the post-war period, states experienced their strongest internal growth due to the development of the welfare state and the associated tax system. But, this internal expansion of states did not challenge the trend towards market liberalization.

The main heritage of the previous period of triumphant totalitarianism remained the consolidation of the USSR as a big power. It had traded its participation to the victory of allied democracies for the expansion of its Euro-Asian empire which, at its maximal reach, covered almost half the world, including its satellites and allies. The conflict between the Allies and the Axis Powers thus gave way to the cold war.

As a consequence, the second twentieth century only really began with the implosion of the Soviet Union and the collapse of communism which marked the sudden and "mysterious triumph of capitalism"[1] over its last surviving opponent since 1917: centralizing socialism.

But everything had begun some twenty years earlier when other shocks had suggested that the world was at the dawn of a new era. 1973 marked the end of the golden age of the post-war economic recovery. The fourfold rise in oil prices decided by the OPEC, the international cartel of oil-producing countries, and the tenfold increase of 1979 that interrupted temporarily the secular downtrend in oil prices, affected severely the economies of oil-importing countries, especially Europe and Japan, which slid into stagflation. This began our era of economic weakness but also of technological and organizational upheavals: it was a time of accelerating opening of national economies thanks to advances in communications and information techniques, of changes in economic policy conceptions, of liberalization and deregulation, of privatizations and break-up of conglomerates.

The last years of the twentieth century saw a clear reversal of all the trends established between 1873 and 1960. These new directions were almost the exact opposite, the inverted reflection, of all those that defined the first twentieth century: de-concentration and disintegration of existing companies, decrease in their average size, dismemberment of heterogeneous states and proliferation of small states, collapse of the last empires, replacement of totalitarian regimes by democracies and development of individualist and anarchist trends supplanting Communist and Fascist mass ideologies, increased control over company managers by owners/stockholders and over state leaders by voters/taxpayers in place of corporatism and dirigisme, economic

---

1. This expression was first used by Paul Krugman in "Capitalism's Mysterious Triumph," *Nihon Keizai Shimbun*, 1998.

opening to the outside world and tougher competition in lieu of state protectionism and collusion. The international monetary order of fixed and managed exchange rates conceived in Bretton Woods in 1944 collapses, unable to resist the growing trade of goods and services and the international liberalization of capital flows, and is soon replaced by floating currencies.

This announced the return of international markets and a global economy. From that point of view, the world is as open and cosmopolitan in 1999 as in 1890 or 1913. For instance, the ratio of merchandise trade to GDP fell from 15.5 percent in 1913 to 9.9 percent in 1960 before bouncing back to 16.7 percent in 1980 and 17.1 percent in 1990. At the same dates, this ratio was 19.9, 14.5, 21.6 and 24 percent in Germany, 14.4, 10.0, 19.3 and 15.9 percent in Italy, 29.8, 15.3, 20.3 and 20.6 percent in the United Kingdom and finally 6.1, 3.4, 8.8, 8.0 percent in the United States.[2]

The dates of all the deep transformations mentioned above are centered around the early 1970s. Given the extent of the changes that they saw, the two decades that followed the trend reversal of 1973 can only be compared to the 1873–1914 period which was marked by the centralizing revolution and the collapse of the economic, social, intellectual and political universe of the nineteenth century.

The evolution of the second twentieth century is the exact opposite of the first. It consists of widespread decentralization and the dismemberment, the fragmentation, of the largest public and private organizations. These transformations directly affect both the firms and the states, thus inverting the secular race for expansion of the size of hierarchies. These changes in the organization of the political and economic relations also modify profoundly the individuals' position in the society, in terms of their relations with both other individuals and the state. It is a decentralizing, democratic, individualist revolution.

2. Robert C. Feenstra, "Integration of Trade and Disintegration of Production in the Global Economy," *Journal of Economic Perspectives*, Autumn 1998.

Already announced in the late 1960s by the success of the anarchist and libertarian ideologies then considered as a consequence of the spectacular baby boom of the post-war period and a logical but turbulent reaction of the young generations attracted—and paradoxically frustrated—by the general increase in wealth, it had in fact much deeper and solid roots.

Underlying technological factors combined to form what some historians and economists call "the third industrial revolution." This revolution relies on the new phenomenon of creative disintegration, explains the striking comeback of the individualist civilization and offers new growth prospects. From an organizational standpoint, the world has taken a quantum leap backward to the pre-1873 era, to the liberal nineteenth century.

THE THIRD INDUSTRIAL REVOLUTION

The revolution that began in the 1960s is in some respects the perfect reflection of that of the 1880s as the mergers and restructurings that it generates make the headlines and worry public opinion. But this is only the tip of the iceberg, the tree that hides the forest. The underlying movements in organizational structures are the exact opposite of what the most spectacular mergers suggest. In fact, they only concern very few companies in specific sectors that have reached their maturity through revolutionary technical advances in other areas of the economy and that are now faced with overcapacity.

Indeed, statistics show that there is a faster increase in the number of small- and medium-sized companies. Instead of inducing multinational gigantism, the Third Industrial Revolution has resulted both in market globalization and a decrease in companies' average size. It is the revolution of small-scale organizations, contrary to what many of our contemporaries believe, as they only follow this trend from a distance in the press and on television.

The Misinterpretation of Mergers

The best analysis on this issue has been made by Michael Jensen, one of the top specialists in the theory of the firm and finance, and a Harvard Business School professor. As was the case during the previous revolutions, a number of ancient activities and companies were made obsolete overnight by technological advances. As the demand for their products and services has declined, they have ended up with much greater production capacities than the markets could absorb. Some of these companies thus had to disinvest or disappear to reduce the overall production potential either through restructuring or through bankruptcy.

But this is only the destructive side of the revolution. The creative side materializes in a burgeoning of new firms, generally small-sized, and shows stunning growth rates.

As Jensen wrote:

> Since 1973 technological, political, regulatory, and economic forces have been changing the worldwide economy in a fashion comparable to the changes experienced during the nineteenth century Industrial Revolution. As in the nineteenth century, we are experiencing declining costs, increasing average (but decreasing marginal) productivity of labor, reduced growth rates of labor income, excess capacity, and the requirement for downsizing and exit. The last two decades indicate corporate internal control systems have failed to deal effectively with these changes, especially slow growth and the requirement for exit. The next several decades pose a major challenge for Western firms and political systems as these forces continue to work their way through the worldwide economy.[3]

And indeed, with the obsolescence of many sectors and big companies, their leaders are faced with a major challenge: switching from expansionary policies and market share conquest to capacity-reducing

3. Michael C. Jensen, "The Modern Industrial Revolution, Exit, and the Failure of Internal Control Systems," *Journal of Finance*, July 1993.

policies, disinvestments and eventually the redeployment of workers and capital into other activities. These strategies are neither thrilling nor rewarding. As big companies' internal management mechanisms—and the behavior they generate—do not easily lend themselves to such an exercise, resistance is strong. One of the ways to reduce production capacities is for the top company in a sector to buy the others and replace their leaders to accelerate the reduction in production, investment and labor volumes.

Technical advances give birth to new industries and lead to the creation of new companies, but paradoxically they also result in mergers in traditional sectors in order to make their collapse less harmful than with plain bankruptcies. As these long-established firms have experienced several years of strong growth and intense expansion, their restructuring is not aimed at making them even bigger but rather removing excess labor and capital resources that are now necessary to the growth of the new activities.

New technologies always generate overcapacity and unavoidable restructurings in the most ancient activities; they do not necessarily increase the ideal size of a company. Technical advances can be of many types: some require big companies while others are most adapted to low production volumes and small workforces.

There is no economic law suggesting that technical advances must always increase the optimal size of a company. And although this ideal or average size tended to grow during the first twentieth century, there is no reason why it should do so today or in the future.

As a consequence, although technological revolutions are always accompanied by waves of restructuring, they can equally result in an increase or a decrease in firms' size depending on the circumstances and the type of innovation. People tend to focus on the mergers induced by the revolution and believe that they necessarily lead to a larger size of all the organizations because the media themselves focus the attention on the largest and thus oldest firms—those precisely that needed to change their strategy and reduce their capacity and the scope of their activities. We keep in mind also the evolution of the Second Industrial Revolution of the 1880s and 1890s, which resulted in the formation of giant corporations. If we combine these two phenomena—the current wave and the memory of the past one—it seems that we are facing a new era of gigantism. But this is wrong as the Third Industrial Revolution is one of disintegration and contraction of firms' size.

The crisis of the 1970s saw the development of many new technologies which added to the existing technical advances such as radial tires, aluminum and plastic wrappings, fiber optics, personal computers, communication satellites, digital techniques for the transmission of sound and images, enhanced telecommunications capacities with new data compression methods, and cellular phones, among many others.

These innovations were accompanied by organizational transformations in companies, reducing the economic advantage that big units with large workforces benefited from. On the contrary, they favored the decentralization of small units thanks partly to more efficient and lower cost telecommunications. This also favored the development of more adaptive "just-in-time" production techniques, "virtual" companies and various forms of sub-contracting. Large-scale hierarchical bureaucracies based on the early-century military model lost their advantage to smaller and more mobile units.

At the same time, the opening of international trade and the progress in a certain number of developing countries increased substantially the world supply of more traditional products generally using poorly-qualified workers. Once again, the eldest companies tended to be the first to migrate towards low labor-cost locations, and this movement accelerated with the collapse of the autarkic communist systems and their inclusion into world markets.

This resulted in a sharp increase in labor productivity and widespread overcapacity in traditional businesses. Excess capacity has four major causes.

First, these technological advances increase substantially the production capacities for a certain capital stock and a given organization. Thus, the power of microprocessors has been growing to such as extent that, with no increase in the quantities demanded, this change implies that excess production capacities must fall by about 90 percent. Logically, prices decrease to stimulate demand, but this is not enough to reduce this new surplus.

Second, technical advances generate overcapacity indirectly by making obsolete traditional goods and services. This is why Wal-Mart spells death for old-line department stores, just like Promodès and Carrefour do with non-specialized convenience stores.

Third, competitive intensity encourages all producers to equip themselves with new technologies, which prompts overinvestment that will only leave very few of them surviving at the end of the process. But none of them could accept to lose this competitive race without even having run it. Otherwise, they would not be entrepreneurs. A good example of this is the Winchester hard disk drive industry. Between 1977 and 1984, venture capitalists invested over $400 million in 43 of these hard disk producers and initial public offerings of common stock infused additional capital in excess of $800 million. In mid-1983, the capital markets assigned a value of no less than $5.4 billion to these companies. Yet, by the end of 1984, this amount had plummeted to $1.4 billion as market openings had been limited by new technical advances in the meantime. Investors and entrepreneurs had been lured by incompatible and unrealistic growth forecasts. The only solution left was to reduce the capacity surpluses accumulated during the period of euphoria.

Fourth, as was the case in the merger wave of 1890–1905, the economic outlook accelerates the ongoing trend. Recessions or economic crisis intensify the movement resulting from technical advances:

> Sharp falls in production costs and prices resulted in widespread overcapacity—this problem was exacerbated by the fall in demand

brought about by the recession and panic of 1893. Although attempts were made to eliminate overcapacity through pools, associations, and cartels, not until the capital markets motivated exit in the 1890s' mergers and acquisitions (M&A) boom was the problem substantially resolved. Capacity was reduced through the consolidation and closure of marginal facilities in the merged. During the decade from 1895 to 1904, more than 1,800 manufacturing firms merged into only 157 consolidated corporations.[4]

The current revolution takes place in very similar circumstances. The tenfold increase in oil prices between 1973 and 1979 disrupted companies' equilibrium conditions—to different extents depending on the sector studied, thus inducing widespread redistribution of labor and capital between the various sectors and companies. The macroeconomic policies conducted to curb two-digit inflation succeeded in about ten years but only at the cost of rather deep recessions, unknown of since World War II. The firms who invested massively during the euphoria of the 1960s to bet on new technologies were suddenly saddled with massive production capacities that markets could no longer absorb.

Indeed, in an industry in excess capacity, where demand does not match the increased production volumes resulting from technical advances, prices tend to fall and companies' profitability deteriorates. When endemic losses accrue, bankruptcy is a major threat. Against these conditions, suppliers have to leave the market through internal restructuring to reduce capacity, bankruptcies or a buyback and subsequent restructuring by the new owners and leaders. This latter solution is easier to implement for newcomers than by the existing managers who conducted the policies which brought about overinvestment and overcapacity. Often, outsiders are the most capable of changing radically the existing policies.

4. Michael C. Jensen, "The Modern Industrial Revolution, Exit, and the Failure of Internal Control Systems," *Journal of Finance*, July 1993.

Bankruptcy or Restructuring: Which Is Best?

Downsizing is difficult to implement as stockholders' internal control is often insufficient to impose the necessary policy changes to the managers who often abhor reducing the size of their company and modify substantially the strategy that they have developed and conducted. This is the "agency" problem that all the companies of which ownership is very diffused are faced with: the salaried company manager does not always share the same interests as the owners/stockholders. The former benefits directly from the development of the company and even more than from large profits. The CEO is better paid in a big firm or group than in a small firm. His numerous and qualified assistants make his work much easier for him. His social prestige depends on the size of the company even if profits are meager.

On the contrary, stockholders do not benefit from the never-ending expansion of their company: what really matters is the profit they get from their property. However, if there are many stockholders each holding only a very small fraction of the company's capital, their direct control on the manager's strategy is quite limited. Managerial democracy is imperfect and imposes itself only very slowly. As a consequence, the manager can make his interests prevail over those of the shareholders during rather long periods. For instance, he will prefer to reinvest the company's profits in new—even though low-profitable or unprofitable—investments rather than redistribute them to the stockholders as the latter course of action may curb its ambitions and limit its power. Thus, companies running on public savings are generally the scene of a conflict between prestigious growth policies and profitability policies.

And the conflict worsens in times of overcapacity:

> In industry after industry with excess capacity, managers fail to recognize that they themselves must downsize. The tire industry is an example. Widespread consumer acceptance of radial tires meant that worldwide tire capacity had to shrink by two-thirds (because radials

last three to five times longer than bias-ply tires). Nonetheless, companies like GenCorp (maker of General Tires) invested heavily in aggressive R&D and marketing programs for their tire business. The response by the managers of individual companies was often equivalent to "This business is going through some rough times. We have to make major investments so that we will have a chair when the music stops." But increased investment seems not to be the optimal response for managers in a declining industry with excess capacity.[5]

Taken to its extremes, this inefficiency of internal control can either cause bankruptcy or trigger a stock sell-off that will drive the share lower and thus leave the company vulnerable to a takeover through which new stockholders buy on the cheap a minority or majority controlling interest and appoint a new board of directors. As it is not a prisoner of previous policies, the new board can make the cost-cutting and size-reducing efforts that were specifically requested by the new owners. Actually the new management is itself interested in increasing the value of the firm as it often gets stock options. The company is thus reformed by reducing its overcapacity.

Sales volumes are crucial to the profitability and survival of companies with high fixed costs. If ten firms share a market and the overall demand in that sector falls by 50 percent, each firm's demand also declines by 50 percent at first. Sales decrease and that is quite enough to convince the firms to cut their prices to limit the damage. The decline can be so dramatic that the selling price falls below the average cost, which implies a loss for the company. However, if the sector has reached its maturity, the price war will be limited, as no company can expect to encroach upon its opponents' market shares given the trust relation with their ancient clients. The sector's balance can only be restored by a number of failures. But the bigger the company, the bigger the social and political drawbacks of a failure (the "too-big-to-fail" argument). These businesses will thus ask for the state's support

5. Michael C. Jensen, "A Revolution Only Markets Could Love," *Wall Street Journal Europe*, January 3, 1994.

and subsidies, try to target other markets or use any other method to avoid the worse. But these techniques often consume resources, including human capital resources, that could have been better used elsewhere.

In some cases, a survival instinct drives the firm to restructure by itself, especially when the manager's compensation is officially tied to stockholder wealth creation. He is thus tempted to increase this value by all means possible, whatever the other human or social costs. For instance, in the post–cold war era of 1991, U.S. defense contractor General Dynamics Corporation appointed a new chairman and CEO, William A. Anders, and a new management team as the company faced declining demand in an industry saddled with excess capacity. General Dynamics stock significantly under-performed the industry and the market, and stockholders had lost 59 percent in the four years prior to his appointment. Anders negotiated a contract that guaranteed him a substantial compensation, total independence, a large pension on leave and a package of General Dynamics stocks and options that were worth respectively $1.4 million and $1.9 million on the day he signed.

From 1991 to his departure two years later in 1993, Anders's strategy was to reduce production capacities, liquidate some of the existing activities and restructure the company totally. From a reference level of 100 in 1991, General Dynamics stocks surged to 653 in December 1993, generating $4.5 billion in stockholder wealth, which represented a dividend-reinvested return of 553 percent. In their financial study, Jay Dial and Kevin Murphy estimated that between $2.3 and $3.5 billion of that wealth increase resulted specifically from Anders's policy.

This example shows that industries having reached their maturity can create wealth through a reduction in production capacities rather than growth. It also underlines the influence of financial packages on the CEO's management policy. In this case, Anders's very lucrative contract was so specified that he did not have to try and increase the company's size, strengthen his position and secure future income. The only target he had to aim for was to turn around the company. Being handsomely paid to do so, he could focus on this problem and leave as soon as it was solved. And so he did. On the contrary, many salaried managers prefer to maintain the company's size and secure their position whatever the cost, and often to the detriment of stockholders.

While company growth is usually a good omen in new activities with growing demand, it often means that resources have been wasted and that the group is losing money in old-line sectors where demand is eroding.

But a turnaround requires that the most ancient shareholders, who have always left uncontrolled managers do as they wanted, pull themselves together and suddenly change their tactics. This rarely happens, especially in companies with numerous stockholders or with reciprocal shareholdings that protect managers from stockholders' demands for returns.

In fact, the most convenient solution is to be taken over by a company governed by an efficient and ambitious manager (the target's stock price is low because of the losses or the low profitability) who will sell whatever can be and rationalize the firm by reducing its staff and incidentally the sector's overall capacity.

And indeed, most M&As only "work" when they are followed by restructuring and staff cuts, by the closing down of the less profitable plants and a refocusing on the main activities. After that, the restructured company is more specialized than the original as it is smaller now that it has got rid of secondary activities and surplus capacities. It is often sold by the new owner, as the acquisition is often followed by divesting.

A study on divesting after acquisitions showed that out of 271 acquisitions made between 1971 and 1982 in the United States, 44 percent of the companies acquired had been divested by 1989. This proves that the main purpose of the acquisition was to change the policy conducted by the management of the targeted firm and not to diversify.[6]

In general however, people find it difficult to understand this mechanism and its social utility. Jensen cites the example of the late nineteenth century political protests against the authors of these reforms that the media and politicians nicknamed "the Robber Barons." The same is true today: people are often scandalized by the shareholders' and managers' wealth that they deem "excessive," as well as by their alleged "short-termism" or short-sightedness in the pursuit of profit, while workers are laid off. For superficial observers it just looks as if workers wealth was simply confiscated and transferred to shareholders and managers.

Because of the economic complexity of all these strategic maneuvers, there is great misunderstanding about the mergers and the recent wave of takeovers and restructurings. Obsessed by the immediate impact of these operations, most commentators do not analyze the broader industrial dynamics. For instance, they note that the joint company resulting from the takeover of a big firm by another is, obviously, larger than any of its components. They generalize this immediate observation and conclude hastily that there is a general trend towards upsizing. But they disregard the more discrete creations of small companies, the spin-offs and the efforts made by the governing company managers to downsize their firms and refocus on their key sectors.

The occasional observers of these large-scale maneuvers only see the most spectacular, but like Fabrice at Waterloo in Stendhal's novel, they never get the big picture. Indeed, this is neither their target nor their job.

They also believe that the purpose of these restructurings is to

6. Steven N. Kaplan and Michael S. Weisbach, "The Success of Acquisitions: Evidence from Divestitures," *Journal of Finance*, March 1992. See also Patricia L. Ansliger, Steven J. Keppler, and Somu Subramaniam, "Après les fusions, les scissions," *Expansion Management Review*, September 1999.

make a lucky few richer—the shareholders—by robbing all the others—the laid-off workers, but this conclusion is also erroneous. There is thus a complete misunderstanding about industrial trends and mergers.

Other recent proofs that the trend is now to downsizing are the dissolution of large conglomerates and the studies estimating the wealth creation resulting from companies' re-specialization, that is their refocusing on their core business.

THE SURPRISING EXTINCTION OF CONGLOMERATES

Remember the extraordinary vogue for conglomerates and the enormous prestige of their managers in the 1960s? At the time, it seemed that the key to prosperity was to build large industrial groups, regrouping various activities according to strategies that were codified in the Boston Consulting Group's famous strategic matrix. But since then, the trend turned towards reengineering, downsizing and refocusing on core business. The time to purchase "portfolios" of diversified activities, administered by non-specialized managers that are supposed to be as competent to work in the banking, automotive and telecommunications sectors and in volume retailing is no more.

The mergers of the 1960s resulted in vast gatherings of companies with very contrasted specializations. The basic principle was that if managers were especially talented for management, they could use their gift for almost any type of production. In other words, the manager of a bank could also administer an airline, a press agency or a steel company.

This is an extreme version of the ideology of the administrative executives who first appeared in the U.S. railway companies in the late nineteenth century. According to this conception, the management techniques were the same whatever the product.

Managers used their "internal" capital market, self-financing some of their acquisitions with the cash flow surplus resulting from other operations within their group (for instance, conglomerates in the United States, keiretsus in Japan, big banks with majority interests in several sectors in Germany and the highly nationalized banking sector under the leadership of the Finance Ministry and Treasury in France). It seemed that internal financing was more efficient than external financing, where the company tapped the market by various means such as floating bond, the issuance of new stocks or bank credit. The group's strategy merely consisted in reallocating the cash flow surplus of its most mature companies towards its promising newly born businesses.

Managers were thus supposed to be universally competent and more capable of reallocating their investments towards portfolios of activities or firms than financial market participants. But the atmosphere has changed so much since then that it is now difficult to explain the origin of the astonishing conglomerate boom of the 1960s.

It is quite unlikely due to the extraordinary superiority of a few managers given the extent of the move: why would the number of competent managers suddenly soar, and why then precisely? But on the other hand, the hypothesis of the superiority of internal capital markets appears vindicated by the stock market appreciation of companies that had announced diversified acquisitions in sectors with no direct link with their key competence. Could so many Wall Street investors have been wrong about their true interests in valuing diversified conglomerates beyond their real value?

In a recent article, finance specialists R. Glenn Hubbard and Darius Palia from Columbia University provide an explanation for the vogue of conglomerates.[7] They explain the financial market's confidence in those conglomeral operations, reflected in an increase in the buying company's stock price, by the superiority of internal financial markets on external financial markets, at the time.

7. "A Reexamination of the Conglomerate Merger Wave in the 1960s: An Internal Capital Market View," *Journal of Finance*, June 1999.

Admittedly, the functioning of external financial markets—stock markets—is imperfect given that information does not circulate easily, financing is scarce, and competition is limited by various regulations (for instance, the forced use of intermediaries such as stockbrokers—although their number is considerably limited by the law—or the legislation regulating stock market listings and public issuance, which are only two of the many obstacles to takeovers). But there remains an alternative that can prove a little more effective: internal financing within industrial groups. A group active in a wide variety of sectors and owning several companies showing cash flow surpluses will reallocate them into the other firms of the conglomerate with cash flow deficits but highly-profitable investment projects. The group's management team is often better informed of the quality of the projects than external investors who put their money in stocks, especially if financial reporting is still limited.

The same is true of countries under development or with incomplete financial structures and imperfect financial markets, such as Japan or Korea. In these countries, large industrial groups (keiretsus and chaebols) systematically use internal corporate financing. There is no need then to finance the company on very imperfect capital markets.

Such was the view of Harold Geneen, one of the most representative figures of the conglomeral universe and manager of International Telegraph and Telephone (ITT), which ranked among the world's largest diversified groups in the 1960s.

> In picking and choosing what companies to acquire [. . .] with our expertise in management and our access to greater financial resources add something to that particular company [. . .]. In most instances, we kept the same management and introduced the company's managers to the ITT system of business plans, detailed budgets, strict financial controls, and face-to-face General Managers Meeting.[8]

8. Harold Geneen and Alvin Moscow, *Managing*, Doubleday, 1984, pp. 206–207.

This means that internal financing was more developed because it was better informed and more reliable than market financing. This also shows that the takeovers of the targeted firms were not disciplinary sanctions: the idea was not to replace a faulty management team and impose new and more wealth-creating strategies, but rather to give to those well-managed firms a financial advantage that they could not obtain by themselves, and moreover to give them the benefit of a centralized managerial control using the methods of private business planning.

Looking at a vast sample of diversification acquisitions conducted in the 1960s, the authors confirmed that the capital gain created is a consequence of the superiority of internal financing and not a disciplinary sanction taken against the management of the targeted firms.

Much on the contrary, in the 1980s and 1990s, companies conducting diversification acquisitions lost money. Conversely, the companies who resold subsidiaries or divisions with activities too distant from their core business saw their stocks pick up sharply.

This marks a fundamental shift: it means that external capital markets became more efficient than the group's internal market over the last decades. This evolution coincides with the various deregulations, the opening of financial markets on the outside world and the increased competition resulting from increasingly cheaper real-time communications, which are the new dominant trends of the past years.

The accuracy of this analysis was also confirmed by studies underlining the still decisive role of internal financing within vast diversified industrial groups in developing countries where financial markets are notoriously imperfect. Subrahmanyam & Titman and Khanna & Palepu thus report the current existence of many vast conglomerates in India, contrary to the structure of the American and European industry, especially since economic opening and modernization of financial markets on both sides of the Atlantic.[9]

9. Avanidhar Subrahmanyam and Sheridan Titman, "The Going Public Decision

Undeniably, this is a good example of the new signification that mergers and acquisitions took, and of the transformations that companies' industrial structures underwent when economies entered the second twentieth century. The trend towards centralization was replaced by the trend towards downsizing although the M&A turbulences that accompanied both may seem identical in the eyes of superficial observers.

Re-specialization and Wealth Creation

Recent mergers confirm that the trend is towards de-diversification and refocusing. They take place in sectors poorly concentrated internationally or nationally and having reached their maturity with market growth rates lower than the country's GDP growth—such as bank, insurance, and pharmaceuticals. As such, their purpose is not to upsize the company but rather to restructure it by reducing the workforce and obtain a more "normal" concentration rate. The economy's financial outlook also has its importance when stock markets are on the rise.

The type of merger depends on the underlying context, for instance new or old industries, economic recovery or slump. They do not all have the same purpose and do not meet the same needs.

The conglomeral merger wave saw upsizing and diversification until its collapse in the 1970s and was followed by a totally different M&A trend in the 1980s and 1990s, when very aggressive management teams started buying exaggeratedly diversified and poorly-profitable firms to resell them piecewise, to cut them into smaller pieces. In other words, to reduce their size.

The aim is opposite that of the 1960s. It was the time of the "chop shop" or company-cutting for the sake of efficiency and profitability.

---

and the Development of Financial Markets," *Journal of Finance*, 54, 1999, and Tarum Khanna and Krishna G. Palepu, "Why Focused Strategies May Be Wrong for Emerging Markets," *Harvard Business Review*, July–August 1997.

Suddenly, "small was beautiful." It was the shareholder's value, the external financing on financial markets, that motivated this desire to refocus on core business, to reduce the field of action of the manager who thus re-specialized in a particular trade. Once again, the shareholders' return was the company's top priority as it had become crucial for its functioning.

The downsizing trend gained momentum. Wealth was created by this fragmentation as it removed the excess infrastructures of companies and their costly and unprofitable equipment. Takeovers and piecewise sales of big companies' divisions intensified as they created wealth by improving the average productivity rate. Now, the total production of ten small independent firms was much greater than when they all belonged to the same conglomerate.

A number of recent studies have estimated the wealth created by these company breakups that also resulted in re-specialization. We have already mentioned the spectacular experience of General Dynamics, but there are many other such examples of substantial wealth gains following de-diversification and refocusing. For instance, Constantinos Markides underlines how companies' business policies shifted between the 1960s and 1980s. Over the first period, one percent of the 500 largest U.S. firms re-specialized while 25 percent diversified. But the trend inverted in the 1980s with 20 percent re-specializing and 8 percent diversifying. And most companies that had re-specialized benefited from stock premiums exceeding normal profitability.[10]

This phenomenon is still hard to understand for the public opinion and the authorities who strongly believe in the axiom that economies of scale are always present so that upsizing always generates

10. Constantinos C. Markides, *Diversification, Refocusing, and Economic Performance*, MIT Press, 1995. These results were confirmed by more recent studies such as Herman Desai and Prem C. Jain's, "Firm Performance and Focus: Long-Run Stock Market Performance Following Spinoffs," *Journal of Financial Economics*, October 1999, which conclude that the spin-offs on financial markets generate more capital gains when they represent a respecialization rather than when they correspond to a simple resale with no specialization strategy.

productivity gains. This idea was fixed in people's minds by seventy years of successful Fordism.

That is why the raiders and the other actors of takeovers and restructurings are so misunderstood. They are often viewed as unable to create "real" wealth and willing to sell off the family jewels, to disperse the existing capital without ever increasing it.

But organizational conditions have changed. Wealth creation through de-diversification is a form of creative disintegration, which has been the dominant trend of the recent years. This downsizing phenomenon concerns both the states and the firms, and gives renewed importance to individuals.

THE RETURN TO SMALL SIZE: CREATIVE DISINTEGRATION

Undeniably, the most striking feature of the late twentieth century was the creative disintegration that resulted from the downsizing of private and public organizations. Companies restructured and re-specialized. States reduced their internal dimensions and often dismantled. Transformations in all organizational structures stimulated the return of individualism which had been announced by anarchist movements and confirmed by the triumph of democracy worldwide. Although the society entered the era of post-Fordism, the previous concepts remained fixed in people's minds.

The pursuit of large size had been the industrial leitmotiv—the organizational credo of the first twentieth century. But it was justified only under particular technological conditions. It was replaced in the 1960s–1970s by the concept of "small is beautiful." For example, in the 1950s and 1960s, mainframe computers were big and costly and could only be bought by large firms and large-scale public administrations. But the invention of the personal computer (PC) gave households and craftsmen the same calculation power. Obviously, they could not buy and amortize cumbersome mainframes nor pay for the large space necessary to store such machines as easily as factories employing thousands and producing several thousand units per month. These high-performance equipments thus had to become smaller and less costly for small firms to buy.

This need was met with the advent of miniaturization, which came as an answer to a progressively more individual than collective demand because of the disintegration of big structures (for reasons that we will study later on). In other words, it is the downsizing of productive organizations that fueled the demand for miniaturization, that was soon met by equipment producers.

Downsizing was everywhere. Craftsmen now had the calculation power that only organizations with thousands of employees, such as the Defense Ministry and insurance companies, could previously afford. Big companies thus lost one of the sources of their productivity advantage on small companies: their exclusive access to high-performance equipments. A very large economic literature has tried to explain this new industrial divide. Small and then micro-companies burgeoned in the new IT and communications services sectors of Silicon Valley, but also in more traditional steel and textile industries of northern Italy.

Economies of scale are no longer a decisive competitive advantage. Size does not matter that much anymore. On the contrary, in these conditions, it becomes a handicap as it is harder (and more costly) to build a cooperation between thousands of employees than among a few dozen colleagues (or less) that the manager of the micro-company will meet every day. Small is more efficient.

It follows that the large business groups, the most heterogeneous conglomerates, are outclassed by smaller-scale companies focused on a core business, and thus more specialized. The small organization perfectly illustrates Adam Smith's theory of the origin of wealth. It is better to be smaller and more specialized than big and diversified.

Despite that, the mergers and acquisitions of the 1990s were often viewed as the expression of an upsizing desire and of the economies of scale made possible by the development of international markets.

Many observers would thus conclude wrongly, but with the appearance of a straightforward logic, that global markets are good for companies because they enable to sell larger quantities of goods and thus to reduce average production costs. Thus, the first company that reaches this advantageous size is more competitive, and those that do not are threatened of extinction insofar as their costs, and consequently their prices, remain higher than the others. In the end, there will only remain one firm in each sector: the world company such as Coca-Cola, IBM, or Microsoft. Yet the misfortunes recently suffered by some of these firms that are among the largest and the most famous should arouse skepticism about the absolute advantage that their big size is supposed to offer them.

World Company or Downsizing?

The biggest area of misunderstanding is undoubtedly companies' growth and globalization. When asked about the motives of the contemporary M&A wave, most people answer that the general opening of markets to the outside world and the worldwide competition resulting from both the removal of tariff barriers and the decline in transportation costs, inevitably force firms to upsize. First, to be active worldwide and second, to benefit from the economies generated by big dimensions ("economies of scale" or "economies of scope"). And the mergers and acquisitions that have intensified in many sectors only confirm this opinion.

More than thirty years ago, in 1968, Jean-Jacques Servan-Schreiber wrote a world-acclaimed book in which he warned Europeans to beware of the "American Challenge" in the form of the "dynamism, organization, innovation, and boldness that characterize the giant American corporations." But in fact this issue had been regularly mentioned in economic literature since the beginning of the century, and more especially, by Joseph Schumpeter who considered that big companies' higher wealth-creation capacity and better quality of management gave them an incomparable advantage on smaller firms.

As a consequence, Servan-Schreiber advocated an industrial policy for Europe consisting of choosing 50 to 100 firms which, once they would be large enough, would be the most likely to become world leaders of modern technology in their fields. They would be the "European champions," a continental and more ambitious version of the French so-called "national champions" which were in such favor with the ministries and governments. Many politicians still dream of that and it is what most of my PhD students answer when I ask them the origins of the contemporary M&A wave: large-scale organizations are a source of creativity and competitiveness in a world economy.

Yet, David B. Audretsch wonders what would have become of the U.S. computer and semiconductor industry if IBM had been selected as the U.S. national champion, say around 1980, and had thus received public assistance to protect it from the competitive threat of Apple, Microsoft and Intel.[11] Would the United States have become the world leader in these industries in the 1990s? Apparently, the conditions of success have changed dramatically since the 1950s, when Charles ("Engine Charlie") Wilson of GM could still proclaim that "what is good for General Motors is good for America." The industries' structure has shifted from stability and concentration to instability and downsizing.

The specialists of this issue have indeed noted a trend reversal in the mid-1970s which now encouraged companies to downsize.[12] At first, it may seem that this is a general move towards the post-industrial society, the service economy, as services notoriously face smaller economies of scale and can be provided by small companies. But in fact the trend is even clearer in the industry than in the service sector.

---

11. *Innovation and Industry Evolution*, MIT Press, 1995, p. 185.
12. Zoltan J. Acs and David B. Audretsch, *Small Firms and Entrepreneurship: An East-West Perspective*, Cambridge University Press, 1993. Gary Loveman and Werner Sengenberger, "The Re-emergence of Small-Scale Production: An International Perspective," *Small Business Economics*, 1, 1991.

And it affects all countries. For instance, if we consider the proportion of small firms (with less than 500 employees) in the overall
economy, we note that this percentage has risen from 30.1 percent in
1979 to 39.9 percent in 1986 in Great Britain. Similarly, in northern
Italy, the share of companies with less than 200 employees increased
from 44.3 percent of the overall economy in 1981 to 55.2 percent in
1987.

And it is interesting to imagine the worldwide consequences that
a policy based on Servan-Schreiber's approach could have had by
looking at the figures of the share of the total industrial production
that came from the 100 largest firms of the most developed countries
during the century.[13] According to this study, the percentage rose
between 1918 and 1970 and eventually declined in 1990, from 22 to
33 then 33 in the United States, from 23 to 22 then 21 in Japan, from
17 to 30 then 23 in Germany and from 17 to 40 then 36 in Great
Britain. A policy of national champions would have handicapped the
United States just like it slowed French growth.[14]

This brings us to a double conclusion: there is no inexorable law
ruling business concentration, and if a trend did materialize during
the two first thirds of the century, it saw a complete reversal during
the 1970s.

If you are still not convinced, there is also the example of the car
industry which is viewed as the best illustration of a mass industry
benefiting from unlimited economies of scale. It is the sector in which
the advantages of upsizing, of the use of global suppliers and of worldwide production is supposed to lead companies inexorably to concentrate into an ever-smaller number of firms. We are regularly told that
there will soon be just enough space left for only five producers in
the world.

And yet, as John Kay underlined in a newspaper article, the con-

13. John Kay and Leslie Hannah, "Myth of critical mass," *Financial Times*, 1999.
14. See Elie Cohen, *L'Etat brancardier: politiques du déclin industriel*, Calmann-
Lévy, 1989, and *Le Colbertisme high-tech*, Pluriel, Hachette, 1992.

centration in the world car industry has been declining since the beginning of globalization.[15] In 1969, the three largest manufacturers in the world—General Motors, Ford and Chrysler—produced one car out of two. In 1996, this fraction had fallen to one out of three or 36 percent of the total. In 1969, there were nine "mega-manufacturers" each producing one million cars a year. In 1996, there were fourteen. In 1969, these nine companies held 84 percent of the market against only 66 percent in 1996. If we define a key producer as one who realizes at least 1 percent of the world sales, then there were 15 in 1969 but 17 in 1996. Whatever the angle under which we look at these figures, we get the same broad picture: the car industry is increasingly less concentrated. The frequent alliances, mergers and acquisitions by which ailing firms were taken over by their rivals were not enough to stop the de-concentration wave. And this trend is deep-rooted. The highest concentration rate in the sector was reached in the early 1950s, when three quarters of the world car production was handled by U.S. companies.

We have thus been living with false ideas for half a century. It takes time to perceive and appreciate fully new realities, and hindsight is needed to conclude a reversal of the existing trends. The supposed advantage of big dimensions and mass production is now considered as an outdated view.

And these restructurings concern not only the private organizations but also the public organizations, the states, considered as political firms.

State Fragmentation and Secession Wars

The conglomeral state is now selling the non-core businesses through which it provided non specific, non "regalian" services. Like private companies who downsized and refocused on their core businesses, the

---

15. "Globalisation, dimension et avantage compétitif," *Le Figaro*, June 26, 1998.

state collected more money by selling these firms than by keeping them. The value—or productivity—of these newly independent firms was higher than what it would have been if they had remained parts of a single giant enterprise consisting of all public sector's industrial and commercial stakes. Unaware of these mechanisms, many opponents to privatization accused the authorities of selling the nation's heritage cheaply to put up with immediate financial needs. But, gradually, people discovered that the firms performed much better once privatized than before.

And this move concerned not only public business firms, but also the states proper, which are giant organizations with all the characteristics of firms except that they are (supposedly) non profit-making. In a similar way, they tried to reduce their external dimensions. Regionalist and separatist claims led to the atomization of the states and to secession—or independence—wars. The growth rate of the newly independent states was often higher than when they were the provinces or regions of a larger country, and this was yet more evidence of the economic efficiency of downsizing.

After World War II, the "world industry of states" tended to decentralize much like the other industries, despite the bipolar influence of the two superpowers at the apogee of the cold war.

The number of nation-states in the world skyrocketed from 74 in 1946 to 195 in 2000. In the language of industrial organization economics, this corresponds to an "atomization" of the population of the firms concerned. Indeed, the steady decrease of the economic weight of the United States in the world economy, and the subsequent collapse of the Soviet Union, transformed the structure of the sector from a duopoly into an atomized competititve structure of small firms, the rivalry of a great number of small- and medium-sized states competing together.

And indeed, most of the new states were very small-sized firms. In 1995, 87 out of the 192 states existing in the world had less than 5 million inhabitants. And among those, 58 had less than 2.5 million inhabitants, and 35 had less than 500,000 nationals. More than half of the world's countries (98 nations) have a smaller demographic dimension than the state of Massachusetts: its population was estimated to 6 million inhabitants in 1990, which represents the median dimension of the state enterprise in the world.

The average demographic size of a state also decreased from 32 million inhabitants in 1946 to 29 million in 1999, despite the world's demographic boom that on the contrary tended to increase the population of the average state.

The atomization of the state industry was partially caused by the disintegration of the empires that essentially took place during the decolonization of Africa and Asia, but also more recently in the Soviet empire when the USSR imploded.

Most colonized territories winning their independence between 1945 and 1965, apparently under the pressure of nationalist uprisings, united into a vast cartel of Third World countries which organized a head-on confrontation with the imperialist West. Denouncing the neocolonialism of the Western world, they tried to spark a North-South economic and political clash while establishing a shared and common management of the world. The duopoly of the cold war turned into a poor/rich duopoly, a sort of Marxist class conflict between nations. But these conceptions faded away in the 1980s when the Third World cartel imploded and disintegrated like the other large geopolitical entities and alliances.

Besides the struggle of the colonized people or their elite, the loss of prestige of European powers during World War II has often been put forward to explain the quick collapse of colonial empires.[16]

But the decolonization wave must also be understood as a movement serving the obvious interests of the Western countries. As Pik Botha underlined, speaking about the end of apartheid in South Africa—a kind of domestic decolonization—"in the end it was simply

16. Touchard and Alii, op. cit., p. 478.

too costly."[17] And most of the European empires had come to that conclusion long before.

Thus, the United Kingdom voluntarily decided to grant independence to its colonies, and in 1962, De Gaulle anticipated the longing for independence of the French colonies in sub-Saharan Africa.

Another reason that is suggested is the increased cost of colonization for the Western powers due to the growing opposition of colonized people and their longing for independence—the guerrillas and the revolts. But in the past, many other rebellions had been quelled or ended in bloodshed.

Finally, another factor to take into account was the decreasing interest in colonization, both in purely economic terms with the re-opening of international markets and in political terms with the decrease of the optimal dimension of a nation.

Whatever the virtue of the other hypotheses, both the new creation of small states and the disintegration of the existing empires can mainly be explained by a series of economic factors such as the development of global markets thanks to the liberalization of trade, but also by the growing social cost of the national tax systems in a world of free movement of goods and people. It is difficult to heavily tax specialists that can easily find a job in other nations or to tax capital that can instantaneously migrate towards more taxpayer-friendly countries. Thus, for a given tax base which remains unchanged, states' taxation capacity tends to diminish. But lower receipts also means lower spending, and first of all, those dedicated to minorities which are far from the center of power (the outlying territories and the colonies) and then the border regions. Assuming that the cost of the public services offered to citizens increases with the geographical distance from the center, large countries are at a disadvantage compared to small ones.

17. Quoted by Ronald Wintrobe, *The Political Economy of Dictatorship*, Cambridge University Press, 1998, as an epigraph of chapter 8.

States chose their demographical and geographical dimension by performing an arbitrage between the economies corresponding to the spreading of the cost of a public good over a larger population on the one hand, and the increasing cost of the supply of these same collective goods to a population that is more heterogeneous when it grows, on the other hand.[18] Hence the diminution of the optimal geographical and demographic dimension of a nation when the cost of the state resources (taxes) increases.

But the domestic dimension of the state, the share of its nation's production—estimated by its spending in the country's overall production—also tended to reverse its trend. That reversal was hesitant at first, but presented by many governments as their new medium-term target.

The reason behind that drop in public interventions—also visible in the broad privatization of public sector firms—was that the cost of the capital invested in that sector had become higher than the likely profits—economic and political profits.[19]

That change in the public sector's balance reflects in the impact of public spending on the growth of national economies. Like private investments or labor, public production contributes to growth by guaranteeing the safety of goods, people and contracts, and by developing material facilities, education and health systems.

There is a level of this spending that maximizes growth.[20] Below it, the productivity of public spending is very strong—higher than its costs. Above it, it diminishes and becomes lower than the costs, which means it is socially unprofitable. And it seems that this is what is happening now. As a result, the impact of public spending on a country's economic growth turns from positive to negative when the dimension of the public sector exceeds its optimal level.

18. I developed more precisely the example of national defense in *Euro Error*, Algora Publishing, 1999.

19. See my article "Nationalization, Privatization, and the Allocation of Financial Property Rights," *Public Choice*, 1993.

20. See the references quoted in *Euro Error*, Algora Publishing, 1999.

Basing their analysis on the example of Canada, economists Johnny C.P. Chao and Herbert Grubel—the latter being a member of Parliament in British Columbia at the time—showed that the effects of public spending on growth have recently inverted.[21] From 1928 to 1960, the increase in public spending as a percentage of the domestic product was accompanied by an acceleration of the growth pace. On the contrary, over the next period from the 1960s to 1996, the correlation became negative: when the percentage of public spending in the domestic product increased sharply, growth slowed down. Admittedly, one could argue that this phenomenon is due to the recent inelasticity of public spending. During the first period, public spending eroded when growth slowed down, with spending adapting to resources, while in the last few years, spending proved incompressible, even in a context of economic slowdown, thus resulting in a negative relation between economic growth and the importance of the state, measured by its share in the domestic product.

But that change must also be explained. Another possible interpretation is to assume that the productivity of public spending changed in the '60s. While before the larger dimension of the state helped to improve economic growth, the same effect is now obtained through the reduction of the dimension of the state. Grubel drew the conclusion that the optimum dimension of the state had been reached in the early '60s, with a share of domestic product close to 27 percent, and had been exceeded since then. But we believe that the optimum dimension itself has changed. Ever larger until the '60s, every increase in spending brought the optimum closer and improved the performance of the economy. Smaller from the '60s on, the dimension of the state introduced a new situation, in which every rise in spending pushed the economy further away from the optimum and reduced growth.

21. "Optimal Levels of Spending and Taxation in Canada," *The Independent Institute,* 1999.

In *Euro Error*, I already provided empirical measures supporting the view of an optimum dimension of the state in the economy. The conclusion we can draw from the study of Chao and Grubel, and above all from the numerous breakups of states and firms, is even more precise: it seems that the optimum dimension changed with time and that it is decreasing since two or three decades.

These changes in the determinants of nation-states' optimum dimension account for the centrifugal and secessionist tensions which are seen everywhere. Not only in Russia and in the Balkans, but also in Spain, Italy, France, Belgium, the United Kingdom—which has just taken a few decisive steps towards regional autonomy—and even in China, Japan and the United States. Decentralization, a limited form of independence, spreads throughout Europe.[22] It also illustrates the efforts to downsize management units.

Finally, because of the newly born organizational, communication, and information economics, large states are left with almost no decisive advantage over smaller ones. Their comparative advantage declines like that of large firms. Companies in small nations or even micro-nations can be as efficient as in large countries because global markets allow them to reach the minimal size that gives them maximal efficiency although the national market is very small.

These factors fuel the disintegration process of the largest and least homogeneous nations. Regional or cultural minorities can now afford a secession because political frontiers no longer need to coincide with those of economic markets. The access to a large domestic market is no longer a major advantage for a firm, as most domestic markets are largely open. The exceptional advantage that the United States enjoyed at the time of the first Ford and the invention of the production line— the large size of its internal market—disappeared during the last decades of the century. The globalization of trade thus fuels the pro-

---

22. John Newhouse, "Europe's Rising Regionalism," *Foreign Affairs*, January–February 1997.

independence and secessionist trends, and makes them realistic from an economic as well as political point of view. It favored the wave of political disintegration, independence (or secessionist) wars and the return of nationalism.

Federalism is merely an intermediate solution in this devolution process and only if the initial pattern is that of centralization and not a multiplicity of nations like in Europe, in which case federalism tends to reduce diversity and generate centralization instead of decentralization—the precise opposite of what is needed.

Parties and Trade Unions: From Mass to Networks

This broad downsizing trend also affected non profit-making firms such as associations, trade unions and political parties. Data about political parties are notoriously viewed as unreliable, but all the comments of the last decades suggest an exodus of their members. The activist parties, the mass parties of the interwar period or the immediate post-war period, all turned more or less quickly into parties of executives and notables, into vote-getting organizations which only rally ahead of the elections. At the same time, mass demonstrations tended to weaken. Parties became coordination networks for electoral campaigns, very much like integrated firms that decentralized, turned into networks with more or less loose relations between subcontractors and other suppliers or ally with similar firms in other countries.

Yet, there are more accurate and quantitative studies about the evolution of trade unions. All conclude that trade unions are faced with a "crisis" or at least an exodus of members. Henry S. Farber and Alan B. Krueger, two specialists of labor economics, studied this continued flood in the United States.[23] They underlined that the unionization rate of wage earners in the non-farm private sector had fallen from 21.7 percent in 1977 to 15.6 percent in 1984 and 11.9 percent

23. "Union Membership in the United States: The Decline Continues," *NBER Working Paper*, number 4216, November 1992.

in 1991. At the same time, this rate increased slightly in the public sector but not enough to offset the decline in the overall rate for the whole non-farm working population from 23.8 percent to 19.1 percent and then 16.4 percent. At the end of their analysis, the authors conclude that this evolution could not be explained by the change in the sectoral structure of the economy, in which the traditionally strongly-unionized sectors would disappear to be replaced by traditionally poorly-unionized sectors. The reason would rather be wage earners' lower interest in trade unions.

The same assessment was made in Western Europe. In a file collected by Janine Goetschy and Danièle Linhart all the authors reported an exodus of members since the mid-seventies.[24]

> The 1980s saw a disaffection for trade unions in most of these countries. . . . [it is] a major turning point in the history of trade unionism in France, Great Britain, Ireland, Italy and the Netherlands.[25]

In France, trade unions lost a quarter of their members (around one million people) during 1975. In 1985, the unionization rate had shrunk to a mere 14 percent and is said to have even collapsed below 10 percent in 1990. In the Netherlands, trade unionism shed more than 10 percent between 1979 and 1986, falling to 25 percent. In the United Kingdom, three million members out of twelve million were lost and the unionization rate thus eroded from 53 to 43 percent. In Ireland, that rate is reported to have decreased from 44 to 36 percent over the same period.

But Germany, Austria and Scandinavia proved more resilient. Outside Europe, the Japanese trade unions experienced a crisis much earlier. While the unionization rate peaked at 55 percent of the working population in 1949, it fell to 35 percent in the seventies and eventually to 29 percent in 1985.

All trade unions went on a diet, a downsizing, at least as intense

---

24. *La crise des syndicats en Europe occidentale*, La Documentation française, 1990.
25. Jelle Visser, "Survol européen" in *La crise des syndicats en Europe occidentale*.

as in business firms. And the decline is not over yet as it was recently reported in the *Financial Times*.[26] From 1985 to 1995, Sweden was the only country to see its unionization rate increase from 83.8 to 91.1 percent although it was already the highest in the OECD. In all the other countries—France, the United States, Japan, New Zealand, Germany, the United Kingdom and Australia—the unionization rates fell further, sometimes by 15 percent or more in the states that were the most unionized initially, such as Australia or New Zealand.

Although the explanatory factors are numerous and distinct, the general trend remains the same: like the other large organizations, trade unions were forced to downsize.

Smaller organizations and less developed hierarchies left a larger room for individual decisions. On the whole, the general wave of organizational atomization seen in the second twentieth century deeply altered social relations, the place of each individual in the society and its relations with the authorities. While he was predominantly subordinated to the organizations at the beginning of the period, the individual returns as a citizen and a sovereign consumer of public services at the end of the period.

26. Robert Taylor, "Collective Responsibility," September 13, 1999.

CHAPTER 4

The Return
of the
Individual

The smallest conceivable social organization is that of a Robinson Crusoe on his island. Individuals are the atoms of society. Does it mean that organizations' trend toward downsizing necessarily implies a trend toward increased individualism? Facts proved that the answer is yes.

All the intellectual and political transformations that occurred everywhere since the late sixties can thus be considered as the materialization of the transformations undergone by all the organizational structures: not only the almost anarchist precursory student demonstrations against the administrative authorities but also the democratic reforms that have toppled the authoritarian regimes—one after the other—from the early seventies onward.

PRECURSORY AND ANARCHIST MOVEMENTS

In the late sixties, student discontent was on the increase in rich countries. They were a good illustration of the individual's revolt against social authorities and established institutions. These were anarchist movements against the bureaucratic order that often tried at first to situate themselves politically—with much difficulty and confusion—

in the traditional early-century divide between the "revolutionary" Left and the "conservative" Right. But for once, they also sometimes criticized the so-called Leftist bureaucracies, that is the state's power in communist countries and the mass communist parties in capitalist countries.

It had all started in Berlin in 1967 with spontaneous student demonstrations. Admittedly, for a few years U.S. students had been expressing their opposition to the Vietnam War and the national military service, and also for a few of them to the racial discrimination against African Americans, particularly in the southern states. The opposition to war and the protection of civil rights, especially those of the Blacks, corresponded to an universal fight for individual rights against the existing society. This is true of all generations but in those years the turmoil was much more intense.

In 1968, riots opposed the students—and sometimes the teachers—of Berkeley and Columbia to the "regents," the deans of these universities. Then, in May, some 150 leftist demonstrators protested in Paris against the working conditions and selection methods of the new University of Nanterre, a Paris suburb, with the support of several hundred sympathizers. One week later, the crisis spread to all the universities and ended in the "Commune of the Sorbonne," an explicit reference to the insurrection of the Paris Commune in 1871. At that time, it was a revolt against the rulers which had caused the defeat of France in the war against Germany. The 1968 revolt was against public authorities, which were accused of having caused the failure of higher and secondary education, and consequently of the students.

During the following weeks, the student unrest spread to the United States and Europe, disrupting life in universities and giving a hard time to the authorities, which often gave in and resigned.

But this phenomenon spread broader than universities and capitalist countries. In July 1968, the Soviet invasion of Czechoslovakia aimed at punishing the Czech leaders who had tried to affirm their independence, which was deemed dangerous and unbearable by the

Russian occupying forces. Pacific but determined resistance arose in the streets. Jan Palach, a student, set fire to himself, like the Vietnamese bonzes who protested against the American occupation.

In 1969, the massive strikes in Poland confirmed the role of protest leader, Lech Walesa, the future president. The same year in August, riots in Belfast put Bernadette Devlin forward. At the same time, fundamentalist terrorism developed in the Middle East.

Anarchists vs. Bureaucrats

The common characteristic of all these events of varying importance was the anti-authority revolt, the decisive role of small groups and individuals and the direct and militant initiative which brought the collapse of the traditional political apparatus. An ideology of protest tried to develop beyond the existing logomachy. It was an anarchist ideology, advocating individual liberty and spontaneous order, and refusing submission to the great hierarchical organizations, armies, universities, governments and centralized bureaucracies. To be spontaneous and express one's own aspirations was the order of the day.

Much logically, the Communists, the greatest supporters of bureaucratic and centralizing organization, were those who aborted the revolution by helping the conservative government. And this is not on a simple whim that Cohn-Bendit especially gibed at the "Stalinian crooks": the Communists were the greatest advocates of hierarchical organization and bureaucratic discipline.

It was not very surprising that the revolt spread so much in France given the extreme centralization of the Napoleonic, military-like, hierarchy that governed universities. Extreme bureaucratic rigidity inevitably leads to occasional but profound collapses. When it collapses, extreme centralization can only be replaced by anarchy, as there is no legal framework that can manage organized decentralization.

The same was true in Germany, where the revolt against the especially heavy hierarchies manifested itself in extreme violence with the atrocities of the "Red Army Faction." A degree of violence that can only be compared to that of the anarchist movements of the late nineteenth century, a period where large hierarchical organizations—both public and private—developed and gained influence.

Beyond the iron curtain, the Prague Spring of 1968 was further evidence of the depth of the nonviolent popular revolt against the Russian army and centralized communism. A revolt that was more individualist and Libertarian than nationalist or economic.

In the United States and the United Kingdom, two liberal economists, James Buchanan and Nicos Devetoglou, tried to take stock of these events which were particularly puzzling for academics of liberal and conservative origins. They published *Academia in Anarchy: An Economic Diagnosis* (Basic Books, 1970), an essay in which they vehemently condemned the destruction of academic institutions that they considered as the guarantors of a certain individualism and of fundamental liberties. And the word "anarchy" that they used in the book's title was the most appropriate, as it meant the most radical reaction possible against the hierarchical order, including that of the large universities, the only organizations with which the students were really familiar, apart from military institutions for a few of them.

In fact, the lack of an organization model likely to replace the large hierarchies called for anarchy. Giving a sociological explanation of the May 1968 protests in France, Raymond Aron stressed that conceptual weakness:

> In the absence of a model that fulfills our aspirations, these bouts of fever essentially appear as being negative, nihilist or destructive. Which model could fulfill the revolutionaries' aspirations given the Soviet model is super-bureaucratic? The true revolutionaries of May 1968 believed in direct democracy, as they were in a sense more anti-soviet than anti-capitalist. However, they presented themselves as Marxists, which is paradoxical given a planned society could hardly be less bureaucratic than a semi-liberal capitalist society. Admittedly, in the latter, there is a bureaucracy within each company,

a state bureaucracy. But a planned society leaves even less room for liberty, people and initiatives.[1]

He was indisputably right, but the subsequent developments, which he could not foresee, then showed that there was nevertheless another conception of social organization, and that there could be a de-bureaucratization and de-hierarchization of the Soviet planned society and of the Western semi-bureaucratic or semi-liberal societies.

Such was the fully justified goal of the revolts of the sixties. They heralded the great return of individualism, liberalism, and markets. All those elements were compatible despite the misunderstanding that appeared in Europe, and especially in France, where individualism was thought to be anti-capitalist. The great tragedy of the "revolutionaries" of that time was that they could not rely on a coherent vision, an alternative ideology as they were—and many still are—obsessed by the traditional divide between "the Right" (favorable to both capitalists and bureaucrats but which advocated markets and individual initiatives), and "the Left" (favorable to both the wage earners and the bureaucrats but which only trusts bureaucratic mechanisms). As they were opposed to the markets, they were eventually rejected by the bureaucratic hierarchy they hated.

That is what makes the success of the Green Party ambiguous today, as it relies on different demands but expresses the same rejection of large organizations. Yet they should note that, although their opponents are mainly the large industrial firms that pollute the environment, these companies can equally be a public company (a nuclear plant) or a private company. The hostility to capitalism, which is expressed through a condemnation of the markets, is mainly due to the fact that the previous period gave the example of a capitalism of large organizations, reducing the role of the market and its individualistic and decentralized functioning.

1. Raymond Aron, *The Elusive Revolution: Anatomy of the Student Revolt*, Praeger Publishers, 1969, p. 47.

Until then, and since the defeat of the fascist regimes, student revolts had resolutely presented themselves as supporters of left-wing parties and ideologies—supporters of the Communist regimes. The domestic protest thus joined force with the external attack of the Soviet empire against the western capitalist-dirigistes regimes.

But with the new anarchist movement, the target changed radically. Political and economic powers, together with political and social authorities, were all lumped together, regardless of their ideologies.

So what did the protesters denounce? A certain organizational mode of the societies that gave a greater importance to the economy and to the markets, or on the contrary the one that gave priority to the community and the political authorities? All the organizations and authorities, all the social powers were a priori suspect. The protesters' ideal was a society of individuals free from any coercion.

The common myth that inspired the anarchist movements was that of the "revolution," on the model of 1917 or 1789. It had the advantage to challenge the authorities, the mandarins, the bourgeois, but also the Communist regimes and their allies, the western left-wing parties, a criticism which had never been heard before. And that myth followed from a romantic conception, which gave to the active individual an excessive role in the social changes. He was supposed to be able to deflect the course of history, just as the governments divert—through constraint and concerted engineering—the course of rivers. This is the myth of the king-individual, the all-powerful individual.

Admittedly, many have objected that this conception was totally immature. But, although the activists spoke with childish words, it seems they well understood that the transformations underway would change dramatically all the societies. It is interesting to note that the former wave of anarchy took place at the very beginning of the modern period, at the end of the (chronological) nineteenth century and at the start of the first twentieth century. In other words, at a time when the society coagulated into a group of centralized organizations: large states, empires, bigger-than-ever firms, trusts and cartels.

Today, it appears in retrospect that the late sixties somewhat marked the apogee of that system. On the world level, there only remained two empires, two superpowers engaged in a more or less latent conflict, while the most profitable firms were also the largest, like Ford or General Motors, state education ministries or even IBM. The big bosses of the world were chairmen of conglomerates, a type of organization that blossomed in the sixties. The standardization methods introduced by Ford in the early century were still in place. Large centralized organizations spread quickly in both the public and private sectors. These large organizations drove growth and sustained the post-war prosperity. The wealth they produced enabled the advent of the consumption society, and above all, the mass consumption of standardized products that Ford advocated for economical reasons, because of their efficiency.

That is what the students broadly "revolutionized" against, as they could not find more accurate words, ideas and targets. They mainly criticized the "mass" aspect of consumption, roughly saying: "If consumption implies being absorbed by an hierarchic, mass society, then given the level of well-being we have already reached, we prefer to renounce to further consumption and gain freedom and individualism."

Commentators focused on the opposition to consumption in general while most of the students' critics concerned mass consumption. It was not an elitist critic of the society either, as some people believe, but only an individualistic critic, with everyone heading their own direction with this slogan in mind: "do your own thing."

Manufacturers got it right, as they managed to fuel ever-increasing sales by offering a very large range of products, given this seemed to be what the population was looking for. There was no renunciation of consumption as a whole but everyone could obtain the variety that enables an individualization of the ways of life. And indeed today, the same basic car model is available in 36 variants, while the number of manufacturers has been increasing in the world.

An Elusive Revolution?

Commenting on the developments of that "elusive revolution," Raymond Aron strongly underlined its anarchist leanings: teachers and students asked the supervision authorities for "true autonomy," "hierarchies, which had always been too rigid in France, suddenly collapsed and were supplanted by egalitarian illusions" and "the only ideology of the student demonstrators [. . .] was to refuse all disciplines. They claimed to follow the anarchist principles, a so-called ideology that was obviously incompatible with the organization of a modern society," and all the practices of the general meetings of the faculties, the scenes of the psychodrama at that time, showed that there was "a symbolic opposition to the apparatus, the administration and bureaucracy."[2]

This is the essential reality that the philosopher and historian has not understood, the opposition to the extreme centralization in all contemporary societies. He indeed assumes that the bureaucratic order of the time was the only possible order in a modern society. So that when he denounced the lack of realism of the anarchistic student protest—which makes good sense—he prevents himself from understanding the legitimacy of the critic that the students direct at a society whose hierarchical system is no longer adapted to the new conditions of the present time.

If revolution is elusive as Aron suggests, it is because its target is ill-defined, which makes its plan wild. The aim is not simply to replace a team of rulers by another at the head of the state but rather to change the world without organizing a substitute power.

In the absence of an alternative or a constructive proposition, the

2. Ibid.

authorities can easily denounce the protesters' irresponsibility, take things in hand again and refocus on serious matters, but not without having somewhat soothed the minds with increased public spending and a few nominal reforms for show. In the United States, the end of the Vietnam War contributed to isolate the student protesters and the former GIs, who were marginalized. In France, the movement was partly taken over by the non-Communist Left, and used to weaken its rivals and partners, the Communists.

Yet the realities that had triggered this international movement did not disappear, and the developments continued in an unexpected but much deeper way than the failure of the anti-authority movements had suggested.

The collapse of communism, the disintegration of large businesses and the political separatisms affected the great pyramids of our time. Individualism made a comeback and large organizations collapsed. Finally, the student protesters were at the origin of a new mutation of which famous liberals like Aron or Buchanan had grasped neither the depth nor the impact, although they had perfectly understood the weakness of the anarchist movement.

And, yet, it is the same individualist aspiration that was at the origin of the triumph of democracy, the crowning achievement of the transformation of the second twentieth century.

THE TRIUMPH OF DEMOCRACY

The three last decades of the century indisputably saw the triumph of democracy worldwide. Whereas the first twentieth century saw the endless proliferation of authoritarian regimes—which all had similar principles and organizational structures despite their declared intentions to describe themselves as "left-wing" or "right-wing," the former emphasizing the interest of the masses and the latter those of the state—the second twentieth century saw their crisis and the collapse of most of them.

In his book *The End of History and the Last Man*,[3] Fukuyama described the new weakness of strong states. He underlined that the crisis of the authoritarian states, that had become obvious to everyone with Gorbatchev's perestroika and the fall of the Berlin Wall, had in fact begun seventeen years earlier with the collapse of several authoritarian regimes in southern Europe: The regime of Caetano in Portugal and the regime of the colonels in Greece in 1974, the end of Francoism with the death of its founder in 1975, then Turkey and Latin America in the early eighties, first Peru in 1980 then Argentina at the end of the Falklands War in 1982, Uruguay and Brazil respectively in 1983 and 1984, followed by Paraguay and Chile at the end of the decade and Nicaragua in the early nineties.

Then the movement spread to Southeast Asia, with the Philippines in 1986, South Korea in 1987 and Taiwan in 1988. In 1990, De Klerk's government in South Africa announced the release of Nelson Mandela and the end of outlawing both the African National Congress (ANC) and the Communist Party, and launched the negotiation process that would later put and end to apartheid.

Like most of the commentators of these evolutions, Fukuyama thought they resulted from an autonomous ideological movement. He thus wrote:

> Both the Communist Left and the authoritarian Right were short of serious ideas to maintain the political cohesion of strong governments, whether they were monolithic parties, military juntas or personal dictatorships.[4]

He then mentions the degeneration that logically took place in authoritarian regimes when the terror regimes—to which nobody could escape—had to give a bit of leeway, with the state then losing the control of the civilian society. But he did not explain why those countries had to reduce the police and military terror, thanks to which

3. Avon Books, 1993.
4. Ibid., p. 64.

they had been able to supervise and control the whole society. According to him, it is only the historical progress of ideologies that lead to the victory of the "idea of liberalism" as it was faced with a decreasing number of rival ideas in the contemporary world. Thus, with enough hindsight, one could realize that the universal history of humanity had a general sense that would lead, despite temporary cycles and occasional reversals, to liberal democracy.

Fukuyama indeed admits that the current trend toward democracy might only be a cyclical phenomenon. And indeed, back in the late sixties, democracy was threatened in various regions of the globe. And we can also wonder whether the current crisis of the authoritarian regimes is not due to a most extraordinary chance that might not reoccur before long.

Indeed, the events of the last quarter century seem to support the cyclical interpretation the author showed in a table listing the liberal democracies in the world.[5] Latin America counted fewer democracies in 1975 than in 1955 and the world as a whole was less democratic in 1939 than in 1919.

Thus, out of 36 developed countries, the author counted 3 democracies in 1790, 6 in 1848, 14 in 1900 and 20 in 1919, but only 9 in 1940, 22 in 1960 and 36 in 1990. When he also took the developing countries into account, he reported a much later apparition of democracy—it was almost non-existent before 1960—and thus a sharp reinforcement of the trend toward democracy in the last decades.

But one must not confuse the long-term global trend toward democracy (when economic advances increase the living standards) with the democratic fluctuations seen during the century in countries already developed. In theory, democracy is linked to economic development. Not because the "democratic or liberal idea" becomes more convincing—as we pointed out in the previous chapter, when we mentioned the opposite trend that leads from democracy to totalitar-

5. Fukuyama, op. cit., pp. 74–75.

ianism—but because a hierarchical society with a centralized organization calls for an authoritarian mode of functioning in which individual liberties are an obstacle to the good functioning of the whole; on the contrary, a decentralized organization where downsizing and markets are the watchwords, requires a lot of independent individual decisions, that is an individualistic functioning based on personal judgments. These are also the prerequisites of democracy.

As, in a democracy, the government is controlled by the masses, all the members of the society regain the right to speak and the power that was monopolized by the center in the authoritarian regimes is redistributed to those members. From subjects, they turn into citizens. Each person is granted the right to inspect, censor and appoint the collective power instead of only being a tiny cog in the machine, subjected to the will of the top.

Democracy is thus the expression of a certain type of individualism, although it is ambiguous given that it consists in taking collective decisions—those of the governments, of the states—that will then be imposed on all the individuals, including the minorities.

Yet it is individualistic since it must necessarily grant the individuals rights so that they can exercise their power of control over the executive: civil law, political rights.

In companies, democracy is represented by the demands of the shareholders who ask for a policy that will increase the value of their shares (their own target) against the managers' personal interests. It is a sign of de-hierarchization and of a development of financial markets. The same is true for the relations between the voters and the rulers, depending on the extent of the development of the political markets compared with that of the political firms that the state and parties are.

It follows that our interpretation of the democratic revolution that took place at the end of the cycle of the twentieth-century organization is based on the transformations introduced by the decentralizing revolution that we have just analyzed. The general downsizing of organizations and the subsequent weakening of individuals' hierarchical subjection enabled the restoration of the central role of individual decisions and judgments, the freedom of choice and consequently, the necessary freedom of thought which is its prerequisite.

It is this organizational cycle, which originated from the hazards of technological progress, that brought the renewal of the democratic and liberal revolution.

Thus, we can conclude with Fukuyama that if the general accumulation of wealth continues, markets are also very likely to develop further (as J.R. Hicks underlined[6]), and with it, liberties and democracy (as our analysis suggests). But if the hazards of technology lead in the future to renewed effectiveness of giant centralized and hierarchical organizations, then democracy and liberties may well decline again, even if wealth accumulation goes on. The second twentieth century thus appears as an exceptional and privileged period that will not necessarily last forever.

That is why democracy and markets are closely related. They are mechanisms for decentralizing decision-making, diffusing the decision and control powers[7] which become widespread when the economic and political markets develop, that is when the hierarchical organizations weaken and lose their importance within human societies.

THE CONTEMPORARY INTELLECTUAL DISARRAY AND THE NEED TO EXPLAIN HISTORY

Two major turning points punctuated the cyclic course of the twentieth century: the Communist challenge of the 1917 Russian revolution—that marked the end of the former liberal and capitalist civili-

6. *A Theory of Economic History*, Oxford University Press, 1969.
7. Eugene Fama and Michael Jensen, "Separation of Ownership and Control" and "Agency Problem and Residual Claims," *Journal of Law and Economics*, June 1983. And also Harold Demsetz, *Economic, Legal, and Political Dimensions of Competition*, North-Holland, 1982.

zation—then the collapse of communism with the second Russian revolution of 1989–1991. In both cases, these turning points occurred after the development of major technological revolutions: first, the centralizing and administrative revolution from about 1870 until the end of the nineteenth century, and second, the decentralizing and democratic revolution that has gained ground since the late sixties.

But today the collapse of one of the two protagonists of the political, economic and military clash between capitalism and socialism deprives us of the traditional framework that dominated all the debates about societies' organization since the Second Industrial Revolution. And the new reversal of all the previous trends that accompanies that collapse only makes that period even more obscure and enigmatic. If contemporary history is no longer based on the uncertain conflict between two nations and two opposed political and economic regimes, what are now the terms of the choices confronting modern societies?

And how could a system, whose flaws were constantly denounced and whose death had been announced since Marx's *Communist Manifesto* in 1848, recover and prevail over its rival—socialism—that most observers in the sixties still praised as obviously superior, morally and economically? In the same vein, several future economic Nobel-prize winners who taught and wrote in the fifties deemed that the dirigisme or state ownership was the only way to organize a national and international economy efficiently, as Andrei Shleifer reminds us:[8]

> Half a century ago economists were quick to favor government ownership of firms as soon as any market inequities or imperfections, such as monopoly power or externalities, were even suspected. Thus Arthur Lewis[9] concerned with monopoly power, advocated the na-

8. Andrei Shleifer, "State versus Private Ownership," *Journal of Economic Perspectives*, Autumn 1998.
9. W. Arthur Lewis, *The Principles of Economic Planning*, London: George Allan & Unwin Ltd., 1949, p. 101.

tionalization of land, mineral deposits, telephone service, insurance, and the motor car industry. For similar reasons, James Meade[10] favored "socialization" of the iron and steel, as well as the chemical industries. Maurice Allais,[11] always a step ahead of his English-speaking peers, argued for the nationalization of a few firms in each (!) industry to facilitate the comparison of public and private ownership. At that time, privatization of such services as incarceration and education was evidently not discussed by serious scholars.

These comments by future Nobel Laureates were part of a broader debate over capitalism, socialism and the role of planning in a market economy, which raged in the 1930s and 1940s. . . . A remarkable aspect of this debate is that even many of the laissez-faire economists focused overwhelmingly on the goal of achieving competitive prices, even at the cost of accepting government ownership in non-competitive industries.

And Shleifer goes on citing Henry Simons (1934), Pigou (1938), Schumpeter (1942) and Robbins (1947). Of course, this was not true of Hayek, but he was for long rather lonely and marginalized. And Friedman, Stigler, Buchanan, Coase, North, Becker and Miller were to make their contributions on the topic a bit later, beginning in the '60s with Friedman's intellectual revolution, monetarist and capitalist, which was at the time deemed "extreme" by mainstream economists.

How indeed is it possible today to escape intellectual disarray when the classical liberals and socialists alike, who all claimed they knew what the best societal organization was, were proved wrong by history one after the other, some during the first twentieth century and the others during the second? Or is it that some were wrong and the others were right all the time but that it takes quite a while to prove them so? But in that case, how could half of the humanity have

---

10. James Edward Meade, *Planning and the Price Mechanism: The Liberal Socialist Solution*, London: George Allen & Unwin, 1948, p. 67.

11. Maurice Allais, "Le Problème de la Planification Economique dans une Economie Collectiviste," *Kyklos*, 1947, p. 66, quoted by Andrei Shleifer, op. cit.

been wrong so long? Or is it that both camps' definition of the ideal society was wrong? In both cases, it appears that misconception is proved to dominate human societies. Hence, the great skepticism about our ability to understand the order of these societies.

This was summarized very clearly by James Buchanan, one of the founders of the public choice theory. He refers to economic systems but his conclusion also applies to political systems:

> We are left therefore, with what is essentially an attitude of nihilism toward economic organization. There seems to be no widely shared organizing principle upon which one can begin to think about the operations of a political economy.[12]

That echoes the aforementioned reflection of Paul Krugman, according to whom the great question with the twentieth century is why three quarters of a century were spent supporting values hostile to markets and free trade, while the latter were on the contrary fully rehabilitated during the last quarter.

Economic liberal ideas, which had seemed definitively dead and buried, made a stunning comeback. The latter is difficult to quantify but unquestionable, as proved by the new tone of the political leaders who marked the eighties, Ronald Reagan and Margaret Thatcher, as well as by the broad recognition of the analyses of Milton Friedman (rewarded by a Nobel prize of economy). The same was true for several liberal economists, including Gary Becker and James Buchanan, after Friedrich Hayek.

Thus, the problem which now dominates the public debate is that of decentralization. Other evidence of this comeback is the striking similarities in decentralizing movements that affect both business management and political management.

It is true that during the first twentieth century even American and British democratic capitalism underwent the general movement of concentration of firms' productive apparatus that led to the devel-

12. "Socialism Is Dead; Leviathan Lives," *Wall Street Journal Europe*, July 19, 1990.

opment of giant companies, large trusts, conglomerates and to the increased weight of the centralized political power that resulted in corporatism. That clearly shows the universality of the factors in play. But today the reverse trend is also seen in the societies that remained rather decentralized. The return of the markets is accompanied by a challenge of the vast state apparatus. Indeed, democracies and markets are linked by the general and parallel evolution of public and private organizational structures. Both are mechanisms that decentralize decision making and diffuse the power of control.

The theoretical and practical acknowledgement of the complementarity between democracy and markets leads us today, in retrospect, to reject or at least moderate the indetermination that Schumpeter mentioned in *Capitalism, Socialism and Democracy*. According to him, the economic centralization of socialism does not depend on the political regime chosen and is not incompatible with a democratic regime. It is true indeed that some kind of economic centralization, mainly private or due to nationalizations, may have occurred in western democracies without pushing them into dictatorship. And, on that issue, the fears of Hayek have not been confirmed by subsequent developments: a greater intervention of the state in the economy does not necessarily, nor automatically, lead to the extremes of totalitarianism and serfdom. But this is because we dawdled on the way, so that the decentralizing revolution caught up with us while we were still in largely decentralized societies. On the other hand, the societies that came closer to full centralization had to abandon the idea of democracy and thus opt for authoritarian regimes. Economic centralization and political centralization necessarily merge when they are taken to their extremes.

These observations lead us to underline the fundamental unity of economic analysis and political analysis, and give the priority to the essential concepts of concentration or centralization of decisions and organizations. The great cycle of the twentieth century is to be understood within this common framework and we have described its general and deep consequences.

Yet, the reason for the ebb and flow of centralization must still be explained. Which factors determined the global movement of the organizations and consequently the fate of our societies?

PART TWO

The Fundamental Question

The upheavals, the political, economic, and military earthquakes that punctuated the twentieth century, brought about significant mutations of the existing social order, the structure and functioning of the society's hierarchical and market organizations. To understand what happened (and what is still happening), it is necessary to analyze more precisely in what respects the social order has changed and what determined (and still determines) these transformations.

During the past century, most observers believed that the trigger was the competition between the political beliefs or ideologies, the drastically simplified representations of the existing political and economic systems. Their common implied reasoning is based on a vision of life that philosophers would describe as "idealist" or "platonic" in the sense that once the intellectual conception of the good society, the idea, has spread among people or among the elite, it influences the political authorities and the rulers who in turn apply it to the social reality to build a regime resembling, more or less, the initial abstract system.

With this process, the rulers' decisions are discretionary when the democracy is neither total nor direct: an autocrat or a government who is not fully controlled by his people's will still can apply the right system or not. The choice of the concrete regime is thus both centralized and discretionary. In turn, this gives great importance to the "intellectuals" which are "system engineers," manufacturers and traders of ideas. And it is because of this vision of their own influence on societal transformations that they are so willing to advise the rulers.

Thus, the twentieth century political and economic debate confronted the capitalist and socialist (or national-socialist) systems, or in other terms, the private and state ownership regimes, since no other form of collective appropriation could be found that would work without a state. It thus reduces the choice of society to a choice between the market and the state, or more exactly, between the markets and private firms on one side and the public administration on the other.

Conflicting Systems or Conflicting Nations?

In people's minds this dichotomy was vindicated by the simultaneous development of the state and its bureaucratic apparatus, and the emerging socialist critique of the nineteenth century "capitalist" regimes. Admittedly, the rise of statism and interventionism was accompanied by a reduction of the market area to the benefit of the administrative economy. But the conviction that a choice had to be made between two antinomic systems was born out of the conflict between two nations, the United States and the USSR, which both seemed to be respectively the ideal type or the elected champion of each of the two systems.[1]

1. This view is based on the conceptions of the nineteenth century socialists who, following Marx, considered the communist system as the natural and designated successor of the economic regimes existing in Europe and in the United States and that they described as "capitalist." Politics thus turned into a dilemma between two opposed and conflicting organizational systems. This view was shared by the Liberals (Schumpeter, Hayek and Friedman) who believed that a binary choice between the market and the state had to be made but criticized the growing control exerted by

According to the ideal type view, all contemporary nations thus had—it seemed—to make the fundamental choice between these two superpowers. This decision was viewed as discretionary and, depending on the personal preferences of the rulers and their people, on their preconceived political and social "convictions," a bit like when a consumer has to choose between two models of cars or two dishwashers. Each one is free to prefer either the "American" or the "Communist" model, or even (for the least courageous or hesitant) a mix of the two in variable (and there again arbitrary) proportions. It thus seems that the societies' political and economic organization is a question of aesthetics. As the ultimate "consumers of social systems" citizens are free to choose them according to taste and color. In the end, they must base their decision on their comparative experiences of the economic and political performances of these representative countries and of their regimes. Ideologies there are but a form of political advertising, each speaking highly of its product but with little credibility.

After a long and indecisive period during which the Soviet system seemed to outperform the American system, the trend eventually reversed. The final collapse of socialism and the implosion of the USSR gave credence to the idea that capitalism was definitely better than

---

the state over the economy all along the century.

According to this common "Marxist-Liberal" vision of history and political and economic systems (in other words, contemporary societies' "fundamental constitution" or "social contract"), private property and markets are the main determinants of the systems' effectiveness, with one side emphasizing the superiority of markets and private property, and the other the superiority of the state and public property. This simplistic conception of political choices became dominant because of the state's growing control over liberal economies, the world conflict between liberal democracies and the more dirigist totalitarian states, and more particularly the cold war between two superpowers, the United States and the USSR, who in the end respectively embodied the capitalist or market society and the Socialist or Communist society. As the cold war dominated world politics after World War II, it reinforced the idea that the main political issue was to chose between the American and Russian systems, between the Liberal and Marxist conceptions of social organization.

socialism and that there was no longer any other option to organize societies. This idea was reinforced by the crumbling and the defeats of corporatist (or hierarchical) capitalism in Japan and Asia, in France and Germany under the combined effects of the financial crisis and the M&A and restructuring wave. The statist "third way" misfired and the new concept of "Rhenan capitalism" became a forgotten page in history books as soon as it was theorized. All this evolution seems to support the idea of a dilemma of the systems that would have described properly this century's developments and conflicts. In this framework it seems that the political issue is for each government to choose, in a centralized way, the best system that should then be fully applied to the real society. This debate was supposedly settled at the end of the twentieth century, when it turned into a survival ordeal that could only leave the really good system running, thus signaling the end of history.

But a closer look reveals that this likely scenario, like Kipling's *Just So Stories*, has the appearance of a serious explanation but cannot be viewed as a rigorous description of reality. Indeed, the dilemma that this conception initially sets between two well-defined systems is basically shaky. It neglects the fact that some organizational characteristics are shared by all nations and does not take into account an essential part of economic realities. Besides, even the idea of being forced to choose all or nothing between two polar systems is proved false by all the experiences of the various countries during the century. And finally, although the idea of a ruler choosing the society's system discretionarily and in a centralized way is flattering for him and his advisers, and seems realistic, it is in fact superficial and does not reflect the real decision-making mechanisms.

This view belongs to the "constructivist" misconception of society that Hayek often denounced, while at the same time took seriously as a real possibility. The Fascist and Communist experiences convinced him that governments really chose the country's social system discretionarily, while in reality totalitarian rulers merely legalized by reforms and coups the ongoing transformations resulting from deep-rooted and uncontrollable social determinants, and claimed paternity afterwards. A more matter-of-fact study of politics leads us to believe, with the sociologist Michel Crozier, that a society cannot be reformed by decree. Like any other, organizational choices result from a multitude of individual decisions that determine the social structures which rulers must take into account.

In chapter 5, we will see how a society's organizational system is chosen and subsequently analyze the economic determinants of these choices in chapter 6. We will then broaden our analysis to the international organization of nation-states and their relations in peace and war.

All in all, this second part of the book will give us a broad picture of the general conditions that explain this century's deep transformations of the internal and external social order. It will also give us a means to sort out, in view of the ongoing events, the possible trends from the theoretically impossible ones, and we will study this issue in a concluding chapter focusing on the competitive state in a global civilization.

A Clumsy Dilemma

The commonly shared "Marxist-Liberal" vision is that of a war between societal organizational systems that expresses itself as a dilemma between two diametrically-opposed models: socialism and capitalism. One would have to choose either the state only or the market only, as a mix would be regarded as a false, inefficient, and intellectually unjustified solution since each of the "pure" systems claims its absolute superiority. However, a dilemma can only exist if its terms do not intersect and together cover all possible choices.

But, in this instance, this dualistic vision born from the military conflicts between capitalist democracies and totalitarian nations does not describe two mutually exclusive alternatives. Real societies are not "all-market" or "all-state" organizations, and nothing indicates that the mixes of public and private economies that most of them adopt (in various proportions) are unstable and forced to evolve towards the most extreme mythical solutions. Even Hayek carefully underlined that he had never asserted, in *The Road to Serfdom*, that democracies inevitably turned into totalitarian states with time. He only warned people against such an eventuality that he thought could be avoided by increasing public opinion awareness.

In any case, the dilemma of the extremes is clumsy. The dichotomy on which it is based does not reflect economic realities: first, because these two categories do not cover the entire scope of social organizations, leaving aside those that are neither state nor market, and also because they share common ground, which is the case of the concepts of capitalism and socialism especially, since the former includes the latter as a special case.

Moreover, the two presentations of the dilemma used in politics are not equivalent. Capitalism vs. socialism? State vs. market? Is it the same? Public and private property of production means is what distinguishes the two elements of the first alternative. The extent to which equity ownership rights are distributed and capital markets are developed is seen as crucial. But there are several types of capitalism, more or less open and bureaucratic, where financial markets are more or less developed and sometimes non-existent, and where capital property is more or less concentrated. In particular, the Asian variety or the European statist banking capitalisms.

The other presentation of the dilemma, state vs. market, makes the distinction between a particular type of hierarchical organization on one side and a decentralized decision-making mechanism on the other, without taking into account all the reality of the private hierarchies that companies are. Many Liberals consider "free enterprise" and "market economy" as equivalents. And it is true that there are more markets in economies where most firms are private than in Socialist statist economies. However, across the world and more especially in the United States, twentieth-century "market" economies were mainly based on a hierarchical institution: the corporation. The corporation is not the market: even if it sells products and buys goods and services on markets, it is built internally on an authoritarian and hierarchical structure. The corporate hierarchy is based on the principle of military command. It functions much more like a public administration than like a market.

From the inside, hierarchical organizations such as General Motors, the Bank of Italy and the World Health Organization have a lot in common. Employees work in similar conditions under the direction of superiors on whom their daily work and promotion depends. This is what William Niskanen, a classical liberal economist and an academic specialist of bureaucracy, underlined after having worked for the U.S. Defense Department and before becoming Ford's chief economist: "A government bureaucrat who joins Ford feels at home and is thus immediately operational." And his colleague Gordon Tullock logically concluded: "In other words, these structures are very similar."[2]

Presenting the dilemma as an opposition between capitalism and socialism is also untenable. While communism is clearly defined by state property and the almost total centralization of production decisions, the opposed system—which is supposed to be unique—is designated by the uncertain and inadequate concept of "capitalism," whose incoherence has frequently been underlined by many economists.[3] In the economic sense, a system is capitalist if it uses inten-

2. Gordon Tullock, *Economic Hierarchies, Organization and the Structure of Production*, Kluwer, 1992, p. 41.

3. Friedrich Hayek: "Generally, the words capitalism and socialism are used to describe yesterday and tomorrow's society. They conceal rather than explain the transition that we are experiencing" (*The Road to Serfdom*, Routledge, 1944, p. 36).

The word capitalism itself only appeared in the early twentieth century long after communism as Braudel underlined (*Civilization and Capitalism, 15th–18th Century*, part 2: *The Wheels of Commerce*, Harper Collins, p. 275). Debating with Bastiat, Louis Blanc gave it a new meaning when he wrote in 1848: ". . . [That is] what I would

sively the capital, the machines and even human capital according to its more modern sense. All modern societies, including the Socialist, are obviously capitalist. Capitalism, which defines as the intensive use of capital, is a notion that applied perfectly to Stalin's Russia and today to all the societies in the world, contrary to the primitive societies that accumulated little, if any, capital. "Socialism" has no other sense than that of state monopolistic capitalism where political authorities own all the country's capital except human capital—although slavery had been partly reintroduced in the Nazi and Communist totalitarian societies. In a rigorous sense, these notions do not define mutually exclusive categories of existing societies.

Among those, some choose state capitalism and the others a form of capitalism that authorizes the private property of companies' capital

---

call capitalism, i.e. the appropriation of capital by some to the detriment of the others." In 1867, Marx still ignored the word. And it is only in the early century political debates, especially in the scientific field with Sombart's *Der Moderne Kapitalismus* (1902), that it gained recognition as the logical antonym of socialism. Braudel concluded: "it is thus a political word" (p. 276).

During a long time, this word was criticized by the economists because it mixes a "hodgepodge of meanings and definitions" (Herbert Heaton). Alexander Gerschenkron simply considers it tantamount to the industrial system ("Capitalism, that is the modern industrial system," *Europe in the Russian Mirror*, 1970, p. 4). And he is undeniably right in the strict technical sense, i.e. that of a capitalistic production system that uses intensively the "technical capital" (durable equipments). In that economically-founded definition, it is clear that all modern economies—which are industrial before focusing on services—use technical capital intensively.

Even Hayek finds it difficult to define the terms of this opposition. While he considers that the concept of socialism is well-defined and a synonym of planning, a centralized economy, statism, he finds no single word to describe the opposite system. He uses one after the other the words "capitalism," "competition," "a society" or "a market economy," "liberalism" or "a freedom society."

As we underlined, all these terms have major drawbacks: (1) the meaning of capitalism is so general that it includes Socialist societies, (2) competition is not always respected on all the markets that can be monopolies or oligopolies, (3) in a market economy, corporate hierarchies play a major role, (4) the definition of liberty or liberties has always been elusive.

The only distinction that designates mutually exclusive categories and that enables us to sort out according to a single criteria all the societies is the centralization or decentralization of decisions and of the organization of production.

and the free trade of these ownership rights on capital markets. Similarly, all modern economies use corporate bureaucracies—whether public or private—to organize most of their productions. In fact, the main difference lies in the degree of concentration of these companies' ownership. When the state owns most of them, it groups all the activities together within a single bureaucracy that manages them all and distributes them the necessary capital while suppressing market exchanges between firms, prices and competition. On the contrary, when there are several private owners, there are also several independent hierarchies whose activities are coordinated by goods and capital markets, competition and prices.

What differentiates the various economic regimes is neither the degree of "capitalism" nor the institution of the corporation, but rather the degree of centralization of property and decisions. The political problem of system choice does not consist in choosing between such polar concepts as capitalism and socialism but rather between different degrees of centralization from an infinite range of possibilities. The Soviet Union and the Unites States only represent two specific solutions among many others.

This assessment cannot be reduced to a play with words. It puts a serious question mark on the rationality of the mythical opposition that rules all the debates and analyses about political systems. If that opposition is incoherent and does not fit with reality, the debate is distorted and has no effect on that reality.

Indeed it is the very incoherence of this opposition between capitalism and socialism that prevents us from understanding the astonishing upheavals of the twentieth century: the initial triumph of statism and communism, and more recently the collapse of socialism and dirigism. Who was wrong then? The dirigist centralizers which were acclaimed from 1917 to 1989 or the Liberals who were pushed aside from the end of the nineteenth century until the last decade of the millenium and only had *in extremis* the marvelous surprise of the collapse of socialism? As the capitalism/socialism dilemma does not take into account the fact that there is real diversity of capitalisms in which states continue to play a major role (a much greater one than in the nineteenth century), it does not enable an understanding of the ongoing evolutions. If socialism was really that better, why did it collapse? If markets and private property triumphed in 1989, why did not the state rapidly lose power and why does it still take a 40 percent to 50 percent cut of the national product in rich countries, as the Liberals wonder?

With the roulette of history, the last winner cannot be sure to continue to cash the dividends of a favorable fate.

Neither does that false dichotomy explain the global decline of democracy during the first twentieth century that resulted in dictatorship and totalitarianism, and its revival at the end of the century other than by the results of World War II and the cold war. This does not teach us anything about the initial triumph of authoritarian regimes and suggests that if these wars had ended differently, democracy would not have reemerged. It leaves undetermined the ambiguous relation between economic systems and political regimes: capitalism can be either authoritarian or democratic and the same would be true of socialism, although to a lesser extent.

Contemporary history will remain incomprehensible if we stick to the Marxist-Liberal alternative between the state and the market that takes no account of the existence of firms, and if we support the theory of an automatic escalation of all regimes towards the extreme cases of total planning or "all market," which has never been satisfactorily justified or confirmed for the simple reason that it does not exist in reality.

Organizational Economics and Individual Choices

To solve these mysteries and address these unanswered questions, economic analyses require a better-defined framework that takes into account the degree of development of not only the state but also the firm. This implies an analysis of the organizational modes of production. The organization of societies is above all the organization of production in the broad sense, including political production, the production of collective safety and goods. And the fundamental choice of any social activity for the production of private or collective goods and services is between the market and the hierarchy, the latter including firms and states as specific cases.

Winner of the 1991 Nobel Prize in Economics for his explanation of the existence of firms in a 1937 article entitled "The Nature of the Firm," Ronald Coase puts the emphasis on the contrast between markets and firms. When companies' ideal size increases, markets tend to decline, and conversely when markets develop, hierarchies shrink. Williamson generalized this reasoning by presenting hierarchies, companies' fundamental mechanism, as a substitute for markets. We can thus infer that, as a consequence, the opposition between the state and the market appears only as a particular case of the opposition between the firm and the market.

In this view, the main determinant of any social organization is companies' optimal size and consequently the area left to markets in societies. But the markets' importance can be reduced by the development of both public hierarchies (and the state which governs them) and private hierarchies, that is corporations.

This economic and organizational view of social system choices easily explains the parallel evolution of all the societies' organizational structures during the twentieth century. Thus, the trend towards hierarchization was illustrated by both the triumph of the Communist regimes, where giant public companies were supervised by a central planning body, and the concentration of the giant private companies that used internal planning in cartellized—oligopolistic or monopolistic—private capitalist countries such as the United States and Germany, and often in cartelized mixed capitalist countries, like for instance in France and Japan. That is why "capitalism" and "socialism" evolved in such similar ways.

That way, the course of the twentieth century seems much more coherent and is provided with a general explanation. The optimization of hierarchies' dimensions drives nation-states into either nationalist and imperialist expansionism and war, or fragmentation, separatism, and world peace at times of downsizing. The same analysis can explain the part played by the state in a national economy of a given size, and adding to that the centralization rate of private hierarchies which evolve in the same direction, also explains the politico-economic system of a nation.

There is thus an infinite range of possibilities: a very centralized politico-economic apparatus results in socialist planning, while a discreet and decentralized state, small companies, and developed markets, gives a liberal capitalism. An intermediate development of public and private hierarchies determines the dirigiste French-style capitalism and a wide range of more or less corporatist mixed systems.

But these choices are not made in a fully-centralized way. That would only be possible in an already fully-centralized society that would ban any activity outside its single hierarchy. In all the other less extreme cases, it is the individuals who choose either to work independently on markets or to integrate the hierarchical pyramids of private or public companies. They make their decision according to the costs and rewards of each alternative. And if we sum up all these individual choices made according to economic opportunities, we obtain pyramids more or less big and numerous and more or less developed markets. A society's organizational structure thus results from a number of decentralized decisions. Generally, the choice of a society is not a "macro-decision" but rather results from a multitude of "micro-decisions."

In Chapter 5, we present the terms and conditions of the basic individual choice between markets and hierarchies that has to be made for all human activities and in all the economic and political sectors. The overall structure of a society depends on the choice individuals make between markets and hierarchies. The overall centralization rate which characterizes that structure also defines the dominant type of human relations, market transactions or subordination. In turn, the organization of the society resulting from those individual choices affects all aspects of people's life and the characteristics of the civilization.

What then are the determinants of individuals' choice between working independently on markets and being subordinates within hierarchies? As usual in economic analyses, the costs and rewards will be the main determinants. Individuals will opt for the most efficient and thus the most profitable mode. Markets and hierarchies will develop until their efficiency falls to the same level of the other production mode.

The more or less general adoption and development of either of those two basic mechanisms within a society thus depend on their cost differentials, which mainly result from the way they use information: markets use a lot of it and hierarchies much less. In the latter, only the decision maker consumes information that he then shares with the other agents. Conversely, on markets, each participant must collect his own information and only for himself.

Thus, in a society where information is rare and costly, hierarchies are a more economical production mode as they require little information. On the contrary, in a society where information is plentiful and cheap, markets can develop as each participant can obtain cheaply the information that he needs to produce and adjust its output to that of its competitors. The "theorem of organization" can thus define the organizational structure and the centralization rate of a whole society according to the availability of information in this society (Chapter 6).

As a consequence, the evolution of politico-economic systems depends directly of the economics and technology of information. A society with little information will be centralized, hierarchical, statist, and even totalitarian. Conversely, a society with abundant information will be decentralized, commercial, egalitarian, individualistic, democratic and liberal. The impact of information on the organizations is the key to understanding the evolution of societies' social order over the twentieth century.

But can that analysis also be applied to the other basic trends of the twentieth century, those that affected the general framework of all contemporary societies, the nation-states, whose size and relations have changed so profoundly over that period?

Well, it can, as our analysis of nation-states' systems shows in Chapter 7. The geographical dimension of nation-states depends on the numerical dimension of public organizations and private companies. Nowadays, an average state employs around 10 to 15 percent of its working population, a little more than 2 million people with whom it controls and provides public services to an average population of 30 million inhabitants (the median dimension of a state is only 6 million inhabitants) over an average area of around 270,270 square miles.

Like in other firms, the size of this administrative hierarchy depends on the availability of information. When information is rare, large states have a cost advantage over the smaller ones, because they amortize the purchase cost of a given information over a larger number of constituents. It is this economy of information sharing that gives their superiority to the largest states.

When information is abundant and cheap, even the smallest states can buy it, so that large states do not benefit from a significant cost-spreading effect. And as small states can answer better the demands of populations that are smaller and more homogenous, they have an advantage over bigger ones. Like big firms, large states will thus disintegrate, fall into pieces, reduce their overall size, and small states will blossom.

But the relations between states also depend on whether the general trend which affects them all is towards upsizing or downsizing (Chapter 8). From conflictual in the first case, they become neutral or peaceful in the second case. Unexpectedly, the availability of information thus defines the structures and evolution of the "world state industry" and governs peace and war between nations.

CHAPTER 5

The
Organizational
Choice

Whether an organization is based on market mechanism or on
the authoritarian relation that characterizes hierarchies, the gathering
of many individuals within organized societies enables task specialization, which is impossible with small groups living in autarchy. And,
as Adam Smith underlined, it is the specialization of labor that makes
wealth production efficient. But specialization also poses the problem
of the difficult coordination of individual activities.

In a collective production process, each specialized and independent producer only manufactures one part, one particular element or,
in other words, a single "component" of the end product that will be
sold to the consumer. It can be a tangible good, like for instance the
engine of a car or the chip of a cell phone, or an intangible one, a
service. The producer of each component chooses independently the
precise characteristics and the production volumes that he intends to
offer to his potential clients. In those conditions, how can the production of all the components of the end product or service be coordinated? How can elements designed and produced separately be
assembled into something coherent—a product whose parts are compatible, properly connected and produced in the right quantity? How
can we be sure that a car or a television works and is aesthetically

pleasing, and that a mobile phone will be able to be connected to all the other telephones of the world network?

The universal problem with collective productions is to coordinate individual efforts and have all the specialists cooperate. It is the problem of how to organize production, to structure the relations between the producers, as organization is precisely meant to define the conditions of cooperation between a group of individuals.

There are only two ways to organize the most basic cooperation, that between two individuals only. These two coordination mechanisms are: voluntary market transactions and hierarchical subordination. What differentiates them is the distribution of the decision-making power, the answer to the question: who decides? In the decentralized mode (market transactions), each individual decides for himself what action he should undertake. In the hierarchical mode, only one person decides and the other accepts the directives and the orders given in return for a given pay.

These two organizational modes are mutually exclusive: if there is a market transaction between two individuals, there cannot be a hierarchical relation between them or within the group they belong to. On the contrary, if one of them accepts to be subordinate, there is a hierarchy, and the possibility of a negotiated market transaction thus disappears between these two people, as long as the hierarchical relationship is maintained.

Hierarchical organizations can be more or less developed and be composed of more or less employees. But each time they recruit new employees, they supplant the market mechanism that person used before to determine and sell its own production.

While the relations between two individuals merely implies a binary choice—all or nothing, market or hierarchy—a society necessarily consists of a multitude of hierarchical organizations of various sizes and of more or less developed market areas. As a consequence, societies' overall level of centralization evolves continuously from absolutely no hierarchical organizations (in a fully decentralized society)

to Stalin's Soviet society which merely consists of one giant hierarchy—a single pyramid that covers all social fields and where all the
decisions are eventually taken at the top.

In this continuity of organizational solutions, the degree of concentration of decision-making, that is the society's overall centralization rate, depends on the size of individual pyramids. The bigger the
average pyramid, the more individuals it contains, the fewer pyramids
there are in a society with a given population. And the fewer the
hierarchical organizations, the fewer the decisions makers, the hierarchical heads, as the other members of the hierarchy do not decide
for themselves. It follows that the decision-making process is all the
more concentrated as hierarchies are bigger and fewer. Moreover, the
development of large hierarchies reduces the market domain where
there are as many decision makers as individual participants. Consequently, the fewer the markets, the bigger the hierarchies and the
higher the society's centralization rate.[1] On the contrary, when the
optimal pyramids are small, there can be many and there will be as

---

1. The centralization rate is not the concentration rate that economists calculate.
In an economy with many companies, the concentration rate measure the disparities
between their respective sizes. The fewer the very big companies and the more numerous the very small ones, the higher the rate. If all the companies have the same
size—whether big or small, the concentration rate is minimal.

The centralization rate measures the concentration of decision making within a
smaller or larger group of individuals. It is the total number of decision makers in
the society divided by the total number of subordinates. For example, if there are 100
companies in a society consisting of 1,000 individuals, the centralization rate is 100/
1,000, i.e. there is one decision maker per ten subordinates. If the number of companies falls to 10, the centralization rate will be 10/1000, i.e. one decision maker per
1,000 subordinates. But, if there are no hierarchies but only independent craftsmen,
the centralization rate is 1,000/1,000 = 1, i.e. there are only decision makers and no
subordinates. The decentralization rate thus ranges from 1 (full decentralization) to
about 0 (concentration of all the decision making powers in a single person within
a society with a very high population).

As such, the centralization rate is directly correlated to companies' average size
measured by the number of employees. When the average company is small, the
centralization rate of decision making is low and when the average company has
many employees, the centralization rate is high.

many hierarchical decision makers. Moreover, there are more market transactions between several small hierarchies than between a few big integrated hierarchies. For the same population and production as in the previous case, the society's structure is thus much more decentralized.

THE SOCIAL ORDER

Politico-economic systems define a social order: a set of stable and established relations that rule the exchanges between individuals. The latter choose to belong to a society because of the production and consumption possibilities that the environment of an organized system offers, in opposition to what can be considered as the natural state in which men lived over a million years, in small nomadic groups of hunters-gatherers. In the numerous sedentary societies that developed since the invention of agriculture, the relations between individuals implied either subordination or consensual negotiations with shared decision-making power. The former result in the creation of hierarchically structured groups for production purposes that are commonly described as "organizations" although this word has a more general meaning of "order" or "system." In the restrictive sense it is considered as a synonym of "hierarchical organization," although there also exists decentralized and non-hierarchical organizations such as markets. In this book, it will have its common hierarchical meaning and if it does not we will specify as often as necessary that the organization we are referring to is a decentralized or a market organization.

An Organization of Organizations

The goal of any organization is production. Each of them is a group of individuals working as a team and producing collectively goods or services. This is true of industrial and business firms but also of athletic associations, universities, political parties, trade unions and public administrations who produce collective services focused on security, justice and wealth redistribution. To this list should be added the conglomeral state which produces a wide range of collective goods, and sometimes even private goods, under the sole leadership of its government and head of state.

Organizations are omnipresent in contemporary societies and have very different purposes.[2] Herbert Simon, one of the pioneers of organizational analysis, underlined their ubiquity:

> Suppose that a mythical visitor from Mars approaches the Earth from space, equipped with a telescope that reveals social structures. The firms reveal themselves, say, in solid green areas with faint interior contours marking out divisions and departments. Market transactions show as red lines connecting firms, forming a network in the spaces between them. No matter whether our visitor approached the United States or the Soviet Union, urban China or the European Community, the greater part of the space below it would be within green areas, for almost all of the inhabitants would be salaried workers and would thus work in firms. Organizations would be the dominant feature of the landscape.[3]

The society, in its contemporary sense of the largest community that an individual can join, is an organization given it is an "association of persons."[4] Its definition is the same as for an "organization" which the dictionary describes as "a group of individuals involved in long-lasting and organized relationships, most often established as in-

---

2. Thus, according to Douglass North: "Organizations include political bodies (political parties, the Senate, a city council, regulatory bodies), economic bodies (firms, trade unions, family farms, cooperatives), social bodies (churches, clubs, athletic associations) and educational bodies (schools, universities, vocational training centers). Organizations are made up of groups of individuals bound together by some common purpose to achieve certain objectives."

3. Herbert A. Simon, "Organizations and Markets," *Journal of Economic Perspectives*, Spring 1991.

4. As Bergson wrote: "Human or animal, a society is an organization."

stitutions and protected by sanctions." In other words, the terms "organization" and "society" describe the same realities.

However, it is convenient to distinguish between basic organizations (groups only composed of individuals) and societies (organizations composed of both individuals and simple organizations). A society is an organization of organizations. For instance, a nation (a national society) is composed not only of isolated individuals but also of a large number of smaller organizations such as regions, districts, trade unions, and families, which can be involved in various relationships. And the largest complex and non-hierarchical organization is the whole group of the world's nation-states as a whole. It is the global society or the society of nations, which accepts as members the organizations of organizations that nations are.[5]

There are thus different strata of organizations who sometimes juxtapose and sometimes stack within one another like Russian dolls. Unlike basic or simple organizations which are only composed of individuals, the society is an encompassing organization, an "envelope" organization consisting of a multitude of individuals and complex (or composite) organizations. We thus concur with Braudel who defines it as the "set of all sets" ("l'ensemble des ensembles").[6]

The national society, the most common and largest type of human societies after the world or global society itself, is mainly governed by the rules or institutions of the state in which it is located and which defines its geographical frontiers, unlike organizations such as firms

5. The national society can even exist without an international legal structure such as the League of Nations of the interwar period or its successor, the United Nations, given its components, the national societies, define its morphology (the number of members they are composed of and their relative dimensions) and accept some common behavioral rules. It is not a hierarchical or centralized society but a society with no common goal, a decentralized society which functions more like a market or rather an anarchic state which, unlike a market, does not follow common rules or institutions accepted by all participants.

6. Fernand Braudel, *The Perspective of the World: Civilization and Capitalism 15th–18th Century.* New York: Harper & Row, 1979, chapter 5.

or families who do not have a major territorial component.[7] The state, the encompassing organization which defines on which territory all the other organizations are, is characterized by a specific goal: the production of collective services which we will call "political production."

But is it really possible to perform the same analysis on profit-making organizations such as business companies and universities, churches or states?

Political production and private production are considered as two distinctive fields of contemporary social sciences. However, the decision to make this distinction is quite recent as economic sciences have given up studying politics since the beginning of the nineteenth century only. But since all organizations, whether public or private, have seen the same transformations during that century, it is necessary to show that the structures and management techniques are indeed the same in political organizations and private business organizations. Organizational economics, which is sometimes defined as the economics of institutions, is a new branch of economic sciences that concerns all organizations. And the recent emergence of an economic analysis of politics, called "public choice," shows that there is a trend towards a reunification of these sister disciplines given their fundamental problems are similar and require the use of the same conceptual tools, those used in the study of the choices concerning the allocation of scarce resources, which are precisely the instruments of economic analysis.

---

7. However, like families and firms, a nation-state's borders can also be defined by the people that it is composed of, that belong to it. Instead of using the concept of territoriality to define the word "national" as it is often the case, we can use the notion of filiation: national societies can thus introduce two types of rights of citizenship based either on kinship or on birthplace. However, they are composed not only of individuals (subjects or citizens) but also of many organizations: families, firms, associations, churches, trade unions, public and private administrations, the state, whose relations are defined by rules or institutions.

Political Production

Politics concern everything that is related to cities (*polis*) and by extension to societies, given cities were the first form of modern society in human history. Since the Neolithic agricultural revolution, when food resources increased suddenly, men have lived in increasingly larger societies instead of staying in small groups of hunters-gatherers. In highly populated societies, politics basically consists of producing a particular type of goods: public or collective goods.

Politics are often opposed to economics as if they were two totally distinct "spheres" of social activity, governed by diametrically opposed behavioral logics and pursuing fundamentally incomparable goals. But in fact the difference between both fields is much less obvious and even becomes insignificant when we consider the evolution of institutions. Just as private companies' organization is studied the same way whatever the sector (aeronautics or banks), the same principles do apply to both business and political firms.

Indeed, like other economic activities, political production necessarily has to answer to the following questions: what to produce, for whom and at what price? It also converts scarce resources into more useful goods and services. Politics are thus no more than a particular branch of the economy given it is also subjected to the laws of supply and demand, and to the selection of the most effective combinations of scarce resources.

Admittedly, each sector of an economy is different from all the others given each product is unique: a car is not a software, a concert or a novel. Production processes differ from one product to another as they use specific techniques, and cars are not commercialized through the same distribution networks as books and concerts.

However, the same economic laws apply to all goods and services. And many products can be classified according to common characteristics in large and more or less homogenous sectors. In its well known classification, Colin Clark distinguishes the primary sector (agriculture and mining) from the secondary sector (industry) and the tertiary sector (services).[8] Here, it is the nature of the product which determines the distinction.

There is, however, another distinction that is undeniably even more important for our societies: public and private goods. Here again, it is the respective characteristics of the products that make the difference. Admittedly, the state can produce private goods such as cars and telephones, goods that can be both bought by any individual consumer and commercialized by private firms. But it is not because that car or telephone is produced in the public sector that it will become a public good.

True public goods[9] are those that cannot be sold or exchanged retail but are produced wholesale for a group of users who do not pay directly for their use: the safety of goods and people, legal order, national defense. These services are states' "core business," the business where states have a decisive competitive advantage and for which they are in fact irreplaceable. Indeed, unlike the goods that are private by nature for which each consumer buys the quantity that he needs and which often differs from that bought by his neighbor, collective services can only be consumed in one quantity identical for all users, the one that is produced for the whole community. Hence, the commonly accepted idea that the public sector guarantees equality in consumption.

Once produced, these services will automatically benefit each citizen. This specificity results from two characteristics: non-rivalry in use and the difficulty to exclude some consumers or give only a selective access to the good. Hence the commonly held view according to which politics is capable of providing free goods.

---

8. Colin Clark, *The Conditions of Economic Progress*, London, Macmillan, 1939.
9. The traditional definition is that of Paul Samuelson: a public good is "one that each person can consume or use without subtracting from the consumption of the same good by others" ("The Pure Theory of Public Expenditure," *Review of Economics and Statistics*, 1954, vol. 36, p. 387).

The non-rivalry of consumption means that the use of a good or service by a person does not prevent this same service from being simultaneously available to other consumers, which is not the case of a private good like bread or books: if someone buys a loaf of bread and eats it, he will prevent other people from consuming the same loaf of bread at the same time. Conversely, the national defense is available to all the citizens of a country simultaneously. The benefits that it brings to one of them does not prevent the others from also taking advantage of it. A new resident can also benefit from this service without stopping the existing population from using it as they did before his arrival. In fact, the same unit of the product is consumed by several people.

The non-excludability results from the fact that once such a good or service is produced, it is available to everyone. Thus, once the Defense Department is created, it is difficult or impossible to prevent a particular citizen from benefiting from it. The state cannot stop him from consuming this protection, except if they expel him from the territory. The availability of this service does not depend on each citizen's capacity to pay. It automatically extends to all the other users from the moment the service starts being produced.

Because of these two characteristics, the private production of such a service is difficult and often practically impossible. As he cannot exclude some of his consumers, the private producer cannot ask for his service to be paid, given each of them can benefit from it for free. It is impossible to negotiate a voluntary payment in this case. To finance such a good, the producer must be able to force the consumer to pay and exclude from this social group (or territory) those who refuse to remunerate this contribution. For that, it is preferable (if not crucial) to have both a means of constraint to tax consumers and a territorial monopoly so as to spread the production costs over a large number of taxpayers. Hence, the necessity to have the monopoly of violence.

As we will see later on, the state, which initially set up through its specialization in the use of violence and consequently granted itself the legal monopoly of violence over a given territory, is exceedingly well placed to produce these kinds of services.

There are only very few "technically" true public goods and the most well known are the defense, the interior security of goods and people, the justice and police, the country's language, the currency, part of the elementary education, and, in contemporary times, some aspects of health—which is said "public" for that reason—such as compulsory vaccinations against contagious diseases.[10] However, we will add to this list the redistribution of incomes that shows the characteristics of a public good in the sense that a given redistribution of income is imposed on all members of a society: by definition, there is only one income distribution per population at a given time.

Although public services' characteristics are thus very different from those of private goods, the state is a producer just as any other productive organization. It finds an advantage in producing services for consumers that it cannot always control and on which it depends. It is thus faced with a demand from its market—the political market— where a government—in a democracy—provides a range of services in exchange for the votes that enable it to exert its management power and finance itself. Votes are indeed a means of payment for the public services provided. They are like many tax direct-debit forms, or credit lines, granted in advance by the taxpayers to the future government.[11]

As for any other firm, the political production rate of the state

10. The fight against contagious diseases is "indivisible" as everyone must be vaccinated to eradicate them.

11. In a dictatorship, the government is not free from constraints: by definition, the dictator is submitted to the control of a smaller group of individuals than in a democracy. Tullock (*Autocracy*, Martinus Nijhof, 1987) and Ronald Wintrobe (*The Political Economy of Dictatorship*, Cambridge University Press, 1998) have analyzed the dictator's strategy who must not dissatisfy the army and the members of the sole party too much if he wants to remain in power. Although the political market is smaller in that case, it plays almost the same role as an electoral market in democracies.

firm is determined by the costs and earnings of the marginal production. The political program—the program ruling the production of collective goods—is developed to the point where the government has reasons to believe that the taxpayers' marginal dissatisfaction is greater than their satisfaction. If it develops its production beyond or below that level, it may disappoint its people and thus be forced to hand over the responsibility for the political leadership to another government team who will perceive better the expectations of citizens regarding the services they accept to finance with their taxes.

The mechanism for the provision of a basket of public goods paid on a lump-sum basis on the political market is thus the same, at the margin, as for a good sold per unit at a given monetary price on a commercial market.

"Economic" and "political" activities are thus fundamentally similar. They are simply two distinct sectors of the economy in spite of apparent dissemblance. Their respective hierarchical organizations and the respective markets where exchanges are made work in the same way. In both cases, human decisions must be taken concerning the production and consumption of goods and services in a situation of scarcity of resources. The same is true when choosing the production's organizational mode. There are private hierarchies and markets in the economy and political hierarchies and markets in the sector producing collective goods.

And yet, the big difference between the political exchanges between the state and its citizens and the private economic exchanges in our ruled-by-law societies is the existence of a right to violence on only one side of the market: the state's side. When private agents make exchanges within a law abiding society, they cannot use violence, precisely because of the state's monopoly.

That is why economic analysis, which consists mainly in the study of private exchanges and monetized markets, did not take into consideration (until recently) violence and coercion. Traditional economics always consider exchanges as being "consensual." As they result from a reciprocal or shared will, they do not require the use of force which is only considered as a pathology, a dysfunction of the economy.

And this is why the economic theory of illegal, unlawful and violent behavior only developed rather recently both for individual acts such as theft and other offenses,[12] and collective acts such as revolutions and coups d'état.[13]

But the new theory including violence is crucial to understand the states' behavior who regularly use violence or the threat of violence between them or against their subjects or citizens. The state is not only a producer but also a predator. And it is as a rational predator that it becomes a producer as we will see.

Before that, we will study the ubiquitous and general choice between the organization modes of team productions—whether they concern public or private goods—that we have just proved similar in many respects. This organizational choice is the universal problem of social order.

THE PYRAMID AND LATTICE ORGANIZATIONAL PATTERNS

Obviously, collective/team production requires some cooperation between the individuals involved, harmonized decisions and complementary production choices: the good produced, the volumes, the methods and materials used, the production cost, the quality targeted, the deadline and the price. But there are two diametrically opposed ways of cooperating: either by centralizing decisions or by decentralizing them.

---

12. Gary Becker, "Crime and Punishment: An Economic Approach," *Journal of Political Economy*, 1968.

13. Gordon Tullock, *The Social Dilemma: The Economics of War and Revolution*, Center for the Study of Public Choice, 1974. Jack Hirshleifer, "The Technology of Conflict as an Economic Activity," *American Economic Review*, May 1991; and "Anarchy and Its Breakdown," *Journal of Political Economy*, 1995.

In a society, the polar organizational modes are total centralization on one side and total decentralization on the other. The relational pyramid of the former contrasts with the lattice pattern of the latter, the market network. As the word "network" generally refers to a number of relations structured around a central point (road network, railway network), we will use the word "lattice" given it makes no reference to a central point or hub, even though it has the disadvantage of evoking a rigid architectural design.

In the centralized mode, one individual makes decisions for all the others who accept to submit to his directives and act in compliance with his instructions. This is hierarchies' basic organizational principle. The coherence of the whole depends on the manager's vision. Flows of goods and services are coordinated by implementing the decisions taken by higher grades, especially as hierarchical order consists in ranking an organization's members according to their decision-making skills. Higher-grade decisions necessarily impose themselves on lower grades or subordinates. It is the manager who selects the characteristics of the product, its price and its delivery date to the producers of the next stage of the value chain. Within a hierarchy, these internal "clients" do not choose their supplier among many others: they always work with the same supplier whose identity is predetermined by its belonging to the organization and its position within it.

On the contrary, in the decentralized mode, each individual makes his own decisions. Cooperation and the complementarity of individual decisions are obtained by gradually matching the production of some to the demand of the others, and by a reciprocal adjustment of individual productions, while no producer dominates the others. It is an exchange between peers. It is a market organization. Markets coordinate flows by expressing and confronting individual supply and demand and the transactions between the various suppliers and demanders. It is those exchanges that define and gradually modify the characteristics of the goods and services, the prices, the volumes and the production rate of intermediary goods at each stage of the value chain. The buyers of goods or services compare the supply of the various producers and chose one of them according to the preferred mix of their characteristics.

It follows that there are only two types of organizations in simple societies, those composed of two individuals: 1) the organization based on exchanges whose terms have been defined by a mutual agreement and where decisions are made by all independent participants ("free" or market exchanges) and 2) the organization based on hierarchical exchanges between a ruler and a ruled, where decisions are only made by the decider (subordinate or hierarchical exchanges).

The two types of organizations are differentiated by the centralization or decentralization of the decision-making process. Within a hierarchy, a common decision will have to be followed by all the members of the organization. The decision is centralized. In the case of the decentralized market exchanges, there is also a common target (to take part to a transaction that will be profitable to both parties) and thus an organization, but no common management as each trading partner retains its decision-making autonomy. The decision is decentralized.[14]

Variants of both mechanisms exist but they fundamentally belong to one or the other category. For example, when a producer is the sole supplier of one or several clients, he stands in a quasi-hierarchical position[15] (a monopoly), given his clients cannot choose other potential suppliers as is the case in a market. And yet, the producer and its clients are independent entities and their exchanges are ruled by the price mechanism. It is often the case with subcontracting as we will

---

14. The concept of "market" is often misunderstood and reduced to the meaning of "monetized" markets but there can be market transactions in all the consensual (or even partly consensual) exchanges between individuals that do not belong to the same hierarchy.

15. It is not a totally hierarchical position given the client can choose the quantity he will buy while this is impossible in a hierarchy.

see later on. Similarly, a single buyer, a "monopsonist," who uses several suppliers experiences market conditions given he can choose between several suppliers.[16]

The two production modes imply very different costs. This is why firms—hierarchies—exist and grow instead of having fully decentralized production processes only. The *raison d'être* of a firm (and more generally, a hierarchy) is to reduce the costs of operating the production process.

Let's take an example that illustrates the difference of costs between the decentralized market production and the centralized hierarchical production.

The Alternative

A computer is composed of many elements such as the screen and the central processing unit which contains the chip and the hard drive among others. With a decentralized market production, there would be screen producers and fitters manufacturing CPUs.

To complete the production process, we would have to assemble the screen with the CPU. But in our example of the industry there are 3 screen producers and 3 CPU fitters. What assembly, which combination of screens and CPUs will we chose? That is the problem of the meeting between suppliers and clients.

There are nine possibilities of transactions between the six CPU and screen producers as shown on page 159:

Each possible transaction, each possible match, between a screen producer and a CPU producer is materialized by a connecting line, which leaves us with a lattice pattern representing all the combinations possible on this market: A-D, A-E, A-F, B-D, B-E, B-F, C-D, C-E and C-F.

There are 9 (3×3) such combinations. Each craftsman must in-

16. Thomas W. Malone, Joanne Yates and Robert I. Benjamin, "Electronic Markets and Electronic Hierarchies," *Communications of the ACM*, June 1987, p. 485.

Market and Hierarchy

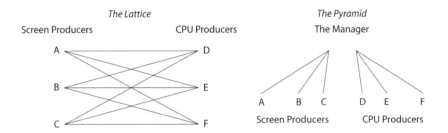

The Lattice

Screen Producers   CPU Producers

The Pyramid

The Manager

Screen Producers   CPU Producers

quire about all these possibilities before signing a contract with a specialist of the complementary trade (screen or CPU), and find out about the characteristics of these products, their prices and the volumes available.

And he should preferably do so for each new transaction. If for example D, E, and F produce one CPU per month, each of them will have to renew his observations each month to choose his partner, given the quality, price and availability of the other products may have changed since the latest transaction.

Each inquiry relating to a transaction has a cost, so that the overall production cost of three computers per month depends on 9 inquiries and negotiations about the 9 possible transactions.

If a production of the same size had been undertaken within a single company, things would have been totally different. The head of this single company would have hired 6 craftsmen to which he would have given precise and uniform directives regarding the production of screens and CPUs. The three screen producers would have continued to produce 3 screens per month and the three CPU fitters would have built 3 units per month but none of them would have to make inquiries to search for clients or suppliers. All this would be predefined and there would be only one supplier and one client: the company itself through its "screen" and "CPU" departments.

The time and money saved on inquiries and negotiations is significant. The process only occurs once, when the 6 craftsmen are hired by the business manager. And if they stay on average 5 or 6 years in the company, as is the case in real life, we see that the market negotiation takes place 60 times less often when the production is organized within the company than when the production process depends on the market (one inquiry and negotiation per month during 5 years equals 60 negotiations on the market, against only one on hiring for the firm).

Admittedly, business managers will have to give precise production directives to the workers manufacturing the screens and assembling the CPUs. But they will only do so from time to time when the product is redesigned or when the production process is rethought.

The number of inquiries and negotiations is thus much lower with a centralized production than with the market: while 9 transactions per month will be required on the market, only 6 transactions every 5 years will be necessary within the firm.

And if the number of producers increases because of a higher demand for computers, this gap will widen quickly: another two producers would bring the total number of possible transactions on the market to 16 (4×4) against only 8 transactions on hiring in the firm. If two other producers join the transactions, the possible matches on the market will rise to 25 (5×5), and then 36 (6×6) and so on.

The number of possible transactions in the market grows geometrically, while the transactions within the hierarchy only grow arithmetically. If each transaction has a given cost, the overall cost of the inquiries and negotiations in the market will exceed the hierarchical production cost very quickly as soon as the number of producers increases.

However, to continue this comparison it is necessary to understand better how the same production can be performed either through a market mechanism or through hierarchical integration even with complex objects. For that, we must go back in time to a period when companies were still in their infancy. A typical example of market production is the manufacturing of weapons in Birmingham in

1860, when the British economy was at its apogee compared with its rivals.

The Birmingham Weapon Industry in 1860

The local light weapon industry, then the most modern in the world, was organized as follows: 5,800 people worked in this field and most lived in a small district next to St. Mary's Church. Workers concentrated in the same area because many craftsmen were specialized in a certain production stage so that they frequently exchanged parts between workshops. It was thus preferable to live close to the other craftsmen. Generally, the gunsmith—the entrepreneur—only had one warehouse where he stored the parts that he bought from the various specialists before delegating the assembly to other specialists, the fitters. Each specialist focused on a very specific task, like producing the barrels, fixing the breechblock on them or manufacturing the triggers or the butts. But there were also polishers, drillers, engravers and adjusters specialized in the machining, assembly and finishing of each part of the rifle. All in all, there were tens of specialized trades and each of them required transfers of parts and market transactions between the producers.[17]

While today the various production stages of this type of gun are centralized within a single firm (Smith & Wesson, Uzi, Beretta, or others), these processes initially implied market transactions. The goods were traded at the successive production stages and prices of these elements at the next production stage were bilaterally negotiated between the manufacturers specialized in each of the element's production.

We can also find in contemporary economies similar mechanisms based on a decentralized production, which is no longer limited to a

17. G. C. Allen, *The Industrial Development of Birmingham and the Black Country, 1860–1927*, London, 1929.

city and its surroundings, but applied to the whole world. In particular, this has become the case with car production.

The Late-Century Car Industry

Recent globalization developments show a return to nineteenth-century-like decentralized procedures. The contemporary example of car production illustrates another version, geographically-decentralized, of this mechanism.

According to the 1998 annual report of the World Trade Organization, the production of a typical "American" car can be broken down as follows: 30 percent of the car's value comes from its assembly in Korea, 17.5 percent from its high-technology components imported from Japan, 7.5 percent from the purchase of the design in Germany, 4 percent from minor elements imported from Taiwan and Singapore, 2.5 percent from advertising and marketing services provided by British companies and 1.5 percent from the purchase of data processing services in Ireland and the Barbados.[18] In other words, only 37 percent of the car's value is produced in the United States.

This also means that independent producers have contributed to the manufacturing of this product in the proportion of two-thirds of its value, with the American producer merely assembling components provided by independent manufacturers. This resembles the totally decentralized methods that were used in Birmingham in the 1860s. The company that "hallmarks" the product mainly acts as a "designer-fitter" of components of various origins that it does not produce itself. This is what many authors call the "virtual firm." In fact, it is a decentralized or "network" firm whose functioning resembles the normal market production process at the beginning of the First Industrial Revolution. This implies that each producer has a lot of information about all the producers of components, equipments or services worldwide.

18. WTO, *Annual Report* 1998, Geneva, p. 36.

But between the late nineteenth century and the end of the twentieth century, all these processes were integrated within a single firm that paid wages directly to each specialist instead of negotiating with them the unit price of each component: their hierarchical superiors now gave them instructions about the quantities needed and the characteristics of the elements to be produced and the operations to be performed. This form of organization developed even more in the United States where markets were larger than in Europe, production volumes were higher, and where impressive productivity improvements accompanied this integration at all the production stages within weapon firms such as Colt or Remington. A different and more advantageous organizational mode replaced the existing one.

A first step toward the integration of all operations within a single firm to reduce the market utilization cost consists in keeping the same supplier faithfully, and by signing a long-term contract that guarantees him exclusive rights, that is a monopoly. But this technique of subcontracting also has drawbacks.

The Limits of Subcontracting

Subcontracting is the intermediary stage between the firm that is fully integrated vertically, from the extraction of raw materials to the delivery of the end product to the consumer, and the decentralized production based solely on the market mechanism.

Between the big integrated firms who produce everything they need and the Birmingham-like market production, there is a wide range of organizational structures that industries and sectors can adopt. In most cases, firms are integrated on a part of the production process that takes place from the extraction of raw materials to the end product. This part of the production process is described by Michael Porter as the company's "value chain" and this terminology is now widely used by strategy consultants. But for the rest of the process they bring in other specialized companies for which they are often the only client (or at least the main client).

With this method, centralization is less intense than with a company totally integrated vertically. In the 1960s, when the advantages of centralization became less obvious but decentralization was not yet widespread, the Japanese firm was taken as a model as it was less hierarchical than European, and more than American firms, had less levels of command and systematically worked with a dense network of subcontracting firms.

But this type of organization was already the rule for the first industrial economies of the early century in America and more especially in Europe.

The case of the automobile producer Panhard & Levassor gives a precise example of this organization in 1890: the firm produced a few hundred cars per year within a single plant, but often with independent suppliers and according to the specifications defined by each client.[19] The company had acquired a franchise to produce Daimler gasoline engines, which were the most powerful at the time. They built several hundred cars per year according to the "Panhard system," a layout where the engine was in the front of the car. The firm was mainly composed of qualified craftsmen who built the cars by hand. These specialists knew everything about mechanics and the materials they used. And many of them were in fact independent producers who worked in the Panhard & Levassor plant or even outside in their own workshops. It was thus a subcontracting system.

The company's two founders and managers, Panhard & Levassor, were in charge of client contacts and defined with them the particular specifications they wanted for their car. They then ordered the necessary elements and supervised the assembly of each car. However,

19. This example was mentioned by James P. Womack, Daniel T. Jones, and Daniel Roos in *The Machine That Changed the World*, Maxwell Macmillan International, 1990.

most of the production (even the design and engineering) took place in their subcontractors' workshops all across Paris.

In these conditions, average production costs could not decline if the volumes produced increased. Indeed, Panhard & Levassor could not manufacture two identical cars. Each of them was unique and thus cost the same to produce the previous and the next. There were no precise standards for each part of the car nor were there machine tools capable of cutting steel and mass-producing identical parts. It was up to each craftsman to produce these elements according to its own methods and measures. Then, in Panhard & Levassor's assembly hall, the hundred of components that composed each car had to be modified and adjusted to each other. They thus produced specific "tailor-made" cars at high costs.

To lower these costs, it was necessary to cut the time spent on the adjustments before the assembly. The solution was to manufacture strictly standardized parts that could be used directly as such, that is to mass-produce them with a single machine. The producers also had to abandon the idea of meeting the specifications of their clients (as Ford did later) as it made each car a unique prototype.

But given the advantages to integrate production costs compared to Panhard & Levassor's extreme form of traditional subcontracting, there were also drawbacks to use the more modern and industrialized subcontracting mechanism where the subcontractor was more than a simple craftsman. This became apparent in the 1920s with the collaboration between General Motors and its supplier of automobile bodies, Fisher Body.[20] The costs that this cooperation implied for General Motors led the firm to integrate purely and simply Fisher Body.

The problem is that, to meet more efficiently and at a lower cost his client's specific requests and standards, the subcontractor must invest in machines particularly adapted to those specific needs. This

20. Benjamin Klein, Robert Crawford, and Armen A. Alchian, "Vertical Integration, Appropriable Rents, and the Competitive Contracting Process," *Journal of Law and Economics*, October 1978, pp. 297–396.

makes him vulnerable to the buyer's decisions as he totally depends on him. If the client decides to work with another subcontractor, he will have difficulty reusing his equipments to supply another company and will be unable to resell them on the secondhand market. He will be a net loser. This potential loss will leave him at the mercy of his client, once he has bought the specific equipments necessary, as he can be forced into cutting prices substantially to the point he makes no profits anymore. This is what managerial economists call the "moral risk" or the "hold-up."

To protect himself against that kind of risk, the subcontractor can ask for a long-term contract that guarantees him the sale of enough products to amortize the cost of these specific machine tools "dedicated" to a single client. This is precisely what had been done between General Motors and Fisher Body. But such a long-term contract cannot take into account all the future developments in the industry. In fact, Fisher Body's contract mentioned the sale price of automobile bodies to General Motors based on the production costs specified at the signature and with the equipments existing at the time, to which had to be added a profit margin representing a fixed percentage of costs that would be paid to the owners of Fisher Body (cost-plus pricing).

But the production techniques of automobile bodies evolved rapidly and it became possible in the late 1920s to produce bodies at lower costs by using the newly-born stamping presses. However, Fisher Body had no reason to make such an investment given their contract with General Motors guaranteed them a profit margin in addition to their production costs with the current equipment. So, why agree to buy new machines to reduce costs when they are sure to get a profit margin anyway? General Motors was trapped and eventually had to buy Fisher Body to modernize its equipments and reduce the cost of its automobile bodies. It was indeed better to integrate this business to its production chain and thus protect itself against possible conflicts of interest between the client and the supplier, and the exploitation of one by the other.

There are thus several reasons to integrate vertically companies and subcontractors in an economy where transaction costs are high. And the upsizing of the average firm resulting from vertical integration reduces the domain of market transactions between specialized suppliers.

Power and the Subordination Contract

Within the firm, transaction costs are indeed minimized. The decision-making power is concentrated at the top, centralized. The definition of the product and all its components are preset, in a coordinated way, and all its characteristics are clearly specified. These standards and directives are then passed on to the divisions and departments of the production line, without any market negotiations. And their proper execution is supervised by the administrative hierarchy.

With the centralized process, the pieces do not need to be adjusted anymore during the assembly, unlike with Panhard & Levassor. The divergences of interest between General Motors and Fisher Body also disappeared. The hierarchical production mode requires no adjustments, negotiations and thus little information. All the information needed by the firm is concentrated at the top, where the decision maker of the whole process lies. The other agents of the firm are either field workers or inspectors and supervisors. All employees are totally specialized in a specific task and do not need information from outside the firm.

On the market, the decision maker can be an individual who decides for himself or represents a group of individuals, such as a firm or an administration. But he cannot impose his decisions on his trading partners. On the contrary, in the hierarchical organization, the decision maker has a right to compel his subordinates to implement his decisions. That is why the basic characteristic of a hierarchy is the relation of subordination. That relation is the very foundation of the labor contract, which governs most inter-individual relations within the hierarchical organizations in contemporary societies.[21]

The distinction is not always made that way in the economic literature as theorists are still undecided about what differentiates a hierarchy from a market. The authority or power relation is often mentioned, especially in the theory of organization, but never clearly defined. Economists have, indeed, always felt uncomfortable with the notion of power, precisely because their discipline is based on the study of markets. As such, they tend to deny the existence of a hierarchical bilateral relation and focus on the market relation, which implies shared decisions and thus rules out a subordination or power relation.

A few authors like Alchian and Demsetz take the market approach to extremes and simply deny the existence of an authority relation, asserting that the relations are the same in firms and on markets.[22] According to them, a customer can "lay off" his butcher or grocer, just like a boss would dismiss his employee, and in return, wage earners can also "lay off" their employer by resigning. All inter-individual relations would thus be perfectly symmetric and there would never be any power relation. The very notion of "power" would be totally meaningless.

But in reality, it is obvious that this symmetry is purely fictitious. A field worker cannot lay off its company head. He can only "dismiss" the whole firm by resigning. To really lay off the company head, he would have to be able to impose his own decision on all the other people concerned—the other employees, the customers, the suppliers

21. In various societies, different forms of "quasi-employment contracts" have existed, each being characterized by a different degree of coercion, serfdom and various forms of slavery.

22. Armen A. Alchian and Harold Demsetz, "Production, Information Costs, and Economic Organization," *American Economic Review*, December 1972, pp. 777–795.

and the shareholders. Thus, he would have to be able to decide for the others, which is precisely the prerogative of the individual at the top of the hierarchical pyramid, and who holds the power, the centralized decision-making power.

And as the people ranked lower in the hierarchy do not have this power, the hierarchical relation is asymmetric. The power does exist. It can be defined as the decision-making power an individual has on people other than himself, and also by the number of these other people on whom the leader can impose his own decision.

Besides, the distinction between the hierarchical and market relations comes from the fact that in a company, a subordinate and his superior both take part together in the production of a same good or a service. There is no such relation between a customer and a grocer. The customer can buy—or not—the pasta he finds in a store, but for all that, he does not take part in the grocer's production.

The confusion between firms and markets is also fueled by the fact that the hierarchical relation between wage earners and their employer within a firm is complemented by market transactions between the firm and its customers and external suppliers. The business firm obviously works on the markets where it offers its products and services. It also acts as a buyer on the commodity market and on several markets of semi-finished goods. For its outside relations, the firm is a market participant and the transaction it makes is a symmetric exchange implying no subordination relation.

That is why many commentators use the terms "business economy" (or "free enterprise") and "market economy" indifferently, although both mechanisms are in fact opposites. The firm is a place of authority, command and subordination. The market is a place of shared decision-making, independence and equality.

The nineteenth century industrial developments saw the creation of numerous firms, plants and factories which gathered together a large and quickly increasing number of employees. As pointed out by Paul Milgrom and John Roberts, before 1850 the Church and the

Army were almost the only hierarchical structures.[23] The few exceptions were in North America, the Hudson's Bay Company, and in England, the East India Company.

However, with the rise of mass transportation, large companies developed quickly. Those bodies followed the principle of hierarchical subordination, with the top issuing compulsory directives, just like in public administrations. These methods, defined and formalized by Taylor, Fayol and Ford, represent the turn-of-the-century "administrative revolution."

The result was what economists call "vertical integration": the firm is under the hierarchical authority of a manager who controls all the transactions made during the production process, from the extraction of the raw materials to the delivery of the product to the final customer, while these transactions and conversions could also take place on markets between firms. With the integration of all these production stages within a single firm, the price mechanism is replaced with command. And thus most of the modern production occurs within administrative organizations rather than through the market mechanism.

It follows that within an economy or a society, we find both market productions and hierarchical productions. The larger the hierarchies, the more employees they contain, the more the authority, the decision-making power, is concentrated since the number of decision makers decreases while the number of subordinates increases. On the contrary, when hierarchies shrink and markets develop, the decision-making power is more widely spread among a large number of individuals.

The more hierarchical the production organization choice, the more centralized the society. The centralization rate thus gives an indication about the society's production system and distribution of the decision-making power. In other words, its political system.

---

23. Paul Milgrom and John Roberts, *Economics, Organization and Management*, Prentice-Hall, 1992.

CENTRALIZATION AND POLITICAL SYSTEMS

The functioning of a society is defined by its political system in its broad sense of the organizational structure of the relations between people. That relational structure provides a clear answer to the question of who decides what is produced, how and at which price. Given these problems are the same for all the hierarchies and markets in the sectors of private or collective production, the notions of "political system" and "economic system" are equivalent.

The centralization rate, based on the choice of the organizational modes of all productions, thus becomes the main characteristic of the political system. It indeed reflects the average size of the hierarchies, and consequently the dominant type of relation between individuals and collective organizations, together with the distribution of the decision-making power in the society. The centralization of power determines the predominance of human relations of subordination, obedience and conformity, as well as the room left for transactions negotiated equally and freely. It thus determines the dominant social values, peculiar to each society. Centralization also defines the role of the individuals in the society and their economic and political rights. It follows that these two types of rights generally go hand in hand as they result from the common operating needs of private and public organizations.

In a society that is not fully centralized, the individuals choose the production mode that suits them: they can either be independent producers who directly intervene in the market or join a hierarchy within an organization. The more or less centralized organizational structure of a society depends on all these individual choices. They are not based on pre-established preferences or political ideologies, but rather on the effectiveness and comparative costs of each production mechanism, market and hierarchy. The choice of an organization is thus economic and contingent: it depends on particular conditions, at a given time and in a given environment, on the respective costs of markets and hierarchies. Thus, there is not only one politico-economic system that is always and everywhere the best. There is an infinite range of organizational structures, and it is impossible to choose by a simple a priori reasoning which would be the most adapted to a particular society at a given point in history. The solution selected can only be empirical and most often decentralized.

Measuring the Systems

Companies' average optimal size within an industry determines, for a given market demand, the number of firms and, consequently, the centralization rate in that sector. The larger the average firm, the greater the number of employees working under a single hierarchical authority and the higher the centralization rate of decision making in that sector. That rate is at its highest level when all the individual producers are headed by a single management team. It is the case of a monopoly.

The subordination rate, that is the number of subordinates/number of managers ratio, increases steadily in line with the size of the hierarchical organization. The more an organization grows, the more centralized the decision-making process is. In a hierarchical organization of 10 people, the manager decides for the 9 others. In a hierarchical society of 100 people, the manager decides for the 99 others. In a society of one million people, the manager decides for the 999,999 other individuals.

The number of managers/number of subordinates ratio represents the decentralization or individualism rate which ranges from 1 (one leader for one subordinate, in the case of independent craftsmen) to 0 when there is only one leader for an infinite number of subordinates (a society organized as a single giant pyramid). As the maximal level of decentralization is also the minimal level of centralization, the centralization rate evolves in the opposite direction from the decentralization rate—from 0 for independent craftsmen to 1 for the hierarchy which counts a very large number of subordinates.

The centralization rate is 0 in a society which only includes individual craftsmen and it reaches 1 when the society only counts a single organization managed by a single leader. It can be calculated for any group of people—for a single pyramid but also for any society that counts a great number of pyramids and markets.

It represents a unidimensional and continuous measure that applies to any type of organizational system. Thus, while the choice of the production's organization is binary or dichotomous for individuals (they can stay independent craftsmen on the market or become employees within a hierarchy), in an organization it ranges continuously from the full decentralization to the full centralization of a unique hierarchy.

That simple remark shows that a society's organizational structure is not chosen the same way that individuals choose their production relations. The latter consists in a radical alternative between a relation of authority or a market relation implying shared decision making.

The overall centralization rate of a society depends on all the organizational choices made by individuals, as these define the size of the private and public pyramids, including the state. The number and sizes of the various hierarchies that coexist in a society comes down to one single figure situated in the infinite range of possibilities between 0 and 1.

Obviously, the centralization rate of a society gives an even more faithful image of these internal structures when all the organizations that it is composed of upsize or downsize at the same time. Otherwise, a constant overall centralization rate might hide opposite trends, for instance between public and private organizations. Yet, there are good reasons to think that the size of most organizations evolves at the same time and in the same direction.

While the various organizations can have different optimum sizes, they are all affected by the variables that influence the respective operating costs of the market mechanism and hierarchical production. Indeed these comparative advantages mostly vary according to information costs, as we will see in the next chapter. As the centralization rate depends on the size of public and private pyramids which in turn depends on information costs, it will follow similar trends in both the "economic" and "political" sectors.

This has a very deep consequence: highly statist societies cannot also have very developed markets. Market socialism is a myth. When the state is very powerful and centralized, the economic sector is also dominated by a few very large private hierarchies, by giant firms, and not by a great number of small firms and craftsmen trading together through market transactions. The large state develops at the same time and in the same conditions as large firms. This typically results in corporatist regimes or in a system of large public firms: a Socialist regime.

On the contrary, when the state is small, the firms are also smaller. The whole society is decentralized. Such was the case with nineteenth-century liberal or competitive capitalism.

There are thus only two extreme cases (liberal and craft capitalism on one side, full communism on the other) and an infinite number of intermediate solutions, each of which admitting a similar level of centralization of its public and private activities. And there are no really "mixed" regimes, with really distinct public and private centralization rates, combining, say, market capitalism (atomized companies) with a very large state holding a centralized political power. Nor is there any regime combining a truly discreet state and vast monopolistic private firms.

The first case of a mixed regime would be that of market socialism. But after the Yugoslavian illusion of the 1960s, one had to realize that there was no real example of market socialism in the socialist galaxy: extreme political centralization including the public ownership of firms is not favorable for the atomization of the production structures. The second case would be authoritarian capitalism. But in fact, in dictatorial regimes, the economic power is almost as concentrated as the political power. Such is the case in the "banana" and "mining" republics of the developing countries. It was also the case with the Fascist and Corporatist regimes of the 1930s in Europe (konzerns in Germany, large public "institutes" and powerful private firms in Italy and France) but also in Asia with the development of the zaïbatsus in Japan after World War I, which peaked with the imperialist "new order" imposed by the military and technocratic establishment on the eve of Word War II.[24] There was even an echo of that general trend in the United States, where large public institutions like the Tennessee Valley Authority, and the Public Utilities in general, emerged and developed during the first twentieth century and above all during the Great Depression of the 1930s, while the federal state grew increasingly influential and the vast industrial mergers continued. Such was also the case with the Scandinavian economies, where the state accounts for a very large part of the domestic product and where the industry is dominated by a small number of giant firms owned by a handful of powerful families.

That parallelism of centralization or decentralization in the public and private sectors has other consequences on social systems. We saw that the hierarchy reduces substantially individual rights, and instead derives its effectiveness from the behavior of subordination and standardization. It is thus reluctant to entrust the employees with a real power of control. It is true for both the state hierarchies, which employ a large part of the working population and thus represent a monopsony in many sectors, but also for the private hierarchies in a position of monopoly which lay off the employees who try to interfere in the company's management. The most extreme cases are the Latin American mining companies which monopolize the job market, the Ford company in its early stages and other giant manufacturers, which impede as much as they can the development of trade unions.

24. William M. Tsutui, *Manufacturing Ideology: Scientific Management in Twentieth-Century Japan*, Princeton University Press, 1998.

Similarly, the great hierarchies which replace the markets with vertical and horizontal integration and reduce the number of firms— a source of competition—also endeavor to discourage external control—the democracy of the shareholders which gives the controlling power to a large number of individuals. The same is true of the big conglomerate-like states which, in practice, try to reduce the controlling power of their electors-taxpayers, the final owners of that collective enterprise. In state-controlled societies, the civil servants, who represent a large proportion of the voters, are also numerous among the elected representatives and thus find themselves collectively in a position of self-control, being both controllers in their capacity as elected representatives and controlled in their capacity as civil servants. In a similar way, as they cannot belong to only a small number of investors because of their huge financing needs (it would require immense individual wealth for a sole ownership, often more significant than the domestic product of many states), very large firms tend to become managerial companies, only controlled by their CEOs and not by their dispersed owners. The same is true of very big states, where democracy—when there is one—is largely monopolized by the executive. The managerial state echoes the managerial firm.

The centralization rate, which is simply the image of the hierarchies' size, is thus the main variable reflecting the general characteristics of the politico-economic systems, given that centralization evolves the same way in all the production sectors.

Counter-currents?

But has the parallel evolution of organizations been confirmed by the facts? Does the decentralization that characterizes the second twentieth century apply to the commercial hierarchies but also to all the other types of hierarchies? Since the late 1960s, the contemporary decentralizing revolution has concerned both the economic and political productions. The largest companies reduce their staff, while the biggest and the most heterogeneous states split into entities with smaller demographic and geographical dimensions.

But haven't we entered again an opposite phase of re-centralization a couple of years ago? The M&As and the multiple takeover bids give the feeling that the dominant trend is for the concentration of labor in an increasingly smaller number of giant enterprises, all striving to attain the mythical "international dimension." Henceforth, we would be living in the "World Company" era and firms such as Coca-Cola, Microsoft, McDonald's and Axa would be the best example of that.

On the economic level, the takeover bids and M&As tend to concentrate the decision-making power. Many observers draw the conclusion that the recent waves of takeover bids will lead us to a society essentially composed of giant firms, where the power will be extremely concentrated.

All that appears to be plain and simple and confirmed everyday by new operations, but it is only an illusion. Although a few firms show spectacular external growth, these are more an exception than a rule. As it was underlined in a recent INSEE survey, corporate downsizing is accelerating. Between 1985 and 1997, in France, the average number of employees working in big companies decreased steadily. If we consider the firms that employed more than 10,000 people at the beginning of the period, we see that the average number of employees fell from 25,408 in 1985 to 13,137 in 1997. In the companies with 5 to 10,000 people, the average retracted from 6,487 in 1985 to 3,797 in 1997. In the firms with 1,000 to 5,000 people, the average declined from 1,964 in 1985 to 1,524 in 1997. And in the 500 to 1,000 employees category, the average also eased slightly from 691 to 648 people.[25]

In percentage points, the reductions of the workforce in these

<hr>

25. *Le poids des grandes entreprises dans l'emploi*, INSEE Première, no. 683, November 1999.

respective categories of big companies were of −48.3 percent, −41.5 percent, −22.4 percent and −6.3 percent over the twelve years under study.

Meanwhile, the average number of employees in small and medium companies increased steadily. It rose by 38.9 percent in the companies employing between 1 and 9 people, 21.9 percent in those counting 10 to 19 employees, 16.9 percent in the 20 to 49 employees category, 14.7 percent in the firms employing 50 to 200 people and finally 3.8 percent in those with 200 to 500 employees.

That movement was general, massive and consistent. The bigger the company initially, the sharper the job cuts. The smaller the company, the larger the increase in the average number of employees. Clearly, there is a global trend toward a reduction in firms' average size.[26]

Furthermore, we must distinguish between the employment dynamics among the population of the companies that survived the whole period (the "perennial" companies, as the INSEE calls them) and the dynamics of corporate demography, which concerns the birth of new companies, the definitive collapses or even the structural changes (mergers and takeovers or on the contrary de-mergers and disintegration). Whereas small companies often collapse and larger ones (over 1,000 employees) almost never die, the creation of numerous small firms also helps to reduce the average size of the company for the whole workforce.

The decrease in companies' average size during the last decade of the twentieth century, confirms the older and international trend mentioned in the second chapter: the downsizing of the production apparatus remains an underlying trend of the second twentieth century.

26. According to the Fortune 500 index, the three largest firms in the world in terms of turnover were General Motors, IRI, and IBM in 1990. They respectively employed 775,000, 416,000, and 383,000 people at the time, but only 756,000, 407,000, and 344,000 in 1992 and 647,000, 132,000, and 268,000 in 1997.

Consequently, the wave of M&As cannot be interpreted as a way to benefit from the advantages of big dimensions. The companies who upsize are the smallest, while the firms of over 500 employees obviously downsize. The takeover bids and other restructuring plans—that nevertheless result in the creation of a merged firm larger than the two initial companies—must thus meet other objectives than just upsizing.

But which are they?

M&As and the Redistribution of Talents

The growing wave of takeover bids and other restructuring plans is less the result of a race for "international" dimension—since companies' average size continues to decrease in all the developed countries—than of the redistribution of the decision-making power to the most effective managers due to increased competition. And indeed, the free movement of goods and people and the development of world trade suddenly increased the number of firms actually competing against one another on a now international or world market.

As the trading area widens with the opening of markets to foreign companies, the competition between the productive hierarchies becomes more direct and harsh, while on fragmented national markets the local firms are, in general, protected against external competitors and can cooperate more easily to sign trade agreements and form cartels. In conditions of reduced competition on narrow markets, the quality of the products and leaders is unequal and often limited. But the intensification of competition will confront the least competent leaders with their best competitors worldwide. The decision-making power is thus redistributed, as the most competent leaders can extend their field of command within their sector, while the least efficient ones are compelled to disappear or accept subordination. The same is true of the show business market, where the superstars widen the gap between them and second-rate artists. Indeed, the information broadcasting techniques make it easier to listen to the best or more popular singers in the world than to the less talented local singers. In companies, the increased competition between a larger population of managers on a worldwide market results in a redistribution of the decision-making power to the "superstars" (who can thus upsize the hierarchies they control) rather than to the less efficient leaders (who must on the contrary downsize the organizations they manage or even hand over the commands to others).

But these localized redistributions of the decision-making power are not incompatible with a general trend toward decentralization. The fact that a few stars manage to increase their audience does not preclude a decentralization of the industry if the number of newcomers setting up only small-sized organizations increases significantly. The space taken by the four or five biggest organizations can grow while the average size of the organizations diminishes, which increases the number of decision-making centers and reduces the overall centralization rate.

In the last few years many authors have explained the differences between the growth rates and dimensions of firms belonging to the same sector by the differences of talent between their leaders.[27] Takeover bids and mergers—the latter often being just disguised acquisitions through which a managerial team takes control of a new unit— are the proof of a manager's confidence in his ability to create more value from the resources of the target firm than its current leaders can do. That manager tries to convince the shareholders of the targeted firm with an overall takeover bid on the equity market. If he succeeds in obtaining enough stocks and voting rights, he replaces the ruling managerial team with his own staff and takes control of the company bought, which he restructures and merges with his own.

    27. Robert Lucas Jr., "On the Size Distribution of Business Firms," *Bell Journal of Economics*, Autumn 1978; Sherwin Rosen, "Authority, Control, and the Distribution of Earnings," *Rand Journal of Economics*, 1982; "The Economics of Superstars," *American Economic Review*, 1981; and Todd L. Idson and Walter Y. Oi, "Workers are More Productive in Large Firms," *American Economic Review*, May 1999.

He then defines new strategies aimed at increasing the prospects of future profits and thus the current value of the stocks of the company bought, which is the purpose of the operation.

General studies about the results of takeover bids show that the value of the target firm increases while the value of the buying company decreases slightly. It is logical that the value of the target rises. First, the bidder must offer a higher price for the targeted stock than the current market price if he wants to convince enough shareholders to sell their stocks. This is called the takeover premium. By nature, it raises the price of the target firm. But the stock will only stay at that level if the new management team and its new strategy turn out to be better than the previous ones. This is often the case because the bidder will only accept to pay the takeover premium if he is sure he can improve the performance of the target company. Takeovers will thus be directed toward supposedly badly managed companies, and are likely to improve the management process and result in wealth creation.

But how can the decline of the bidder's stock price be explained? And why do the leaders launch these takeover bids that impoverish their shareholders? How are those operations possible on competitive financial markets? Why would the shareholders not systematically punish the managers who throw themselves into such hardly profitable ventures?

Well, actually, they do. The fall in the price of the purchasing firms means that the owners deem that the current value of the expected flow of future benefits has decreased. That decline represents sanctions against the ruling team, which it makes slightly more vulnerable to a possible takeover bid. So, why are there takeovers? That phenomenon can be explained by the leveling out of the managers' marginal productivity in the various firms. The talent of a leader enables him to control efficiently a company of a certain size, but that size is limited as we will see in the next chapter. The leader of a small company probably is, all things being equal, less talented than the manager of a big firm. By purchasing a new company through a take-over bid, the leader of the buying firm can dedicate his talent to a broader, more difficult management process but he also replaces a less talented leader. All the losses of control inherent in a large size hierarchy will increase within the newly merged unit he is in charge of. It follows that the competence of the leader will reach its limits, which means that his managerial productivity in terms of wealth creation will decline. It can nevertheless remain higher than that of the former manager of the target firm. But by devoting himself to that additional management, he necessarily manages the first firm—the bidder—less efficiently. The profitability of the target firm increases while that of the bidder diminishes.

The takeover bid is thus justified insofar as the new leader's decreased productivity in the management of the initial firm remains nevertheless higher than that of the previous manager of the target company. He thus dedicates his superior talent to that company, whose future gains and present value increase correspondingly. All in all, that superior talent will be devoted to a larger field of action and replace the inferior talent. The society as a whole and the economy's productive apparatus come off better. The value of all the companies together has globally increased in that case. The decision-making power has been centralized, the resources of the previously independent firms being concentrated under the leadership of the most efficient manager.

The same mechanism is seen in the sectors in overcapacity, where the demand stagnates or even declines. The least competitive companies show a lower-than-average profitability. Then, they have to leave that sector or buy out customers through the takeover of a competitor, whose production capacity will eventually be reduced. To do so, it is better to resort to superior talents. Since some companies have to limit their activity or disappear, it is better for them to reallocate their resources to the best managers and thus to replace the less gifted managers by more efficient ones.

The way these capacity-reducing takeovers take place illustrates the improved allocation of resources in the economy, the (rare) resources of the badly-managed firms being passed to those who can use them the most efficiently after the merger. The decision-making field of action of the most efficient managers thus develops until their "decision-making productivity" decreases and becomes equalized in all the companies. The takeover bids and other restructuring plans are thus a means to reallocate talents and responsibilities.

The productivity of all the leaders, in terms of wealth creation, thus tends to become equalized in all the firms as it is also a function of the differences of size between these companies. The productivity of the most talented manager will fall to the level of the least talented because of the sudden expansion of the former company. He will thus reach the limits of his competence and the profitability of his firm will be reduced to that of the smaller companies managed by less efficient leaders. At a given time, if the economy is competitive, that allocation of talents and resources tends to reach an equilibrium.

In conclusion, it appears that the growth or shrinking of the hierarchies in terms of employment, and consequently their increasing or falling number in the society, results from a process of allocation and efficient use of scarce resources—here, the leaders' talent.

The dimension of the hierarchies and of their opposite, the markets, and the economy's overall centralization rate result from that quest for the most efficient leaders.

The same factors are at play in the hierarchies producing public goods, and they have the same consequences. Thus, the whole structure of the politico-economic system depends on this quest for optimization. There must thus be objective organizational factors that determine the adoption of such politico-economic system. We are thus very far from the traditional conceptions according to which the ideologies—often despised as erroneous—would lead the societies to adopt a structure of political organization that would in fact be arbitrary and possibly unfavorable to the pursuit of prosperity and of the most recognized human values. This is an explanation by the absurd and irrational which implies that the political systems evolve according to a succession of ideological mistakes.

Before suggesting a more rational explanation, let us complete the picture of the social consequences implied by production centralization. It does not only determine the allocation of the management skills, it also explains the varying degrees of development of rights and liberties. The preferred legal order depends on the ethical and political priorities of each individual, whether in favor of liberties or of centralized redistribution of incomes. But whatever the subjective preferences of each of us, which can be both different and legitimate, there are objective factors determining the system of rights adopted by a society at a given time.

Centralization and the Two Types of Rights

The economic and political rights directly depend on the organizational structures. In the first stage of the great cycle, the dimension of all the organizations increased—including that of states—while the number of independent states in the world declined due to imperialism. The latter denies the right of peoples to self-determination. It denies the colonized the civil and economic rights that the citizens of the imperialist nation can benefit from, although those latter rights are themselves often reduced by the internal centralization of power.

During the second twentieth century, the increase in the number of nations and, within the nations, in the number of smaller organizations, led to an increase in the number of decision makers, which resulted in the decentralization of the decision-making process. This trend marks the return of democracy, human rights and economic liberties, as shown by the various editions of the *Economic Freedom of the World* report published by Raymond Gastil and then by James Gwartney, Robert Lawson and Walter Block. Based on the classification of countries according to their level of civil liberties provided by these reports, Robert Barro measured an average indicator of democracy in the world out for about a hundred countries between 1960 and 1994. That average index ranges from 0 to 1. It fell slightly from 0.65 in 1960 to 0.60 in 1994 but after passing by a low of 0.44 in 1975.[28]

In the first (decreasing) phase, the trend is towards a totalitarian society where a growing number of decisions affecting all individuals are made by only a few of them. In the second phase, the trend is towards an individualistic society with personal liberties, where each can decide by himself and for himself.

This is because human relations are very different within the hierarchies and markets. To run smoothly, the hierarchies need virtues such as subordination, obedience to the superiors, a single thought guiding the organization and the devotion of the individuals to the community. On the contrary, individual initiative, originality, personal autonomy, non-conformity or even deviance,[29] the recognition of the worth of a person and of his/her rights within the community, are essential to the good functioning of markets. Recent financial studies have shown for instance that financial markets are more developed and hierarchically-organized banks less significant in the countries where legal systems more generally and more effectively guarantee the rights of the creditors.[30]

Depending on how much a society leans toward hierarchies or markets, it is more or less gregarious and conformist, hardly inclined to define legal, commercial and civil guarantees or, on the contrary, individualistic and egalitarian by nature, supporting the legally constituted state and the constitutional guarantees that represent an explicit social contract.

28. Robert Barro, *Determinants of Economic Growth: A Cross-Country Empirical Study*, MIT Press, 1997.

29. Many authors define the entrepreneur as a deviant innovator, disrespectful toward customs and traditions.

30. Rafael La Porta, Francisco Lopez-de-Silanes, Andrei Shleifer, and Robert W. Vishny, "Law and Finance," *NBER Working Paper*, no. 5661, July 1996.

Rights are guarantees of the liberties, whether negative or positive. They indeed protect the individuals against the attacks and predations of other individuals or organizations. But they also define which actions are authorized and enable the individuals to perceive and retain the benefits of their actions, efforts and investments.

As a consequence, the political system takes very different shapes in very hierarchical societies and in very market-oriented societies. Even when they are very largely guaranteed on paper (for instance, in the Soviet constitution), political rights are difficult to implement in an extremely hierarchical society and can prevent its effective functioning: not only are the usual behaviors within a pyramid organization inimical to those rights, but also the expression of the debate, the confrontation of the opinions and ideas, becomes difficult or impossible in practice when all the media activities (editing, press and television) are concentrated within the hands of a small number of owners (if not a single owner), whether private or public. This is the argument against state control that Milton Friedman convincingly put forward in *Capitalism and Freedom*. Clearly, Soviet dissidents could not have had their work published and distributed by publishing houses as they all belonged to the state. They had no access to the radio or the public television channels. They were banned from the conferences and the universities. On the contrary, in the United States or in Europe, the protesters against the ruling order easily found a radical university or a non-conformist publisher to express and spread their ideas. In France, however, where the public monopoly of television has long been maintained without any economic justification, the political opposition has always had difficulties making itself heard—like the proponents of ideas too remote from the consensus of the dominant intellectual circles, generally opposed to the market mechanism and to competition.

Of course, the issue of private property—the individuals' right to property—and individual rights in general, depend on the development of hierarchies. Indeed, to work properly, the market and the price mechanism require the prior existence of a sophisticated system of rights on goods, services and the production factors (capital and labor) that are necessary to implement that production. This prerequisite to good functioning had always been underestimated until recently because the industrial and culturally-advanced countries had benefited from it for so long that people had forgotten that the same was not true of all the societies. But the recent de-hierarchization of Russia has shown what happens when markets and price mechanisms are implemented without having a legal and institutional system that actually guarantees rights. The economy does not function or gives deleterious results. Then comes anarchy and its law of the jungle.

Conversely, we can also conclude that a system of rights as sophisticated as that needed by a market economy is not essential to a hierarchy. In the latter, the individuals have less rights than an independent entrepreneur on a market. The subordinates must submit to their superiors. To work efficiently, a hierarchy requires that the decisions made by the superiors be implemented without being constantly discussed or modified. That implies a restriction of the subordinates' room for maneuver and right to dissent, that is, of their individual rights. Indeed, the easiest way to avoid protest is to ban criticism. Rights and hierarchies are not easy bedfellows, whereas markets can function only if individual rights are defined, extended and defended by the authorities.

That is why most observers have presented the system of rights, and especially property rights, as the main difference between capitalism and socialism. Having in mind a capitalism of small units, not very hierarchical and mostly market-oriented, they noted that it required a precise definition of the (property) rights of the ones and the others, especially concerning the private property of capital. On the contrary, the hierarchical socialism could abolish these rights or concentrate them in the hands of the leaders.

In the view of many liberal economists, political rights are less important than economic rights because they have no direct impact on growth and on wealth production. Some of them even suggest that political rights and democracy are obstacles to prosperity because they encourage the various social groups to ask for a greater redistribution of wealth in their favor, which weighs on the tax system, encourages greater state control and slows growth. Democracy is sometimes accused of being responsible for the atrophy of the economic liberties, the hypertrophy of the state and the reduction of the general well-being.[31]

We will show later on that the growth of the state-controlled pyramids admits much more convincing explanations than the autonomous—and so far unexplained by those authors—development of political rights. The most striking element is the parallel development of the public and private hierarchies which can be no simple accident, but also their similar consequences in terms of economic and political rights.

In fact, all the hierarchies, public or private, reduce the need for a sophisticated system of rights. In a hierarchy, the wage earners abandon some of their individual rights—though temporarily and in various proportions. The same is true of the political systems based on authority rather than on the democratic decentralization of rights. In the hierarchical systems, "some are more equal than others," as the leader holds most rights. As Molotov once declared, "law is not meant to protect individuals against the state but rather to protect the state against the individuals." And for Hitler, rights had to be subjected to policies.[32]

31. As Robert Barro (op. cit.) underlined, economic growth increases with democracy in the countries where the latter is underdeveloped but then the increase of the already large political freedom results in slower growth. According to Gerald W. Scully (*Constitutional Environments and Economic Growth*, Princeton University Press, 1992), over the 1950–1985 period, economic growth and the various indicators of economic and political freedom were positively correlated, while the state's role in the economy affects growth negatively.

32. Mazover, *Dark Continent: Europe's Twentieth Century*, Penguin, 1998, p. 31. The author also underlines that the German legal customs of the late nineteenth

The gradual development of markets in the Western societies, which had been evolving from hierarchical organization systems and customary authority, was accompanied by the development of people's rights—human rights in the broad sense, especially in the towns where markets developed the most. This, in turn, made possible a greater development of the markets. When the room for maneuver of each individual increases and becomes more discretionary, it is necessary to predefine its limits. In a hierarchy, everything that is not authorized by the superior is forbidden. In the market, everything that is not forbidden by the law is authorized.

There is thus a fundamental parallelism between the development of markets and the development of individual rights, including the capital ownership rights, but also human rights in general: the right to think, to speak and to criticize. There is a deep and necessary connection between markets and democracy, the latter being understood as a legal system increasing individual rights and reducing the discretionary rights of the central authority.

Indeed, in a hierarchy, individual efforts and productivity are encouraged by the wages and the administrative supervision. The purpose of the whole administrative hierarchy is to make sure that the orders coming from the top are followed and to supervise the productive performance of the subordinates.

In a market, the producer is watched by the consumer. But, if he is dissatisfied, the only action a consumer can take is to choose another supplier. The current producer is only affected to the extent that he is the legitimate owner of the possible gains resulting from his activity. Indeed, ownership rights have the effect of making each individual bear the full consequences of his actions. If the careless producer wants to offset the lower income that results from the disaffection of his clients, he has to improve the quality and efficiency of his production.

---

century encouraged the judges to view law as a protection for the state rather than for individuals.

Similarly, on the political market, democracy gives the consumers of public services the possibility to withdraw the confidence they had placed in the "producers," the politicians, through a vote. But this is only possible if all the users and taxpayers are guaranteed the right to give their opinions and elect their representatives.

So that capitalism, which is based on individual capital ownership rights, is a system which requires more rights than socialism, where there is no need to share the decision-making power. And in general, any system that relies on the price mechanism and on the decentralization of decision making to several agents must encourage individual initiatives. But initiatives can only be taken if a code of conduct defines rather precisely which individual behavior is acceptable and which is not.

Thus, it is true that the presence or the absence of individual ownership is what determines the fundamental choice of a society's organizational mode. But keeping to that view prevents realizing that in a society of private property and market, production centralization also leads to an atrophy of individual rights, or in other words, to characteristics increasingly similar to those of the societies in which individual ownership rights are banned. There is a continuity of systems, starting with the almost complete market capitalism, where the firms remain at the cottage industry stage, the great hierarchical capitalism, then corporatism and finally socialism, with or without any residual individual property.

Thus, the revival of shareholders' rights—and of ownership rights in general in the "capitalist" societies of the eighties and nineties—is due to the return of decentralization and markets which require a more developed legal system to function. On the contrary, in *The Managerial Revolution*, published in the 1940s, Burnham described a society in which owners' and shareholders' rights declined. That theme was taken up later by Galbraith in *The New Industrial State*.

The relation between the organizational structures and rights also accounts for the "excessive" increase in legal actions and for the major role of lawyers in the U.S., the most market-oriented system. Only the negative aspect of that system is usually focused on, but legal actions and disputes are meant to define more precisely people's rights or what actions individuals can take legitimately without wronging other people. This is one of the prerequisites to an improvement of the functioning of markets and of the price mechanism.

But the fact that the rights—including ownership rights—are correlated to the development of markets and nonexistent in the highly-hierarchical societies does not mean that the specification of rights determines the development of markets. A legal system is a prerequisite of a market's good functioning. It must even precede it, it seems, as the Russian experience of the last decade tends to prove. But a legal system is not enough to create markets. Rights can become reality and actually encourage the development of markets only if the fundamental economic conditions are met. It is not law that creates organizations, but rather the economic conditions—which we will analyze later on—that lead to the choice of such or such organization and the introduction of the economic or political legal systems that the architecture of organizations implies.

THE EVOLUTION OF POLITICAL REGIMES

We have seen that politico-economic systems are characterized by their centralization rate, which evolves similarly to whatever the type of goods produced, private or political. That rate is also influenced by the presence or absence of individual rights and liberties in the societies considered.

But can we explain why the systems are what they are and what makes them evolve? In other words, can we determine who chooses the system and what motivates that choice?

In the political debate, that question is often presented as if there was a clear-cut answer—as if the point was to decide between the terms of a relatively simple alternative. For instance, between capitalism and socialism, the market and the state.

But in fact, it is impossible to answer—and even ask—such a question because of the existence of an infinite range of politico-economic regimes, each corresponding to a different centralization rate. It is indeed inconceivable to try and find a definition of "the" best regime when we are unable to specify all the details of the precise organization of only one of them. Must we draw up a list of all the activities in which the state is involved, of the structure of its administrations, of its possible industrial holdings? And can we determine what the optimum structure and the number of firms of each industry must be? Can we compare and rank by preference an infinite number of organizations, when we do not even know the concrete differences between them? Obviously, the answer is no. But practically that does not prevent a government from deciding—if it wishes to—to fully nationalize the whole economy and to manage it in a centralized way with a Gosplan. We have good reasons to think that such a system will not be the best from a wealth production point of view. Yet, we are unable to say how much the government should interfere in the economy.

Hayek maintained that the overall structure of a political system should not be designed following a preconceived plan due to a lack of information, although firms often do so to define their own organization. The reason behind that assertion remains quite obscure. He accepts the principle of a "non-spontaneous" organization that would result from a conscious and constructive effort in the case of the firm, but rejects the "constructivist" organization of a very big public firm the size of a country. Yet, some commercial firms, private or public, have larger production volumes and workforces than some small countries. Besides, we make most of our decisions in a situation of incomplete information.[33]

33. If we understand Hayek's "spontaneous order" as an order resulting from

The argument we maintain here is quite different. It is very easy to imagine the development of a social system from scratch, from a common plan—if the opportunity arises. In that case, the process is very similar to the setting up of a firm. But, in both cases and because of the lack of complete information, we are unable to say which organization is the best, which dominates the whole range of other solutions which we cannot describe nor evaluate. We do not know how to solve such a complex problem of inventory and classification.

The task of the ideologists gets even more complicated if they take into account the fact that the definition of the best political regime might well change with circumstances and through time. Indeed, can we reasonably think that the same system could be optimal in third-dynasty Egypt, in Rome at the beginning of the first millennium and in twenty-first-century England? Obviously not. Indeed, suggesting that a centralized choice of social system, or social contract, could be made comes down to suggesting that the society is already fully centralized. So, the answer is in the question.

A Moralistic Caricature

To that impossible question about the best system in the abstract, ideologists currently try to reply in terms of individuals' moral preferences. That answer postulates the existence of moral preferences directly regarding the mechanisms of coordination of production activities. Thus, the very functioning of a market would only express selfish aspirations, while the mechanism of the state hierarchy—that allegedly implies democratic control through the political market—would meet the generous aspirations of solidarity and altruism.

That is pure nonsense. Although Adam Smith showed that the

---

many *decentralized* decisions, then the transmission of the information to all the society's members can account for the superiority of a "decentralized" order on a hierarchical, centralized, order or, in Hayek's inadequate terminology, a "constructivist" order.

market mechanism did not need altruistic motives to meet our demands, it accomodates them nevertheless and thus reflects the diverse nature of our longings. After all, it is thanks to the market-originated economic development that living standards improved spectacularly in the world since the Industrial Revolution, thus doing more for the human well-being than all the public redistribution of income. It would be as utterly ridiculous to claim that the Soviet Union or Nazi Germany were ethical models of solidarity and altruism because they chose the hierarchical mechanism. And it would be even more absurd to suggest that the people working on markets and those working in public administrations are not the same: are the former only motivated by money and the latter by solidarity with fellow citizens?

In fact, the decision-making mechanisms have nothing to do with ethical motivations. What differentiates the hierarchical mechanism from the market mechanism is the productivity and efficiency of the allocation of resources. It is likely that the self-claimed "ethical" ideology suggesting a priori individual preferences for markets or for state hierarchies comes from the fact that each mechanism is often used to produce different goods: on the one hand, the private goods, purchased and consumed by individuals and, on the other hand, the public goods which require a production taking into account the aspirations of all the members of the community managed by the state, as they can only be consumed in the same quantities by all individuals. Hence, probably, the idea that the former satisfy pure selfishness while the latter meet a need for solidarity. Quite a convenient confusion. We will see in Chapter 7 that the modern analysis of the state does not vindicate such a motivation among governments.

However, we can accept the idea that some individuals prefer, on principle, collective goods, while others prefer private goods. But sometimes the same goods can be produced both by public and private mechanism. For instance, in the insurance sector, health insurance is supplied both by public insurance and private policies. The two types of producers, the private companies and the public administrations, are thus potentially in competition. In these circumstances, the assertion according to which public insurance policies only meet a need for solidarity while the same insurance, in its private form, is only a source a profit, sounds like a misleading advertisement in a competition for the same clients. Which is precisely the case.

Can we then accept the idea that the choice of a society simply reflects individuals' preferences no longer between market mechanisms and public hierarchies, but between truly public or private goods. There again, we cannot. Economic analysis shows that this explanation is also false.

Indeed, preferences—whatever their nature—are not enough to determine choices. For instance, each of us can like both going to the movies and reading books. The extent of our preferences for these two activities is not enough to determine the time and money we will devote to them in our monthly budget. We must also be aware of the respective prices of these two consumptions and of our disposable income. The classical theory of consumption—largely supported by abundant empirical works—indeed shows that the levels of consumption of books and movies depend on the result of the arbitrage between our preferences and the costs that we have to incur to satisfy them. The changes in our consumption habits are determined not really by changes in our tastes and preferences for the two activities, but rather by changes in their respective prices: when a book becomes cheaper than a ticket to the movies, we tend to go less to the movies and buy more books instead.

Thus, if we assume that each of us has preferences for specific private or public goods, it is reasonable to think that we will adjust our demand for the former or the latter not because our conceptions inexplicably vary with time, but because the costs of private goods and public goods evolve differently. Even though we still prefer private goods, it is possible that if the fiscal cost of collective goods falls sharply compared with the price of private goods, we will consume more public transportation because the cost of car maintenance, insurance and parking becomes prohibitive.

Then, it is not our preferences that determine the evolution of political systems, but the conditions on which prices depend, that is, the evolution of productivities.

In that view, we switch from a conception based on inexplicable and unexplained changes regarding individual preferences for political or private production (How? Why? Under which influences? Are there evidences of that?), to the idea that political systems evolve according to the changes in the costs and efficiency of these two production modes which can be empirically quantified and tested.

If we assume that the changes in the respective costs of hierarchies and markets are the main determinant of political systems' evolution and of the state's influence, then the periods of decline in state power—and thus of relative market expansion—must also be periods of decline for all hierarchies, including big corporations since they are organized according to the principle of authority, just like states. This can be considered as a preview of our theory that can be—in this precise form—confronted by real and observed evolutions.

Although we have been focusing on individuals' ethical or pre-conceived preferences so far in this chapter, ideologists generally present the choice between political systems as a single and global issue, likely to have a single solution: 100 percent state, 100 percent market or a mix, which looks more realistic and reasonable but is much more difficult to define concretely, as we pointed out earlier.

This approach is built on the concept of "social contract," a kind of implied fundamental pact modern societies' actual constitutions are supposed to be based on. Nothing whatsoever resembling such a founding contract has ever been observed in historical or ethnographic reality. Maybe the Magna Carta was the closest we got to it, but it focused on fiscal issues only and evolved from an existing distribution of wealth and power. The notion certainly gained more credibility with the adoption of the American Constitution, then with the French Revolution and the adoption of the first French Constitution. But there was a big difference: the American and French constitutions were essentially designed to organize state power and public hierarchies. And in that view, they corresponded to a true internal logic. As the hierarchy is managed by the top, it can be reorganized from the top by a single act.

But the same approach cannot be applied to a whole society, which is an organization of organizations, as we underlined at the beginning of the chapter. A society includes both decentralized organizations, such as markets, and centralized organizations, that is hierarchies. But markets are not subjected to a central plan nor can their development be preconceived. They need a legal system that a state can set up easily and efficiently, but they do not require a central and unified structure. They develop according to the decentralized actions of their numerous participants.

Thus, trying to imagine the appropriate politico-economic system for a whole society (even if we give up the idea that one can know and choose the best) amounts to asking a self-answered question: if we can decide—even democratically—what a good organizational system for the whole French society would be, it is because that society is already fully centralized. If it was not, the question itself is impossible, meaningless. It has no theoretical answer. Nobody is able to know in advance what the detailed choices of millions of people will be as they act independently and adjust their choices each time the respective costs of the various alternatives diverge or converge.

The social system will be the outcome of a wide range of rational decisions and will not result from the implementation of a centralized project designed by a few individuals. Despite that, in extreme circumstances, if the relative functioning costs of markets and hierarchies reach exceptional ratios, all the decision makers can choose simultaneously to opt for the 100 percent market or 100 percent state solutions. But this is highly unlikely. As always in economics, the choices reveal a preference for diversity and mixed solutions. And after all, nobody chooses to spend his whole life watching movies or eating burgers!

Thus, we suggest to forget the existing ideological approaches of societal choices for a simple reason: choosing a political system (in a centralized or decentralized way) amounts to choosing an organization of organizations. And as it is a choice, it must be analyzed according to the science of choices and decisions, that is economics. The choice of an organizational system must be analyzed with the very tools of organizational economics.

As we showed above, the choice of the economic system is based on a series of individual and collective decisions which, whatever the underlying preferences, are influenced by the relative efficiency of the decision-making mechanisms on which organizations are based. It is thus the comparative efficiencies—and thus the comparative costs— of markets and hierarchies that determine the size of hierarchies, their number and, as a consequence, the space dedicated to the market transactions between individuals and hierarchies, and between hierarchies.

We are thus led to a more realistic approach of the evolution of political regimes. They change according to a multitude of decisions and to the modifications of the relative efficiency of the two fundamental mechanisms. This results in variable systems, whose centralization rate evolves with production conditions. There are an infinite range of possible systems. It is impossible to describe them all and to determine which is the best, just as it is impossible to calculate ex ante which is the best budget structure of a given household. What we can say is that the relative cost of markets and hierarchies will influence political systems' structure. Thus, there is no single system that is always better than the others in all countries and under all circumstances. But there is a trend towards more effective systems that evolve in line with comparative costs.

The question we must ask ourselves at this point of the reasoning is what the nature of these costs is and what determines their evolution. That problem will be tackled in the next chapter.

CHAPTER 6

The Decisive
Role of
Information

The organizational architecture of a society is a mix of pyramids, in variable proportions, more or less numerous and high, and of more or less developed markets. It is determined by all the choices made by individuals between these two production modes. Their decision is influenced not only by their personal preferences but also, as usual, by the costs and benefits of each mode.

The costs implied by these two mechanisms differ because they do not rely on the same amount of negotiated transactions and individual information search. Markets use transactions intensively and require the processing of large volumes of information. Conversely, hierarchies economize on transactions and limit the access to information to a few specialists and decision makers. And transactions, exchange and information have a cost.

Transaction costs are defined as all the resources that people or companies need to bring an exchange to its conclusion. They include the transportation costs of goods and people and the information search costs. All actions require a view, a mental image, a good knowledge of the environment, or, in other terms, some information about the conditions in which the decision may be made (here, the potential transaction). In a society that is now moving towards electronic trade, a service society where the transportation costs of goods and people fall constantly, the main component of the transaction costs is information cost.

When information is costly and rare, the market mechanism is so expensive to use that the polar hierarchical mechanism is more attractive. But when information costs are very low, transaction costs decline and the market mechanism becomes more tempting. Thus, it is the quest for the most effective production conditions that will influence organizational choices and favor the development of either hierarchies or markets depending on the availability of information in the society.

Abundant information encourages a broader distribution of the decision-making power, which will in turn cause the collapse of hierarchies and the rise of markets. Scarce information results in more concentrated decision making and thus encourages the development of hierarchies. That relation is what we call the central theorem of organization.

It implies that no single organizational structure is unconditionally better than all the others, whatever the time and place. The most efficient organization can only be chosen according to the respective costs of the two possible production modes. This explains the developments and radical changes that transformed politico-economic systems during the twentieth century. They first caused an information shortage as capacities of production and transmission of information improved much less than industrial production. But the trend recently reversed, when information became much more abundant with the information revolution.

In this chapter, we will first study the components of markets and transaction costs, then analyze the determinants of the costs of hierarchical management to explain the central theorem of organization, and finally conclude on how the recent flood of information has changed so deeply social and political organizations.

MARKETS AND TRANSACTION COSTS

Strangely enough, the economists—whose work mainly consists in measuring the cost of everything—have often considered markets as a gift from heaven, an equivalent of the famous free lunch which Milton Friedman views as a myth: according to the traditional treaties and textbooks, supply and demand always met without any difficulty as if an invisible auctioneer was able to find the price at which the bidders would accept to buy the precise quantities offered. Thus, it is not surprising that the Socialists were tempted to replace that invisible trader by a real trader, standing at the head of the Gosplan or any other centralizing bureaucracy, who would also define the price of everything in order to balance supply and demand at the level requested by the government.

And it is precisely in reference to the Socialist experience and to the giant western firms that Ronald Coase first drew attention to the real cost of the market mechanism. The good functioning of the market has a cost. It requires that bidders and askers travel, collect information, negotiate, sign agreements and really deliver the goods in the predefined conditions.

Those transaction costs mainly consist of the transportation costs of goods and people and the costs of collecting and processing information.

Transportation and Information

By definition, market production implies multiple transactions between the independent manufacturers of the products that are complementary or competing in the production chain, which starts with the extraction of raw materials and ends with the delivery of the end product to the consumer. The typical example of the Birmingham weapons industry in 1860 shows that the number of potential transactions between the specialized producers of each component can be very high. And each operation implies several cost factors.

The buyers must first make inquiries about the presence of sellers on the market and find out about their names, locations and specialties. They must also check the product range, quality, prices and reputation of their potential trading partner. Once they have selected a product and a supplier, they must enter into negotiations in order to reach an agreement on the quality, prices, deadlines and delivery conditions that will satisfy both parties. They will then draw a contract either instantaneously and implicitly in the event of a cash purchase, or explicitly and often in writing in the event of a large forward order. Finally, the buyer must accept to bear the expenses necessary to monitor the execution of the contract according to the predefined terms.

These various activities require time, efforts and either traveling costs (if people have to go and hunt for information) or information costs (if people receive the information through the mail and telegraph or, more recently, by telephone, fax or e-mail). Not to mention the cost of the transportation of semi-finished goods from a specialized craftsmen to the actor of the next production stage.

Transportation costs fell substantially after the First and Second Industrial Revolutions and many have forgotten how they slowed activity in pre-industrial societies. In the past, they increased sharply the price of the transported good and limited long-distance trade to light and small objects of great value (for instance, precious metals, jewelry, spices and other goods long viewed as luxury products such as oil and wine in Antiquity). Part of these costs resulted from the high risks incurred, whether natural (shipwrecks) or human (pirates at sea and highwaymen on roads).

Those costs are much lower nowadays. First, because of the ever-increasing land use and the development of state power and their legal order.[1] But also due to the gradual urbanization of all societies, the

1. James D. Tracy (ed.), *The Political Economy of Merchant Empires: State Power and World Trade, 1350–1750*, Cambridge University Press, 1991.

improvement of transportation infrastructures, and the physical or economic compression of the distances between trading partners. For instance, medieval fairs and markets reduced temporarily the transactions costs by bringing together the supply and demand in a same place. Towns have the same permanent effects.

As transportation costs fell constantly during the twentieth century, information costs have become the main component of the overall transaction costs.[2] At the same time, the economic distances between the various areas of the world have decreased sharply over the last decades. For instance, advances in shipping technology have reduced average ocean freight charges per short ton from $95 in 1920 to $29 in 1990 (in 1990 U.S. dollars). Between 1930 and 1990, average air transport revenue per passenger-mile fell from 68 cents to 11 cents, and the cost of a 3-minute phone call from New York to London dropped from $244.65 to $3.32 (again in 1990 dollars).[3]

Moreover, as most production activities have been reoriented toward services rather than tangible goods with the increase in living standards, the importance of transportation costs has decreased. And twentieth-century technical advances have reduced them even further. This reflects mostly in the contemporary tourism boom.

It follows that, in modern economies, transaction costs mainly depend on the cost of information and thus on its availability in the society.[4] Indeed, all the other operations that transactions imply are

2. This was underlined by Axel Leijonhufvud who wrote that "data storage, processing and transmission costs have replaced transportation costs which had long existed." In "Information Costs, and the Division of Labour," *International Social Science Journal*, May 1989.

3. Economic Report of the President, 1997, p. 243.

4. Many economists (and especially Williamson) have tried to analyze the complexity of transaction costs, the consequences of a negotiation depending on the trading partners' commitment to the contract, on the possible abuses of monopoly positions. In short, the cost of the commitment to the trading conditions despite all the uncertainty about the future economic environment and the partner's behavior once the agreement is concluded. The detailed analysis of the contracts is much too for-

information collection processes aimed at identifying the products and partners available, finding out about prices and quality, or even at entering into a negotiation that would not have been necessary if both parties had been perfectly informed about the other's capacities and income and about the conditions applicable to all the other market transactions.

Meanwhile, the higher consumption of the growing population also increases the trading volumes between the suppliers, which are themselves more numerous. Indeed, trading volumes generally grow faster than output volumes, which is especially striking when we compare the respective charts of world trade and national products during the last few decades. And the recent globalization of markets has resulted in even greater task specialization, as Adam Smith had suggested.

In an economy where decentralized production is carried out by increasingly specialized craftsmen, growing production volumes necessarily lead to a rise in the number of individual producers. Consequently, each supplier or client can also select his trading partner from a wider range of possibilities. This increase in the trading volumes, number of producers and possible combinations of the semi-finished products of the various suppliers creates a growing need for information collection and processing.

The development of production and urbanization thus had opposite effects on transaction costs with, on one side, declining transportation costs (thanks not only to technological advances but also to safer movement of goods and people) and, on the other side, a wider range of possible transactions due to the increase in both the number and volume of goods available and the population living in this larger market area. As a consequence, the overall demand for information rises significantly and the second component of transaction costs (in-

---

malized and often fruitless.

Much more simply, most transaction costs are due to the cost of obtaining information.

formation costs) gains importance. The massive increase in the volume of information demanded must increase its cost if its production and transmission techniques remain unchanged.

Information costs have thus become the main component of transaction costs. They deeply influence the organizational choice between pyramids and lattices, given both organizational modes do not require the same volume of information. With market production, every participant must collect information intensively, while the purpose of the hierarchical production mode is precisely to limit transactions, and thus information collection within the production unit.

Participants select their production mode according to the availability of information. When information costs are high, hierarchical production is most likely to be chosen, given it is less information-consuming. On the contrary, when they are low, market production is selected.

These choices between the market and hierarchical mechanisms are made by individuals. The higher efficiency of either production modes, which depends on the transaction costs (in other words, on the information costs), is thus a function of individual information costs.

The Cost of Individual Information Production

As the notion of "information" concerns a wide range of goods and services, it is difficult to give a general definition that will take all of them into account. Following Shapiro and Varian, we consider that this concept should be taken in its broadest sense.[5] According to their definition, information is anything that can be expressed in numbers and more especially 0 and 1, that is all things that can be coded in bits, with the bit ("*binary digit*") being the smallest measurement unit of the volume of information. Thus, the score of a tennis match,

5. Carl Shapiro and Hal R. Varian, *Information Rules: A Strategic Guide to the Network Economy*, Harvard Business School Press, 1999, p. 3.

books, databases, magazines, movies, music, stock prices and website pages are all examples of information.

Information is required for all sorts of reasons (for instance, pleasure, business, military purposes), and by all kinds of people. Information is costly to produce and to collect.

According to the traditional economic analysis of perfect markets, information has the same characteristics as public goods since it is available to all participants in the same quantity and freely. As such, it cannot be sold and has no price. Coase was the first to question that postulate, showing that the transaction costs resulting from the functioning of the markets are mainly information collection costs.[6] Hayek added, in two famous articles published in 1937 and 1945, that the information about the production, consumption and trading conditions varies according to the good and place considered. However, it is spread in the participants' heads, and can only be brought together through multiple market transactions. In its most compact and summarized form, it translates into prices. Stigler has reformulated the mechanism described by Coase and explained it in detail, showing how, given the wide range of prices offered by the various sellers,[7]

6. According to Coase, "the most obvious cost of organizing production through the price mechanism is that of discovering what the most relevant prices are. This cost may be reduced but it will not be eliminated by the emergence of specialists who will sell this information." Ronald Coase, "The Nature of the Firm," *Economica*, 1937, p. 326.

He added that "the costs of negotiating and concluding a separate contract for each exchange transaction which takes place on a market must also be taken into account," but we felt that those costs also amount to information costs. Indeed, if two trading partners are perfectly informed about the other's preferences, its capacity to pay, if he generally honors his commitments and the overall market conditions, they do not need to negotiate or even sign a contract. The negotiation which determines the terms of the contract that will be signed is meant to force each party to reveal its preferences according to the other's desires. It amounts to a mutual production of information.

7. George Stigler, "The Economics of Information," *Journal of Political Economy*, 1961, pp. 213–225.

consumers must devote time and effort to identifying the best price if they want to use their resources as wisely as possible.

It follows that information is not immediately and completely available on real markets. And it has in fact a price or cost for the buyer, whether he decides to collect it by and for himself (he does his "shopping") or prefers to buy it from a specialist of information production who has already collected it (an expert, a journalist, a producer of directories or of comparative tests for each category of products) and who sells it to consumers in various forms, such as newspaper articles, specialized magazines, books, radio or television productions and website pages.

Information Costs in Terms of Time, Effort, and Attention

Conceiving information as a public good is wrong; this does not take into account several aspects of its production and trade. In fact, no information is truly free, for the simple reason that a reader, auditor or spectator cannot assimilate information without spending at least a little time, devoting efforts or, in any case, paying attention. But these human resources are only available in limited quantities. Time is obviously a rare resource and its scarcity increases with living standards.[8] An executive with an hourly wage of $30 will pay $15 for any "freely available" information that will take him half an hour to read.

The total amount of attention that each of us can devote is also limited. And we live in such a complicated world, where consumer goods and activities are so varied that there is permanently fierce competition to catch our attention. Can we pay special attention to the evening news, to what the members of our family are telling us, to the plot of the novel we are reading, to a concert, to the content of the file we brought back home to study "at one's leisure"? That is the

8. Gary Becker, "A Theory of the Allocation of Time," *Economic Journal*, September 1965, and Staffan Burenstam Linder, *The Harried Leisure Class*, Columbia University Press, 1970.

problem raised by Linder and we do not believe it is only a question of time. We can pay more or less attention to a particular activity like reading the newspaper and at the same listen to music, watch television or speak with someone sporadically. And we can also read an article carefully or skim through it. When we pay attention to an activity, we cannot concentrate on the other activities. All activities thus imply an "opportunity cost," a sacrifice, a price in terms of time and attention. And obviously this is especially true of information-collection activities.

It follows that useful information is never universally nor immediately available even if it has (almost) no market price. It is not transmitted automatically nor freely to all the market participants. It is acquired through experience and after a deliberate and expensive hunt in terms of resources. The individual quest for information requires time and efforts that add to the purchase price of the information traded and sold in the form of national and local newspapers, various publications, directories, market surveys and studies, or simply by means of commercial and industrial espionage. And then individuals still have to choose between these information inputs, find out about prices and quality, select those that will be the most useful, assimilate it and possibly store it. This confirms that information has a production cost for the private economic agents who intervene in the market and must collect it and adapt it to their own specific needs. The price itself is one of the easiest pieces of information to find in modern economies, as it is widely and often freely displayed in companies' price tables, adverts, equity quotations and consumer guides. But it quite often requires a comparative study given the large range of products available and the diverse qualities offered by the various market participants.

In other words, useful information is never free, given it must be produced by each of its users. When it is general and undifferentiated, it has little value for decision makers. A wine producer does not care if there is generally little rain and no hail in the region of Bordeaux in autumn. What he needs to know is if it is going to rain on his land and during the third week of October to decide if he should harvest the grapes earlier or later than usual. Moreover, information must be unique to generate wealth, not easily reproducible and thus privately appropriable. If all the engine builders knew in detail how to manufacture fuel injection engines, it would be impossible to patent and sell the concept to another producer. Finally, information must concern precise places and people as the decisions of each consumer reflect its particular needs and unique conditions.

Assimilation Costs and Human Capital Investments

But it is not the only cost of that "public good" that is supposed to be free. The proper and useful assimilation of a piece of information requires prior knowledge and efforts. It is impossible to understand an economic article, even if it is published in a non-specialized newspaper, without having first devoted a minimum of effort to the learning of economic mechanisms by reading studies or accumulating practical experience. The depreciation cost of our knowledge (that is of our intellectual capital) in this field should thus be included in the acquisition cost of the current economic information, especially as that investment has proved very costly in terms of time and efforts in the past. The same is true, say, of a foreign language or the study of science and technology. In economics, the same unprocessed information concerning the latest inflation data does not have the same meaning and use for someone who has invested in economic analysis and someone who knows nothing about it. Useful and productive information is costly to obtain.

Without competence, a kind of intellectual "software" that is also very costly to acquire, the unprocessed information collected in an article will not be understood and thus useless and unusable. Not to mention the cost, the intensity, of the effort made to understand the new elements of the article itself, which is almost always necessary.

Contemporary analyses of human capital, the competence capital, show that it contributes to making people use information more productively in both market and non-market activities.[9] This is why the best trained people are more capable of treating themselves and thus obtain a higher health capital than those who have little education. Medical information is less costly for the former and thus used in larger quantities and more efficiently.

Information is thus never free for its user, even if he has not created or conceived it by himself. He will nevertheless have to choose his pieces of information from a growing range of available data, assess their quality and, because of the limited amount of time and efforts he can invest, select the information inputs he will examine. This first selection process is in itself costly, as shown by the theory of information-seeking behavior that Stigler was the first to develop. He concentrated on price dispersion but many other fields of application were then found, especially in the study of job search.

As a consequence, individual information production is always specific. Each of us must search our own even if others have already found it and each decision maker must bear the cost in terms of time and other resources. Any market production first implies the simple cost of the search for information about the trading partners and their products. But the resulting negotiation between the supplier and the client is only costly in terms of time and efforts because of the scarcity of information. Its main purpose is indeed to define the precise terms of the transaction (characteristics of the goods and/or services, prices, deadlines, delivery conditions, guarantees). And it would only be costless if the information about both parties had been completely and perfectly collected. Each trading partner would then know precisely what the other wants and what he can offer or pay, how his rivals are faring, the current prices for a given quality, the guarantees the other

---

9. Finis Welch, "Education in Production," *Journal of Political Economy*, January–February 1970, and Robert T. Michael, "Education in Non-market Production," *Journal of Political Economy*, March–April 1973.

partner usually offers and so on. In that case, none of the parties needs to hunt for information: the agreement is immediately reached. We will see later on that such conditions almost exist on financial markets. And that is why the latter lend themselves so well to the classical analysis of pure and perfect competition which precisely implies exhaustive and costless information that is freely available to all participants. But this model remains a borderline case that is rarely if ever seen in real life where individual information is always rare and expensive.

As it always has a cost and goes through a "final individual production stage," even if it consumes free public inputs on the same occasion, information remains the sole property of the one who has produced it for its own use, if he wants to. He can spread it or keep it for himself. As such, it is a private good, which does not necessarily fall in the public domain. Its price for the producer-user is the cost borne to acquire it, which is always strictly positive. Its quantity and quality are different for every buyer and producer, especially because its cost in terms of time is never the same for two individuals. Consequently, information is thus a product like any other that can be analyzed with the usual economic tools and does not require the development of brand new methods of analysis, a trap into which many economists fell when they tried to study it.

The gist of the problem is that to be usefully associated with actions, decisions or choices, the piece of information must be processed by a brain or a cerebral substitute, an artificial complementary brain such as a computer and its software. Assimilation and processing are thus necessarily individual-specific operations. They remain private, confined to that particular brain or computer unless the latter is stolen or hacked, or the former, if the expert or decision maker is "grilled" to obtain specific information that he was unwilling to share.

It is totally unrealistic to pretend that information is a public good simply because it can, in some specific cases, cost little or nothing for someone to transmit it—verbally for example. The transmission cost can be equal to zero but the reception cost will almost never be.

Neither is information necessarily a public good nor its price equal to zero because, technically, two people can use the same piece of information at the same moment. Generally, the information producer does not gather it in public. He works in his workshop, his office or in the depths of his mind. He has several ways to retain his exclusive rights. If he decides to transmit it freely, it is most often because he has already used it intensively or to reap the fruits of his efforts, for example, by becoming famous in the case of scientific research. It can also be to advertise his products, which are already patented in the case of applied research. Thus, most often, the transmitter had to "pay" for the "free" information he is disseminating.

Finally, it is also false to assume that there is no rivalry between two people using the same information. If my investigations and analyses show me that, say, Amazon is likely to announce benefits in its earnings report that will only be unveiled by its management at next month's press conference, I can make money out of my information by taking position on the company's stock. When the other participants will be informed in their turn, I will cash profits that will pay for my exclusive information. If on the contrary, other financial analysts obtain the same information or if I tell them about it during a conversation, they will also take position, the stock's price will change immediately and my potential gains will be much more limited or could even vanish. Information is the object of rivalry. Information loses value as soon as it is transmitted. The information acquired by some reduces the value of those held by others. This phenomenon is less concrete and more gradual, qualitative, than it would be with tangible goods: if I use a photocopier, nobody else can use it at the same time. There is total rivalry for its use. But this is also true of the information about Amazon: if other people use the same information at the same time, it is much less useful to me. The value of that piece of information is reduced proportionally, less severely but in the same way, as when someone wants to use the photocopier at the same time as I do. In the first case, I can lose 50 percent of my potential gains on Amazon's stock, while in the second case I lose 100 percent of my gains because of the use of the photocopier by someone else. In other words, the difference with other goods is not a question of nature but a question of degree.

We can thus conclude that information is most often a good that can be produced and privately appropriated just like the other goods and services. This significantly changes our view of organizations.

Information Costs, Profitability, and Imperfect Markets

If transportation and information costs are equal to zero, markets are perfect and everybody is fully informed. There is no transaction risk, no cheating, no complicated negotiation concerning quality and prices, as everything is known from the beginning. The negotiation becomes useless and there is full decentralization.[10] The system is self-regulated: there is no central power, no conscious organizational decision making. It is the organizational optimum or the "ideal society" according to Hayek. But such a society with perfect markets requires the availability of a maximum, if not infinite, amount of information.[11]

As pieces of information are always costly for the end user (who is also the end producer), they always remain rare and expensive in that society. All the potential, "complete," information will never be collected nor produced, and the level of "full" information will never be reached. It follows that markets will never be perfect, contrary to what the theory of the perfectly competitive economy had suggested, as all suppliers and consumers cannot have infinitely abundant information at their disposal at any time and no cost.

---

10. Harold Demsetz, *Economic, Legal, and Political Dimensions of Competition*, North-Holland, 1982.

11. See also Martin Shubik, "Information, Rationality and Free Choice in a Future Democratic Society," *Daedalus*, vol. 96, 1967, pp. 771–778, mentioned in D. M. Lamberton (ed.), *Economics of Information and Knowledge*, Penguin, 1971.

On the contrary, in real life, information is rare and often hard to find. It has a cost which can be prohibitive. Markets are always more or less imperfect. The individual production of information by both the consumers and producers will never be maximal given its production and assimilation costs.

As that information reflects in the prices, the latter will never summarize all the information spread throughout the society. They will themselves be imperfect. This leaves room for the other production mechanism, hierarchy, which requires much less of this costly information than the market.

Information production always stops before reaching the extremes of full and free information, which is characteristic of perfect markets.

The more imperfect the markets, the more varied the prices for an identical quality of the good or service considered. Information collection is thus necessary to make a choice. Conversely, the more perfect the markets, the less useful the negotiation. In a perfect market, the buyer does not have to negotiate the overall price of a car given all manufacturers will sell an identical product at the same price because of competition. It is no use either for the seller to try and obtain a little more than the market price as he would automatically price himself out of the market. Any available information is priced in and it is no use for the buyer or seller to try and differ from it in a situation of competition.

This market efficiency theory has found its best application in finance. The price of a financial asset, a share, for instance, is determined by the right to receive a fraction of the future benefits that the company will realize all along its economic life. These future benefits cannot be known in advance but they are estimated by each buyer or seller of this stock. New information about the whole economy, the sector the firm belongs to or the company itself that influences its potential benefits (now or in the future) immediately alters the stock's price, as it alters the present value of the expected gains.

On a perfect or "efficient" financial market, the least information is captured and used by an investor or another and prompts him to buy or sell the stock, if possible before all the other investors, in order to make a capital gain (the positive difference in the stock's price). Thus, as soon as the information is available, the stock's trading volumes and price vary. And the new price reflects it. We can thus conclude that market prices reflect all the information available in the economy. At every moment, the market price is the "true" price which mirrors the fundamental value of the company. In such a market, we can only hope to make a gain on the current price if we have fresh information that the other investors do not have yet. If not, it would make no difference to buy with complete confidence at the current price, given it would reflect all that is known for the moment about the future benefits of the company. It is impossible to do better than the thousands of participants who all try to determine as well as possible the company's financial outlook and hunt for fresh news.

Thus, professional financial analysts are paid full time to find fresh news. Their very success is an incentive to develop their research activity to the point where an additional piece of information requiring another week of work will cost more to produce than it is worth in terms of increased precision about the exact price of the stock compared with the current market price, and thus in terms of capital gains. As a consequence, a financial analyst earns as much as any other specialist who has the same skills, and both of them rarely, if ever, become millionaires. If other analysts entered the trade, the production of information would increase but at the same time the markets' degree of perfection would improve while the analysts' gains would decrease. The market's informational imperfection will thus be determined by the "normal," competitive salary that an average analyst considers he should earn in view of his education and skills. The higher the average analyst's salary, the more imperfect the market.

However, if the financial research was totally stopped because financial markets were perfect and it was consequently possible to buy and sell at the current price without having to find more information about the stock, equity news would soon stop being produced. The market would become imperfect. Stocks' prices would no longer reflect the information available in the world. And it would thus be possible to make a lot of money by hunting for better information.

Consequently, the production of financial information and surveys would reach its equilibrium level, which would correspond exactly to the normal profitability of the production of an additional information. As the salary of the analysts is not equal to zero, the market cannot be totally perfect. If the market was perfect, the analysts' work would have no value. They would no longer be able to give pieces of advice that would be somewhat profitable and the trade would disappear as we explained above. On the contrary, if the analysts were well paid, the market would be very imperfect.

Real markets are thus characterized by a certain degree of imperfection which depends on information's production cost. This determines the cost of using transactions, that is, the cost of the market mechanism, as it requires that each participant collects large volumes of information.

Because of the existence of positive information costs, the other production mode, hierarchy, is often less costly than the market. When the markets are less perfect, the hierarchical solution to the production coordination issue seems more attractive.

HIERARCHY AND THE COST OF MANAGEMENT

The hierarchical mode is the other way to coordinate production between a large number of specialized individuals. But what makes it information-saving? How does the hierarchy produce and use information? Basically, the information held by the manager is first replicated and then combined to the human capital of the various subordinates, of which it amplifies the efficiency. It follows that there is a sort of leverage of the manager's information and competence which is multiplied by the number of subordinates who use it.

This production mode does not imply the same transaction costs as the market. First, because it reduces the number of transactions and second, because it spreads the cost of a given piece information efficiently by replicating it and transmitting it for free to the members of the hierarchy who will thus not need to hunt for information by themselves.

Consequently, the hierarchical production mode reduces the cost of information per unit produced. Each unit produced is the result of very few transactions. And as each transaction requires a certain volume of information, each unit produced in the hierarchical mode only requires a small quantity of information (and thus low information costs) given hierarchies manage to transmit information at a low replication cost.

But in that case why are there not just hierarchical productions and no markets? This extreme situation will never materialize in real life as hierarchies suffer information and control losses which increase with the size of the organization. The efficiency of a hierarchy thus decreases with size, which means that its production costs increase with size. When the managerial (or hierarchical) unit costs reach the same level as the market mechanism, the firm stops growing. It has reached its maximum efficiency.

The Hierarchical Advantage

While market production requires that all participants, bidders and askers, hunt for information, the hierarchical production needs very little information: only the decision makers at the top of the pyramid have access to it. They then use it to make decisions concerning the characteristics of the product, its production process and the distribution of tasks among the specialists, the quantities to be produced, the terms and conditions and the selling price. They then transmit the information collected and paid for only once to all their subordinates in the form of directives which define the actions the latter should undertake without having to hunt for information individually.

Now, only one member of the hierarchy, the manager, seeks information. The advantage of this technique is that information is transmitted to the rest of the hierarchical pyramid at low cost. If each information seeker-producer must bear its overall cost individually, a hierarchical organization consisting of 100 employees (but where only one of them buys the information) has information costs 100 times lower than a market composed of 100 producer-buyers where each of them must collect identical information individually. For example, the books in a library are bought once and read by hundreds of readers. They can also be photocopied at a rather low cost and selectively. The use of information will thus be less costly for both the company and the library than for an individual consumer.

The hierarchical production mode thus amortizes information costs first by reducing both the number of seekers and the number of inquiries each of them will make, then by replicating and transmitting this information at a low cost and in a reduced form easier to use.

In a hierarchical mode, the list of suppliers is mostly limited to internal producers. While information about the clients and suppliers is frequently looked for by each specialized producer in the market production mode, that search is only performed once and by one person in the hierarchy: the manager hunts for the best specialized producers in the economy and hires them to create a rather stable production team. He then specifies the tasks that each team member will have to perform (instead of letting them define by themselves the production conditions of each component of the end product) and the assembly procedure through a long consultation process.

The hierarchy thus avoids several costly information-seeking processes that are inherent in the decentralized market mechanism. First, by giving to the manager and his specialized employees the sole responsibility to seek information about the producers that the company should work with, instead of letting each independent producer hunt for his own. Second, by selecting only one group of specialized producers that it integrates into its organization and it will not have to constantly negotiate with all the others to define the characteristics of the product's components and the assembly procedures.

It creates a "production chain" that now remains unchanged over several periods and uses it repeatedly to mass-produce an item. It thus amortizes, over a large number of units produced, the cost initially borne to collect information about the specialized producers that were worth recruiting and the characteristics of the production process and the distribution of tasks. It is the high cost of information that encourages companies to make a scarcer use of decentralized exchange procedures based on the price mechanism.[12]

The hierarchy also implies higher task specialization by distinguishing between the production tasks, strictly speaking, and the informational or supervisory tasks. On a market, each participant is both the specialized producer of a product or component and the producer of his own information (technical specifications or information about the markets and his clients, suppliers and rivals). In a hierarchy, the manager does not himself participate in the production process. He only focuses on the tasks for which he is the most productive: using information—that he is the sole to obtain—for the definition of the overall characteristics of the product and all its components and making sure subordinates follow his directives strictly during the production process.

The latter are thus exempted from the design and marketing tasks they had to do on top of their production activity when they were still independent producers on the market. They can specialize in the transformation of products, devote all their time to it and consequently improve their productivity.

12. However, it can increase the production costs given the internal supplier is not necessarily the most efficient among all those who offer their products and services on the market as Malone, Yates, and Benjamin underlined, op. cit., p. 486.

That is why the technologies of information—or, more precisely, its production cost—determine the choices between the two exchange mechanisms: hierarchies or markets. It also conditions the size of hierarchical organizations and society's organizational structure.

Indeed, in a hierarchy, the high cost of information is an incentive to limit its use to those capable of making the most of it. This represents for the community at large the optimal allocation of a scarce resource as we saw in the section about M&As. And this explains the very principle of the hierarchical order as only those who have the information can make effective and sensible decisions. It is thus necessary, when information is restricted to a few, that the decision-making power must be given to the same few. The other producers must not decide for themselves but rather follow the instructions given by the informed.

However, the hierarchy must be able to remain the sole user of the costly information it has collected or bought. Information is thus made more profitable to seek and produce as it gives the firm an advantage over its rivals. It must also manage to amortize the private cost of this information over a large number of production processes.

Command and the Replication of Information: "Managerial Leverage"

According to the principle of command or hierarchical authority, the manager is the only one to collect information and then to transform it into precise directives which will eventually be transmitted to the subordinates. As their exact content and coordination is decided in advance by the manager, the subordinates are given clear and easily understandable indications that do not require a large investment in human capital nor further investigation.

As information is costly to collect or "produce" and to develop by assembling the partial elements that the ones and the others hold, it is logical to try to use it as rationally as possible and produce it and make it more easily available by reproducing it at the lowest cost.

Obviously, in real-life hierarchies, the manager is not the sole information producer. He is assisted by several employees whose work consists of collecting, sorting out and processing the information as efficiently as possible to help the manager make a choice. But, in the end, that information is stored for the sole use of the latter. It is only transmitted to the other members of the firm once it has been included in directives and instructions, in the existing knowledge and savoir faire, in specific techniques presented as procedures or recipes, and in specific equipment. Once reprocessed and disseminated, it is neither recognizable nor really traceable by the team members. It thus remains the private property of the firm and is difficult to recover or reuse outside it, except in the case of industrial espionage where a rival company would try deliberately to reconstruct it by assembling its various components ("reverse engineering"). Such a dissemination of information at every nook and cranny of the organization guarantees its exclusiveness and private appropriation to the company which produces it. Incorporating information is the key to competitiveness.

Incorporating Information

The best way for a company to retain the monopoly of the information it produces is to structure the organization so that the information collected is incorporated into the machinery and into the specialized tasks. The organization thus forms a matrix for the individuals' behavior, guiding employees without giving them access to all the information disseminated in the whole structure. The matrix is designed only once, as if it was durable equipment, and is then used by all the employees who are successively appointed to a same position in the organization. The information is more integrated to organizational capital than to human capital. It can thus be used and reused at various production stages and be substantially amortized.

That way, the company retains its exclusive property and protects itself against the low replication costs that often characterize information. Once information has been integrated into the production structures and equipment, the specific procedures and the "home-made" directives, it becomes opaque for all the team members as none of them gets a broad view of the system. It cannot be copied in its entirety. It is implicit and private. It cannot be cloned and freely disseminated by rival companies.

But this process, where unique information is integrated into various recipes, procedures and products, does not only apply to firms. For instance, each of us builds his own knowledge about the interaction of chemical molecules or the spread of malaria and the resistance of the various types of germs to medicine. We let specialists who invest in medical research deal with it and we then use their conclusions in their popularized, basic, simplified forms—as it is less costly to assimilate than the original—when we are reading, watching a documentary or using an anti-malarial drug prescribed by our GP. Generally, we do not check in detail the quality of the original information, as we suppose that this has already been done by other specialists who have better access to the original information, a field into which we do no try to venture. For us users, this integrated scientific information is opaque and we cannot trace it. Similarly, a field worker in a firm cannot rebuild all the information he uses every day and that he receives in the form of instructions, equipment or organizational procedures. It makes him more productive but he cannot take the credit for it and use it elsewhere.

There is thus a specialization in information's production levels and fields. We simply apply the directives of our GP or the pharmaceutical company that produces the drug. Similarly, when we are preparing meals, we do not try and understand why we must mix these ingredients and cook them at that temperature nor what physical and chemical reactions this implies. We just apply a partial information that we consider to be reliable by relying on the knowledge and fame of the cook who wrote the recipe book.

Some cooking recipes are also integrated in "cooking machines" such as electrical ovens. We just have to select a function that the oven then automatically applies during the chosen length of time at a given temperature. The same is true of all the modern equipments which contain information that is much more complicated than what the user is supposed to know, for example, the GPS navigation devices in cars which show you the best way to reach your destination and guide you where you want. IT people would say that these devices are "user-friendly."

Similarly, in a company which accumulates specific information, the directives that are given by the top manager—once he has collected and sorted out the external information from the information that has been created by the internal R&D departments—are "user-friendly" for the subordinates that have to follow them. They are passed on from one grade to the next until they reach the field producers in their most specific and simplified forms. These subordinates need much less knowledge than the designers of these products or directives. However, they need some competence or human capital, a "software" or in other terms a "business culture," that enables them to understand and apply efficiently those directives. There, as in any human activity, human capital improves the worker's productivity or its use of information. Culture is productive. Thus, the business culture shared by all the employees has the advantage of helping them use easily and quickly the information integrated in the directives coming from the top, without having to know or understand completely its precise content to apply it efficiently. A good knowledge of the firm's methods, habits and organization scheme is useful to deal with the sometimes not completely specific directives given by the management.

The information obtained by the manager is thus disseminated so that all the members of the firm can use it in various forms. That way, all the subordinates can share their knowledge and competence, which is kind of reproduced and reused in as many copies as there are subordinates in the firm.

This method of reproducing the same information is a way to make it much cheaper to use for a layman, a person that has not made the human capital investments that would have helped him understand directly and completely the original information. It also enables the specialist to disseminate his incomparable competence by combining it with that of its subordinates or of the people that buy his recipes in the market. It thus makes the employees more competent at every level of the hierarchy. It represents "managerial leverage." And the larger the informational gap between the bottom and top of the hierarchy, the stronger the managerial leverage.

In a market, the information produced does not benefit from such a leverage effect. The buyer can use the one pre-selected by the specialist and thus benefit from their high competence and productivity to improve his own. But he must first seek information—about the information specialists (for instance, doctors, cooks, financial analysts). In hierarchies, the search is much more limited as each of its members directly submits to the decisions made by his superiors without having to choose between several of his superiors' prescriptions. All subordinates accept in their job contract to submit to the instructions coming from the top of the hierarchy concerning the definition of their task and the methods that they should use to accomplish it. And each of them in turn imposes its informational production and knowledge to the following grade of the hierarchical production process.

He thus abandons the idea of producing his own information and only relies on the information he gets from the company's specialist (who is generally his superior). As it is the superior that makes the final choice at each decision-making level, it is in fact the decision maker at the top of the hierarchy that integrates his own information in the decisions of all his subordinates. His information, which is deemed the best, is then used by all the members of the hierarchy. In that process, the manager will need the help of information producers specialized in marketing, production and finance. But he is the only one to collect all these particular data about the company's environment to transform them into simplified and ready-to-use directives.

He is the only one through which all the information used in the company flows. He thus replaces—with the help of a few specialized advisers—all the individual decision makers in a market that would have had to hunt for information if it had been a decentralized production process like the one of the Birmingham weapons industry in 1860. A same directive coming from the top can thus improve the productivity of tens, hundreds or thousands of employees just because of its informational content.

The total volume of information that needs to be collected is thus much lower in a hierarchy. Admittedly, it is bad news given information will be much less varied and choices will be less justified and consequently more risky. But, on the other hand, it avoids costly searches for information and, as the manager's capacity of assimilation is limited he will rapidly reach a saturation point, which will reduce even further the volume of information bought and the total purchase cost.[13] Because of his reduced information-processing capacity, the manager will probably not make the best decisions. But the money saved is worth some deterioration in the quality of decision making.

Hierarchies are thus less information-consuming decision-making devices than markets. And it is because information is rare and costly that this low consumption of information is advantageous. The hierarchy allocates this scarce information to the employee that uses it the most efficiently, the most productively or, in other words, that makes the most of it. And it is logical that the person who uses information so efficiently and for whom the company collects it, be also

13. Martin Shubik, op. cit., wrote that it is charitable to consider human beings as a channel for information transmission. It is more of a bottleneck, according to him.

the one that makes the main decisions that will then be disseminated to all those in the company who do not have access to such information. The ultimate information and decision-making specialist is thus the manager. He must make sure that the other members of the productive team properly implement his directives.

Thus, when information is scarce, hierarchies contribute to spreading it optimally in the economy. The concentration of the decision-making power depends on how information and the people that use it efficiently are distributed between the existing companies. And this allocation mechanism plays a major role in M&As, as they are aimed at obtaining the optimal management skills (the optimal management of information) in the economy by changing the number of companies, and thus the number of decision makers.

Replication or the Economy of Memes

Before going through the details of this process, we would like to underline the great similarities between the mechanisms of information replication in the hierarchy and information duplication in biological life. Alfred Marshall saw economics as "a branch of biology" and not of physical sciences. And the economics of information within firms proves him right.

All the directives and conceptions of the company managers, on which are based the products and the tasks/activities of the subordinates, are ideas: ideas of products, ideas of production processes and organizational methods. According to Paul Romer, ideas—which are an informational structure, a coherent group of information—are crucial for technical progress and thus for economic development.[14]

But ideas are immortal. They do not depreciate with use. They can be indefinitely reproduced and reused, depending on the variable success they have in different environments.[15] Although ideas that met

14. Paul Romer, "Ideas and Things," *The Economist*, 150 Economist Years Issue.
15. Thomas Jefferson anticipated the partially public good characteristic of ideas

the expectations and needs of the Greek society in the fifth century BC can be of little interest for the Chinese society of the twenty-first century, some can also be reused indefinitely in all kinds of societies, as is the case of plane geometry, for example.

As Richard Dawkins underlined, ideas have exactly the same general characteristics—replication, productivity, immortality—as genes in biology.[16] Genes are immortal. They replicate indefinitely and identically. They contain information that enables the development of organisms and the metabolic processes of which they are the essential complement. Economically speaking, genes are life's production factors. But they are faced with more or less favorable replication conditions depending on the environment.

Like genes, the development of ideas will depend on the success, the degree of replication, of the vehicle that conveys it: the phenotype, that is ourselves in the case of the genes, and the organization and the products in the case of ideas. The ideas of products and production methods, which favor the growth of the hierarchical organizations within which they are developed and implemented, spread within the society at large at the same time as the products and processes they have given birth to.

It is a similar mechanism that explains the endogeneity of ideologies that we have previously underlined. Ideologies propagate according to the development of the organizations that they represent and which expansion favors. In other words, they are the instruments or auxiliaries but not the source or the prime factor. A market society will first spread a market ideology. A hierarchical society will first (and sometimes only) propagate an ideology of command and authority.

---

in some limited personal interactions when he wrote in 1813: "He who receives an idea from me, receives instruction himself without lessening mine, as he who lights his taper at mine, receives light without darkening me." "No Patent on Ideas: Letter to Isaac McPherson," August 13, 1813. In *Writings*, New York, Library of America: 1286–94.

16. Richard Dawkins, *The Selfish Gene*, Oxford University Press, 1976, Chapter 11: "Memes: the New Replicators."

However, ideas blend together and evolve. New ideas appear because of a mutation of the existing ideas or their application to new fields. They also cross. Given they resemble genes so much, Dawkins decided to brand them "memes" by analogy. Ideas and concepts indeed influence the development of the social organisms or products that are the vehicles that convey them and enable them to replicate. They spread from one brain to another where they are blended with other ideas to develop tangible goods, services or organizational methods. However, the selection of phenotypes determines the selection of their memes.

Hierarchies' productivity is thus due to the replication of rare and useful information through the most efficient organisms, managed by the people the most capable of using productively this costly information.

But the savings on information costs that are made with hierarchies are not boundless. The propagation of information to a growing number of subordinates generates information losses, a distortion of the messages and control losses, as employees are increasingly hard to supervise because of their rising number. Beyond a certain size of hierarchy, managerial costs increase and limit the optimal size of the hierarchy by offsetting information savings.

The Loss of Information, the Cost of Management, and the Firm's Boundaries

The hierarchical team production mode thus saves money on information costs compared with the market production mode, but it implies specific costs that we will call the cost of management. Team production poses problems of cheating, control and supervision as it is not easy to measure the productivity of each team member when the production is the fruit of mutual efforts.[17] It follows that cheating

17. Armen Alchian and Harold Demsetz, "Production, Information Costs and Organization," *American Economic Review*, 1972.

and laziness become tempting as the economy of efforts that they allow correspond, for a given monetary salary, to a rise in the real pay received. Indeed, in a wage-earning system, each employee is paid according to his expected productivity. If he manages to reduce his effective productivity and his efforts, he will increase the effective remuneration of his work-effort unit accordingly.

If everybody did so, the production would stop and the firm would have to file for bankruptcy. Team production is thus only viable if there is a control and supervisory body in charge of cutting these losses. But the supervisory body itself has flaws. First, it propagates imperfectly the directives coming from the top, like a message which is whispered from ear to ear by twenty successive people becomes incomprehensible or a document that is Xeroxed thirty times becomes illegible. Moreover, cheating cannot be ruled out in the supervisory body itself.

Monitoring the Employees

The remedy against cheating in the productive teams is the administrative body proper, the hierarchical pyramid whose members are not directly producers but whose work consists in supervising the producers and making sure that they follow the manager's directives. In fact, they produce information about the performances of direct producers.

Monitoring is easier and more efficient when the workers' tasks are simple. Only a lawyer can supervise another lawyer. But with the standardized and simplified assembly line production designed by Taylor and introduced by Ford, one person can supervise the work of ten, fifteen or twenty field workers performing basic tasks. The hierarchical pyramid and task simplification are meant to make supervision more effective.

The methods of Taylor and Ford thus result from the information shortage on two counts. The choice of hierarchical production rather than market decentralization is justified by the fact that information costs make the latter ineffective. But then, as it is difficult to produce information about the performances of individual employees in the hierarchical production mode, work is made as simple, repetitive and measurable as possible so that it becomes easier to supervise the producers and realize the required performance.

This is true not only of industrial hierarchies but of any other hierarchy, especially in private or public services. This transposition of the Taylorist and Fordist methods to the bureaucracies was made by Max Weber. When he described the bureaucratic organization of work, he simply applied Taylorism to service companies.

Bureaucracy as a Service Factory

Bureaucratization is basically the equivalent of assembly line work in the service sector. It improves managers' control and thus reduces managerial costs, that is the productivity losses that can result from teamwork. Max Weber indeed suggested both that the hierarchy's productivity could be increased and that managerial costs could be cut. According to him, bureaucratization (the development of hierarchical pyramids) enabled processing information better, while rationalization (the representation of people as standardized files) enabled using less of it. The latter method consists in destroying or ignoring the useless part of the information to make it easier to process the essential part. This selection simplifies the information and thus reduces its processing cost. This is especially true of the management of personal relations by means of a series of objective and impersonal criteria, for instance, by using forms.

But in fact, bureaucratization is essentially meant to monitor the transmission and implementation of information. It increases managerial costs but reduces the user's cost of information. Like in the large car plants that symbolize twentieth-century industry, it is the standardization and simplification of the administrative tasks that reduces the supervision costs of the vast bureaucracies of which Kafka described the prototype: the insurance company he worked for in Vienna.

The Agency Problem and the Capital Market

The monitoring problem concerns not only the field workers at the bottom of the hierarchical pyramid and the intermediate supervisors, but also the manager, who is often also a salaried employee in big modern businesses. Because of their huge size, the latter require a lot of capital to guarantee the fulfillment of contracts concerning large volumes and significant amounts of money. In most cases, the amount of capital necessary to run General Motors, Pepsi-Cola or the French car maker Renault is much higher than the amount of savings amassed by private individuals. That capital must thus be fragmented by spreading it between a large number of savers who will each hold a small share of the firm's equity. In the end, shareholders are too numerous to manage the company themselves. Because of their number, making a common decision would be a very long and expensive process. There again we are faced with the problem of the cost of market transactions and negotiations.

The solution is to have the stockholders appoint a representative—the manager of the enterprise—at their general assembly or, more indirectly, a board of directors which will appoint its representative: the chairman or CEO. The latter can hold shares in the firm he manages, but his main financial compensation is a wage. He is thus, in theory, a subordinate of either the shareholders or the board of directors. But, in practice, neither of them can make collective decisions and convert the information they have into ready-to-use directives designed to influence the manager's strategy. In fact, it is the manager who gathers the information, makes the decisions and manages the company by issuing directives, whose good implementation is then controlled by his own staff.

But, being an employee, he does not share the same targets as the owners-shareholders. Their aim is simple: they purchase stocks to receive a share of the company's future gains during its whole life cycle. Thus, they want the present value of that future expected flow—which determines today's stock price—to be the highest possible. They want the manager to maximize the stock's value, that is, the firm's market capitalization.

The manager wants both high wages and significant fringe benefits: a company car or even a company plane, pleasant working conditions, comfortable business trips and many efficient assistants and colleagues who relieve him of some of his work. But wages and fringe benefits depend on the size of the firm. First, because large companies have often been growing quicker than the others—because they were the most effective initially—and can consequently pay their managers more. Second, because a manager's financial compensation is a fixed cost which will be all the lower by unit produced that it will be spread over a larger output volume. Finally, because the management of larger firms requires greater skills which justify a higher pay. The same is true of fringe benefits: it is easier to amortize a company plane on high output volumes, while the cost per unit produced can be prohibitive for a small company.

For all these reasons, the salaried manager will often set growth as his top priority, especially as he will gain more social recognition and prestige from managing a big firm than a small one.

He will then focus less on achieving the highest possible stock value for the shareholders. This is the problem when the manager is not also the owner of the firm. It first appeared with the advent of giant companies, especially in the United States in the early twentieth century, and was identified by Berle and Means in their famous 1932 book *The Modern Corporation and Private Property*. This is called the "agency issue" in modern literature. The owner indeed gives the manager—his "agent"—the mandate to manage his capital in a way that best serves his interests. But given the divergence of interests, he must supervise his representative's management strategy.

In a big firm owned by many shareholders, it is difficult for them to avoid losing some control. Small shareholders have at most a weak financial motive to devote their time and efforts to the analysis and supervision of the leader's management. It is not in the advantage of someone holding three shares in a company for a total amount of $240 to spend a dozen hours studying the balance sheets and business plans if his own hourly wages are $20, because that study would cost him his full investment. And even if he did and ended up criticizing the management of the company head, his three voting rights at the general meeting would hardly give him a chance to be heard by the board of directors or the manager, and his investment in time and information would then be lost. Thus, the shareholders' "rational ignorance" is economically justified. On the contrary, a big shareholder, whose votes—put together—can thwart the plans of the firm's head and even force him to resign, would have good reasons to have a close look at the management strategy because the cost of the analysis could be amortized on his significant investment in stocks. Besides, such a study can be beneficial to him as he can change the CEO and the management strategy to better serve his own interests.

The drawbacks of separating ownership from management—because of a large number of shareholders—can be limited by various means. First, by giving the managers a share of the profits in the form of company stocks or stock options. If they amount to large sums of money, the manager will start thinking like a shareholder rather than as an employee since he will earn more from his shares than from his wages. Second, by making the board of directors more independent of the managers through all the means of control, better known as "corporate governance," that have emerged because of more mobile and increasingly competitive capital markets. That way, the shareholders regain some of their decision-making power. There are also the legal measures that make takeovers easier and thus put the managers in competition with other management teams for the control of the firm. That competition encourages managers to offer more than their rivals in order to be chosen by the shareholders. Thereby, the managers are compelled to meet the shareholders' demand, that is, to increase as much as possible the firm's value. Finally, the re-concentration of the shares into the hands of a few persons by financial intermediaries such as pension funds, gives the managers of these funds a real control over the managers of the firms in which they have invested and of which they hold a large fraction of the capital. The managers of these funds are themselves faced with harsh competition on transparent stock markets, where their performances are easily comparable and where investors are quite mobile.

All these techniques reduce the agency problem. And since that problem usually worsens with the size of the firm, they should in theory improve the company's efficient size.

But as they are all imperfect, the size of the firm will be limited by the control losses of managers over subordinates and of shareholders over managers.

There will also be differences of size between firms belonging to the same industry, as managers do not all have the same competence and skills. A more efficient manager will collect information better and at a lower cost, make better strategic decisions and supervise the employees' productivity more efficiently. Thus, he will be able to increase the size of his company more than the others because he will be more productive and will enjoy a cost advantage that will be reflected by larger sales.

A more efficient manager will gain permission to manage a larger volume of human and capital resources. That greater efficiency in collecting and managing the information, which justifies the existence of the firm, will thus result in a larger allocation of resources to the most efficient managers. Consequently, the human and capital resources available in the economy will be distributed between the companies proportionally to the information processing abilities of the various managers. That distribution changes either with the internal growth—or shrinking—of the existing companies or with the external growth of a firm that results from the full shrinking of another company which is taken over by the former.

Thus, in a competitive economy, the decision-making power is optimally allocated between the managers. The mechanism of that competition for the right to decide on the use of the resources is clearly visible during M&As and explains some of their aspects that had long seemed enigmatic.

We can thus explain organizational choices by looking at the respective, relative or comparative costs of the two existing coordination modes: the pyramid and the lattice. Their operating costs—which directly depend on information costs—are different because they use information differently. As a consequence, it is the cost of information that determines the choice of the production structures: either the market model or the hierarchical model.

THE CENTRAL THEOREM OF ORGANIZATION

As for all the other goods and services, the quantity of information depends on its price or cost. For a given demand, if its availability increases, its price falls, or conversely if the price declines, the quantity demanded increases. That inverse relationship between price and quantity, all other things being equal, is the law of demand, which is the cornerstone of economic analysis.

Since information is mostly an economic good like the others—we showed previously that it was indeed a private good—it follows the law of demand in its traditional form. But as information is also the result of a final user's individual production, one cannot observe its price directly on a market. The production of information has a different cost for each individual producer, for each of us, depending especially on the value of time for us, which is usually not the same as our neighbor's.

But what we can study is the price and volume of the informational inputs traded and of the objects containing information: books, newspapers, videotapes, subscriptions to databases and storage means such as hard disks. We can also measure the exchanges of information like for instance the amount of mail, the number and the length of the messages by phone, fax or modem and the radio and TV broadcasts.

Digital Production

Ideally, all these items could be measured the same way, since any information can be translated into "bits," that is, zeros and ones. The total number of zeros and ones circulating in the society would be recorded during the storage or transmission of information and would thus give us a global measure of the overall quantity of information, of its stock and flow. We would thus have a quantitative estimate of the society's "digital production," which would give us an idea of its informational production.

For lack of such a knowledge, which will sooner or later complete the data already provided by the national accounts, we can nevertheless assert, in view of the evolution of the partial data on the volumes of information produced and of the decline in their price and the price of data transmission and storage, that the information revolution often mentioned since the 1960s has resulted in a surge in the volumes available and a sharp fall in the price.

The increase in the quantity of energy available after both Industrial Revolutions, and the concomitant plunge in its price, transformed all the modern economies and societies dramatically. So, in what respects is the current information revolution changing our economies and societies? How can we understand these deep changes and evaluate them? So far, we have only limited ourselves to stating the obvious about the most visible direct consequences: over-information, or rather the saturation of our minds with second-rate information, the invasion of entertainment and the virtual, the plethora of possible choices if you want to read, see pictures or communicate.

But the increase in the global quantity of information in circulation can be analyzed more fundamentally by looking at its effect on all the productions and exchanges that characterize life in society. We have indeed seen earlier on that the purpose of any social organization is production, whether public or private, goods or services. The very choice to live in large societies and not like Robinson Crusoe or in small groups of hunters-gatherers that had to be made since the beginning of human history a million years ago can be explained by the search for a greater number of exchanges and a higher consumption of tangible and moral goods—"mental nourishment" being obviously as important as tangible consumption once the subsistence level has been reached.

But the study of production choices belongs to the realm of economic analysis. Especially as information, as a non-freely-abundant resource, is a decisive production factor, just like labor or capital. It is simply impossible to produce or consume without information. If the Neolithic societies did not produce TV sets, computers or plastic materials, it is because they had not created the information necessary for these productions. Yet, they had labor and the same availability of raw materials as the twenty-first century societies. That is why information is an essential production factor.

If tomorrow all the objects of the post-industrial civilization vanished from earth, would it be a greater catastrophe than the disappearance of all the libraries and the loss of collective memory? Certainly not. Within a few months or years, technologies would reemerge and all the objects that would have vanished could be recreated. On the contrary, the loss of the information stored, the overall knowledge, would take us back, and maybe forever, to the "natural state" of the Paleolithic hunters and fishermen.

In that view, the information revolution can be defined as a swift and sharp increase in the storage and transmission capacities of this production factor, which is the most essential for human activities. We must analyze the consequences of that increase just like we would do for the other production factors. A job for the economists.

Information as a Production Factor

For instance, we know what impact an increase in the quantity of a production factor can have on the structure of a country's activities. Given the production technologies and when the prices of goods are relatively stable, an increase in the quantity of capital available in the economy leads to the development of all the capital-intensive productions, the quantity of labor remaining unchanged.

That is why the European and American economies, which have a lot of technical and human capital and relatively few unskilled workers, produce a growing number of sophisticated goods which require top-range equipment and higher skills, and handed over the easiest productions, such as saucepans, traditional textile and mass-produced clothes, to the economies that have less capital and skills and thus more low qualification workers. Economists will have recognized the "Rybczynski theorem" named after the British economist who rigorously expounded the conditions of that mechanism.

That theorem, which completes Heckscher-Ohlin's classical theory of international trade, shows how an increase in the available quantity of a production factor can lead to the decline of the sector that uses it scarcely, and simultaneously to the development of the sector that uses it intensively.

This analysis of the impact of the sudden abundance of a production factor can also be applied to everyday life. When tangible goods abound, a defining characteristic of our consumer societies, while the time we have at our disposal cannot exceed twenty-four hours per day, how can we take the best advantage of the new relative availability of these ingredients necessary to the fulfillment of our satisfactions? As Gary Becker showed, all consumers are, as such, also producers. We do not consume the meat and vegetables in the state they were when we bought them in the local supermarket. We use our time, skills and equipment (for example, an oven or a food processor) to transform the food (raw material) in order to obtain a higher gastronomic satisfaction than if we had consumed them without a personal finishing touch, that is, without what Becker calls a "domestic production," which uses the following production factors: time and marketable goods, domestic appliances and raw food.

When goods become increasingly abundant (for instance, domestic appliances) while the quantity of our time remains the same, then we will make an increasing use of these goods by unit of time. And indeed the structure of our domestic production becomes increasingly "good-intensive." As a consequence, we concentrate on the activities which make an increasing use of goods and we give up those which mostly take time.

Swedish economist Staffan Burenstam Linder analyzed in depth and with great skill the adaptation of the ways of life to the new abundance of goods and to the resulting relative time shortage.[18] We try to use as many goods as possible by time unit when we read a newspaper while we are watching TV, having a drink and smoking a cigar while our meal is heating up in the microwave and both the washing machine and the dishwasher are on. We call people with our mobile phone as we drive our car. And our spare time is less and less spent resting and thinking: during our leisure we use things, such as a house in the country, tennis rackets, skis, TVs, boats, planes, books, magazines, bikes, sportswear, in short, all that can enable us to use more of these abundant tangible goods per rare unit of time.

All these aspects of our behavior are typical to the modern civilization and result from the abundance of material goods, which is the other component, besides time and competence, of our personal production function.

18. "The Harried Leisure Class," op. cit.

The Theorem

The example of our "personal production of consumption" (or of satisfaction) thus concurs with the Rybczinski theorem concerning international production and trade. And the very same reasoning can apply to the use of all the production factors and especially to the factor we are analyzing here: the information factor.

We can thus conclude that, like for the more traditional production factors (labor and capital), the conditions of use of information in the various types of production vary according to their relative abundance in the various countries.

We will call this the "central organizational theorem,"[19] according to which the choice between centralization or decentralization depends on the quantity of information available. When the quantity of available information increases, the overall structure of the production activities will shift toward the most information-intensive, and especially the decentralized structure, the market mechanism.

The theorem first indicates that we will use goods and services containing an increasing amount of information. This is the case, for example, of the intelligent machines or other robots. Nowadays even the plainest car incorporates microprocessors which regulate the consumption of fuel, the transmission of the engine's power to the wheels according to the state of the road and the risk of skids. It also manages the brakes in the place of the driver and is often equipped with an on-board computer that calculates the distances and the consumption, the time of arrival together with the latitude and the longitude thanks to the GPS system. A contemporary car certainly takes on board a greater calculation and data-processing power than a World War II aircraft carrier. It becomes, above all, a computerized machine.

But the second and most important consequence of the organizational theorem concerns the choice of the production's organizational mode.

19. Or the "Coase-Rybczynski theorem."

As we saw earlier on, goods and services can be produced according to two different modes: the market mechanism, which is very information-consuming, and the hierarchical mode, which only requires small volumes of information as it aims at using the least possible.

When the price of information diminishes relatively to all the other goods and services or, in other words, when its quantity increases even quicker than that of the other goods and services, a direct implementation of the Rybczinski theorem to the two types of production activities—decentralized and centralized—reminds us that the information-consuming process will develop constantly while the information-saving process will be less and less used. As a consequence, the decentralized production mode will develop to the detriment of the hierarchical production mode that has become comparatively more expensive and less competitive.

The theorem indicates that the hierarchy will replace the market each time the cost of information increases, and conversely when it diminishes. It thus fundamentally explains, in a general way and in compliance with all the other economic laws, the worldwide development of the market organization and the parallel decline of the hierarchical organization that characterizes our time.

It also stipulates that the new balance of organizations will remain, as long as the capacity to produce goods will not develop quicker than the capacity to store, process and transmit information. The information society must be a decentralized society, a market society where the hierarchical values are given a pounding, simply because the hierarchies decline and are no longer able to impose on public opinion the moral criteria the most appropriate to their functioning.

All in all, the information revolution has deeply altered human societies' organizational system. Until now, authors have always tried to explain this with a multitude of incidental reasons, but without discovering its profound unitary origin. Some of them, like Dudley—

who completed the precursory work of Innis[20]—have tried to explain the geographical expansion or shrinking of states through history by various types of technical advances. Depending on its characteristics, each innovation would have different effects: either the increase or the reduction of the organization's size. That explanation is thus not really satisfactory because we have to explain in detail why each given innovation should increase or reduce the organization's size, so that no general effect of innovation can be inferred.[21]

The analysis we propose is much more simple and general. Whatever the innovation, its effects will result from the ratio between the quantity of information and the quantity of the goods produced in the economy. Any innovation that increases the ratio leads to decentralization. Any innovation that reduces it leads to centralization. So that it is not necessary to wonder about the mechanism—which would be different each time—through which an innovation affects the organization size. Here, the mechanism is always the same and the question is whether the innovation makes information more abundant than goods or the other way round.

The transformations undergone by firms, the new cultures, and the growth and decline of states and political ideologies are all consequences of the new abundance of information generated by the digital technologies invented in the second half of the twentieth century.

The Critics

That relation is sometimes criticized on the grounds that the mere advances in information technology and especially one machine—the computer—cannot affect all human activities. But that would be disregarding the universal influence of information, which directly im-

---

20. Harold A. Innis, *Empire and Communications*, 1950.

21. Moreover, Dudley distinguishes between two types of techniques which, combined, determine the size of the states: the administrative techniques and the military techniques, so that a new analysis is necessary for each historical case.

pacts all the individual and collective choices, all the personal and commercial productions, and whose cost depends on the storage, processing and transmission techniques, that is, above all on the effectiveness of the computers and telecommunications. The universality of the search for information explains the universality of the social upheavals generated by the progress of these seemingly limited and specific techniques.

The speed of these transformations is spectacular but not unprecedented: in the past, technological progress has often been at least as sudden as is the case for example of the invention of telegraph, railroad, car, television, plane and chemistry. But the current advances concern a small number of techniques that are used in all productive activities. Their impact is only comparable to the energy revolution that replaced human and animal muscles with the steam engines in the early nineteenth century, and later on with the fuel and electric engines. With the information revolution, the human brain needs much less to memorize, calculate and even think. It is above all a cerebral revolution, which thus impacts all the social activities even deeper than the "muscle revolution."

After a brief reminder of the scale of the revolution under way, we will clarify its deep organizational consequences in contemporary societies as a decentralizing revolution succeeds to the long centralizing phase of the first twentieth century.

We thus propose an economic and rational explanation of the great cycle of the twentieth century that resulted in exceptional advances in living standards, health and demography, but also in the conflicts, revolutions and mutations that represent the major intellectual challenge of contemporary social sciences.

THE INFORMATION REVOLUTION AND ITS
CONSEQUENCES ON THE ORGANIZATIONAL SYSTEMS

About an Apparent Cultural Paradox

Because of its growing abundance over the last two or three decades, information has been used in a less and less productive way. As its cost has been falling constantly, marginal information has also become less and less interesting and useful. Like for all the other goods and services, the latest unit used tends to produce an utility that adjusts to its cost. When that cost is lowered, the marginal utility is also reduced.

That fits in with the most basic economic law according to which the scarcest resources must be used parsimoniously and as efficiently as possible. Efficiency is obtained when these resources are allocated to the users who make the most of them, who use them in the most productive way.

On the contrary, more abundant resources can be allocated to less wealth-creating, less productive, uses. And immensely abundant resources are nearly costless and can be wasted almost without any drawback. They can be used without caring about their productivity or efficiency.

Hence, the constant deterioration in the quality of information because of its recent flood. This explains the so specific characteristics of communications in the contemporary society and its marginal cultural poverty, although this is not in contradiction with the highest average level of culture ever reached by human societies.

The Information Revolution

The demand for information to coordinate collective productions increases with the number of exchanges possible, that is, the number of people and the number and the variety of the available goods.

Thereby, the cost of a transaction that did take place increases with the number of potential transactions, that is, with the number of products and the number of market participants, since we must inquire about a larger range of possibilities before making a choice. But each of us can only assimilate a limited volume of information. As Martin Shubik wrote:

> Men live in an environment they know very little about. They ignore not only how to estimate the range of possibilities that is offered to them but also its existence. Their perception skills are rather limited; their calculation power is in most cases smaller than that of a computer and their ability to search, process and memorize data varies with time. Given the rising speed of transmission and the volumes of messages, individual skills are increasingly limited compared with those of the society as a whole.[22]

The information revolution increases those limited capacities and take them beyond their natural limits.

The very expression of "information revolution" has been commonplace for long.[23] Since the Industrial Revolution, firms have always tried to have more information at their disposal. They increased their internal information about their own activities by developing accountancy and other bureaucratic techniques such as files, forms, charts, reports and other circulars, and by adopting new technologies such as the typewriter and the calculator. But they also improved their external information thanks to the telegraph or the telephone. And that will to control and coordinate dates back to the first civilizations, as Jack Goody showed in his book about the origins and the function of writing.[24] But today, these cumulated efforts have given birth to the "information society."

22. Martin Shubik, in Lamberton (ed.), op. cit., p. 359.
23. Jacob Marschak already considered the notion of "information revolution" as being well-known in 1968 in "Economics of Inquiring, Communicating, Deciding," *American Economic Review*, 1968.
24. Jack Goody, *The Domestication of the Savage Mind*, Cambridge University Press, 1977.

The concept was first introduced in the late fifties by economist Fritz Machlup, who was the first to understand the importance that new sector would gain in the U.S. economy and which would play a major role in the "production and distribution of knowledge."[25] He listed about thirty information industries classified into five categories: education, research and development, means of communication (the media), information-processing devices (such as computers) and information-providing services (finances, insurance, housing sector). The sector first employed more than 10 percent of the working population in the late 1880s and this rate then reached 25 percent in 1930, 42 percent in 1960 and more than 45 percent in the 1970s.

At that time, the information sector boomed thanks to the combined development of several technologies: mass media, telecommunications and computers. At the same time, digitization (the binary encoding of any information) blurred the boundaries between the various forms of information (words, figures, drawings, charts, pictures and sounds), and the progress is such that one day it will be possible to digitize, store, process and transmit in a binary form all the human feelings, tastes, smells and touches.

Many authors pointed out that acceleration of the information revolution long ago, like McLuhan and his global village (1964), Phillips and the communications age (1975), Evans and the Micro-Millenium (1979). Touraine and Bell spoke of an information-consuming post-industrial society in 1971 and 1973 respectively, and Mead underlined the increasing importance of information and knowledge in modern culture (1970).[26]

25. Fritz Machlup, *The Production and Distribution of Knowledge*, Princeton University Press, 1962.

26. Marshall McLuhan, *Understanding Media: The Extensions of Man*, McGraw-Hill, 1964; Kevin Phillips, *Mediacracy: American Parties and Politics in the Communications Age*, Doubleday, 1975; Christopher Evans, *The Micro Millenium*, Pocket Books, 1979; Alain Touraine, *The Post-Industrial Society*, Random House, 1971; Daniel Bell, *The Coming of Post-Industrial Society: A Venture in Social Forecasting*, Basic Books, 1973; and Margaret Mead, *Culture and Commitment: A Study of the Generation Gap*, Doubleday, 1970.

As in all the other industries, the advances concerned the conversion, storage, and transportation of basic products. In the case of information, this overall process amounts to encoding (a form of conversion and processing), storage, and transmission (a form of transportation).

Encoding, Storage, Processing, and Transmission

The advances in encoding, storage, data processing, and transmission began long before the modern technologies of the information revolution. The invention of writing and numbers was one of the first stages. The art of writing was even the first administrative technique according to Goody.

The same was true much later of the Morse code and the telegraph. In the information technology age, the main encoding means are the screen and keyboard, which have replaced the punch cards devised by Joseph-Marie Jacquard in 1801 for his looms, and later perfected by Hollerith for his tabulators in the late nineteenth century. These cards were still commonly used in computers in the early 1970s before the PC boom.

Progress continued with the invention of the scanner and the voice-recognition devices: the former allowed to decode (and thus encode) written texts by transforming them into zeros and ones and the latter did the same with language, which is indisputably the first information encoder and transmitter.[27]

In terms of storage, semiconductors' memory capacity has been increasing at a stunning pace since the early 1970s, while their price has been falling quickly.

The number of components on a memory card has increased by 50 percent every year since that date and there is no sign of a slow-

---

27. See Michael S. Scott Morton (ed.), *The Corporation of the 1990s*, Oxford University Press, 1991, and more especially the chapter written by Joanne Yates and Robert I. Benjamin, "The Past and Present as a Window on the Future," pp. 65–67.

down.[28] At the same time, the cost per megabyte fell by 35 percent every year. The steady reduction in the size of transistors allows continuously improved performances of these memory cards. Mass storage is made on hard disks or floppy disks, whose cost per megabyte collapsed by 38 percent every year between 1983 and 1994. The capacities are such today that storage is costless. Besides, with the new optical disks, it will be possible to store information much longer than with the current magnetic disks. In the future, digital disk storage will probably supplant all the other methods, even for videos. So that in the future, the libraries, especially with the e-Books which begin to appear on the market, will be contained in a few hard disks, floppy disks or movie archives.

But having such large-scale storage capacities would be useless if it was too costly to hunt for information afterwards. Hence, the decisive role of the new data-processing techniques. It must be possible to give a few search criteria to a computer whose data-processing speed is high enough to scan these huge information reserves and then find, file and extract the data likely to meet the request. And in that field too, the progress has been—and still is—remarkable.

From the very start of the revolution, in the mid 1960s, one of the pioneers of the Silicon Valley, Gordon Moore, CEO and founder of Intel Corporation, the world specialist in semiconductors, reported that, extrapolating the recent experience the number of transistors on a single silicon chip would double every year. Since then, it has been noticed that the doubling takes a little longer: about eighteen months. Yet, data-processing capacities thus increased geometrically, in a relation whose never-denied stability justifies its name of "Moore's Law."[29]

28. Lars Groth, *Future Organizational Design: The Scope for IT-based Enterprise*, Wiley, 1999, p. 193.

29. Stephen Cohen, John Bradford de Long and John Zysman, "An E-economy?," *Brad de Long's Home Page*, December 1999, www.j-bradford-delong.net. The original Moore contribution is: Gordon Moore, "Cramming More Components onto Integrated Circuits," *Electronics*, 39 (8), 1–4.

One of the most used microprocessors, the Intel 80-86 saw its calculation power increase by 50 percent each year between 1978 and 1997, while the price of a MIPS (Million of Instructions Per Second)—a unit measuring that power—fell by an average of 25 percent each year. As a result, the power was multiplied by 200 over twenty years, and the price/performance ratio improved three-hundred fold. Above all, these advances allowed the miniaturization of hardware, from the first ENIAC computer which weighed 30 tons to the latest palmtop of less than 300 grams. In 2010, computers' data-processing capacities will most certainly be ten-million fold higher than those of the 1975 computers. That evolution over such a short period of time led some science-fiction authors to predict that a computer would reach the data-processing capacity of a human brain between 2030 and 2040. But that will undoubtedly remain science fiction.

The progress was just as impressive with regard to communication and information transmission. Although mail already existed in Sumer, it is not until the invention of the optical and then electric telegraph in the eighteenth and nineteenth century that information technologies really took off. But the telephone, the radio and the computer gave them another dimension. For instance, the time necessary to transmit one page of text from New York to Chicago—over slightly less than 1,000 miles—fell repeatedly and at an increasing pace between 1840 and 1850 (before the railroads), and then after 1850 (advent of the railroad) and again after 1988 with the communication of computer data. From 252 hours initially, the time fell to 48 by rail, then to 0.083 by the telegraph and to 0.0019 by modem. At the same dates and with the same means, the speed of transmission was respectively of 3.37 mph, then 17.7, and eventually 10,240 mph with the telegraph and 447,000 mph with computers. The cost of the transmission of that page was 0.35 dollar in 1840, then 3 cents by rail after 1850, 7.50 dollars by the telegraph and 31 cents by computer and modem.

That results, all in all, in a performance in terms of miles covered per hour and per dollar of 13.5 in 1840, 590 in 1850 by rail, 1,370 at the same date by the telegraph, and 1,440,000 in 1988 thanks to computers.

Under such circumstances, it is not surprising that all the curves representing communication volumes have expanded relentlessly in the recent decades. The phenomenal decline in costs generated exponential demand. The number of words, pictures, figures and sounds exchanged in the world is soaring. Already between 1960 and 1980, the number of words displayed in the various media had increased by more than 8 percent each year on average in the United States and by almost 10 percent each year in Japan.[30] Because of that accelerated fall in costs—in fields where figures play an essential part, like for instance finance—the "end of geography"[31] was even evoked. Thus, while the cost of a transaction in a retail bank is 1.07 dollar when it is performed in a branch, it falls to a mere 68 cents by telephone and 8 cents by Internet.[32]

As a production factor, information is just as necessary as capital and labor. It is a complement to both of them for their coordination in production. But it is used more intensely in the decentralized market production mode than in the hierarchical mode. When it becomes more abundant relatively to the other factors and the other goods and services, it is logically used more intensively. And the cost of the information-intensive production mode will decrease more sharply than that of the information-saving production mode.

---

30. Ithiel de Sola Pool, Hiroshi Inose, Nozomu Takasahi and Roger Hurwitz, *Communications Flows: A Census in the United States and Japan*, North-Holland, 1984.

31. O'Brien, *The End of Geography*. Conversely, although it recognizes the importance of the decline in the cost of transportation of people, goods and information, the new economic geography shows how the localization of several activities in the same place, and especially in cities, increases companies' comparative advantage and attracts investment. Far from being insignificant, localization becomes essential to explain investment flows and economic growth.

32. Larry Downes and Chumka Mui, *Unleashing the Killer App: Digital Strategies for Market Dominance*, Harvard Business School Press, 1998.

That surge in the volumes of information, thanks to its falling costs, also reduced the coordination costs in the economy. Thus, it lowered the relative cost of the information- intensive coordination mechanism—the market—compared with the information-saving coordination mechanism—the hierarchy. The information revolution explains the organization revolution.

The Downsizing of Corporate Hierarchies

Cheap information does not need to produce large cash flows to be as wealth-creating as scarce and expensive information. Its lower cost makes it easily profitable, even in less productive uses. Thus, it is no longer as necessary to save it and limit its use to a few people who know how to make the best of it. Its use becomes more widespread, more democratic. The decision-making power can thus be more widely distributed and the number of decision makers can increase.

In these new economic conditions, the great monolithic hierarchies tend to be replaced by a multitude of small pyramids which have given up the idea of producing everything by themselves. Instead of integrating the whole production process, from the extraction of raw materials to the delivery of the end product to the final consumer, they specialize in a particular stage of the production process. That vertical disintegration marks the resurgence of the 1860 Birmingham model. While in the late nineteenth century, the U.S. weapons industry had replaced a town and its hundreds of craftsmen by hierarchical corporations such as Colt or Remington, the reverse process is under way today.

In our aforementioned automobile example, a contemporary U.S. firm purchases various car components that it sells under its brand to companies all over the world, in Japan, Korea, Italy and Germany. It is thus almost in the same situation as the boss of a small firm in Birmingham who had only one warehouse, where he stored the various components of the rifle that a specialized subcontractor would then assemble before marketing the end product under its own brand.

The substitution of the Birmingham model for the Colt or Ford type 1911 models has recently resulted in a pick-up in market transactions between the smaller pyramids that have replaced the vast autarkic hierarchy. Today, when General Motors or Ford purchase car components in Europe or Asia, the transaction takes place on an inter-firm market. The market develops when the pyramids get smaller.

The Disintegration

But the decentralization process takes many other forms than just vertical disintegration. That disintegration concerns the choice between manufacturing the "inputs" of the production process internally and purchasing them externally. But the company can also choose to have its own distribution system—as car manufacturers, bankers and insurers used to—or to use the services of independent distribution firms, as it is often the case with food and domestic products. It can also create joint subsidiaries with its competitors to exploit a particular product or market. Finally, it can opt for a strategy of diversification which almost turns it into a conglomerate, a kind of portfolio of businesses that have but few things in common, except the financial resources of their "internal capital market," and are managed rather independently.

Thus, depending on the starting point, the disintegration of the large pyramids can use different de-conglomeration processes: (1) joint-ventures are created to replace formerly fully owned foreign subsidiaries, (2) the exclusive distribution network is abandoned, (3) some of the departments dealing with specific products are sold, (4) part of the capital of some subsidiaries in which the company nevertheless holds a stake can be listed on the stock exchange ("spin-off"), (5) some of the managers can buy back the subsidiaries ("management buy-out") or (6) internal profit centers with a decentralized management can be created and function almost like independent firms.

We must thus keep in mind the fact that the erosion of the pyramids is a protean phenomenon. With the decline of large-scale hierarchies, the company's external boundaries first tend to blur. We no longer know exactly the limits of its business. The disintegrating pyramid company first takes the shape of an amorphous group. Hence, the current fashion for "networked firms," "alliances," "participative organizations" and "virtual companies." They only mirror the loss of power undergone by the hierarchies and their effort to get closer to a decentralized market organization. But the latter is in reality only an extreme case.

Indeed, nothing suggests that we will fully return to the Birmingham model. As always in economics, the optimum solution is a mix of the extremes. Nobody wants to eat only steak-fries or pizzas. The optimum most often lies in variety. The decline of hierarchies does not lead to a world of craftsmen only. But the age of the Taylorian and Weberian administrative giants—public or private—is over.

Thus, the total number of decision makers and hierarchies in the economy has increased, but each hierarchy now has a smaller size on average. Hence, the reduction in the number of command levels. Businesses become "flatter," less hierarchical. In fact, less intermediate administrative managers are required to supervise a smaller number of field producers. Since each supervisor can control a given number of subordinates—which has not changed significantly—the structure resembles that of very small companies, where the boss manages and supervises his employees almost on his own.

Obviously, the relation between the information revolution and the decline of large-scale organizations has been underlined by many observers, if only because both phenomena occurred simultaneously. But so far there has been no convincing explanation about possible causal relations between the two phenomena. The development of markets is often explained by a change in political or economic ideas.

And the restructuring and downsizing of companies is justified by financial markets' and shareholders' greater demand for high profitability—while before, they were thought less concerned by this issue or were not entitled to their say—but without giving the reasons for such a reversal. Besides, despite many studies that belong to the Coase-Williamson tradition, very few specialists view the development of markets as the necessary complement to the decline of hierarchies since both mechanisms are substitutes. But we must say we still lack really general data about the overall reduction in firms' average size. This explains why current misconceptions survive. All in all, the general conception is that markets developed because of the ever-increasing greed of the capitalists, while firms restructured to become larger and not smaller.

Obviously, the first interpretation is no explanation: it is difficult to understand why the market supporters would have suddenly let their greed awaken in the 1980s. The second is contrary to the facts, as shown previously.

A few authors admit the causal relation between information and organization but without explaining the reasons, however. For instance, Malone, Yates and Benjamin have published an article about "electronic markets and hierarchies," in which they explained that the new information technologies reduce the coordination and transaction costs as these activities require an intensive use of information flows. Taking up Coase and Williamson's market/hierarchy alternative, they indicate, like Coase, that markets involve high costs due to the numerous transactions they require. Consequently, "an overall reduction in the *unit costs* of coordination would reduce the importance of the coordination cost dimension (on which markets are weak) and thus lead to markets becoming more desirable in situations where internal transactions were previously favored. In other words, the result of reducing coordination costs without changing anything else should be an increase in the proportion of economic activity coordinated by markets."

This intuition is right, but there remains to be proved the reasons why the markets are "weaker" than the hierarchies in terms of coordination costs. It was empirically confirmed in a very interesting 1994 study carried out on several companies of various large U.S. sectors from 1975 to 1989 that their IT investments were negatively correlated to their size.[33] The larger volumes of information and the reduced costs that this equipment involves thus easily explains the choice of smaller hierarchies. That corroborates the previous assumption.

We have thus a first confirmation that the evolution of information costs does account for the downsizing and disintegration of large hierarchical structures but also for the refocusing on core business, for the dismantling of conglomerates and for the secession movements in the most heterogeneous nations. This latter assertion follows from the fact that basically a state is, in economic terms, a firm, a production team run by a hierarchy (a bureaucracy) offering a range of services, even if these are not individually priced on markets but offered as a block-selling proposition for a single, compulsory, fee. Indeed, "Max Weber has pointed out that all hierarchically structured organizations (bureaucracies) are run by managers whose functions are broadly similar, whether they manage government bureaus (civil servants), corporate business firms (executives), churches (clerics), armies (officers), political parties, labor unions, hospitals or other modern organizations (functionaries)."[34]

While commercial, for profit, firms downsize by the means of carve-outs, spinoffs, and breakups, states, which are basically territorial firms, downsize by privatization (refocusing on their core business) and/or by divestiture from colonies abroad or whole regions at

33. Erik Brynjölfsson, Thomas W. Malone, Vijay Gurbaxani, and Ajit Kambil, "Does Information Technology Lead to Smaller Firms?" *Management Science*, December 1994.

34. Martin J. Beckmann, *Tinbergen Lectures on Organization Theory*, Springer-Verlag, 1988, p. 54, quoting Weber's *Wirtschaft und Gesellschaft*, 1925, part III, ch. 6, pp. 650–78, translated in English as *Economy and Society*, Berkeley: University of California Press, 1978.

home which obtain some management leeway or complete independence, that is, secession.

Just as some middle managers in commercial firms take over parts of their firms through LBOs, local and regional political managers see an opportunity when the size of the centralized state does not fit anymore the equilibrium range. They become advocates of secession because they believe that they can run more efficiently, and with greater benefits for themselves, a former region of a large state as a newly independent entity. This is the reason why secessionist movements acquired such a growing following in recent years. Many of them represented a winning proposition.

The cause of the decline of hierarchies and the great comeback of markets is the new abundance of information, whose quantity grows faster than that of any other good or service. As a result, the ratio between the quantity of goods and the quantity of information decreases, so that a larger amount of information can be included in each unit of goods produced. As the relative cost of information falls, its use increases and the most information-intensive production modes see their comparative advantage develop.

Markets develop to the detriment of hierarchies and especially to corporate hierarchies. But the effects of the information revolution are not limited to business firms. They also concern the state as a firm and consequently political organizations and regimes.

The Explanation of the State's Growth and of Privatization

Analyzing the relative efficiency of the hierarchical organization gives a simple and direct answer to the widely-debated mystery of the century: the growth of the state. Many economists have tried to explain it, but all their analyses were strongly criticized.

At first, in the early twentieth century, the "welfare economists" developed a theory about market failure that prefigured the analysis of public goods made later on. The state was supposed to step in

whenever competition was imperfect, when there was a private monopoly or when the markets were unable to produce a good or service
by themselves. But in retrospect, it appears that this argument is faulty.
The simple fact that markets do not work very well or fail to produce
certain goods or services is not enough to justify public intervention.
As Harold Demsetz underlined, state intervention can itself be imperfect.[35] Then, it must be proven that the state is less imperfect than
the market. But in many cases it is not the case. Many authors of the
public choice school supported the opposite view: generally, policy
makers focus on the short term given the brevity of their tenure. They
have no time to bother about the efficiency of the public administrations and, besides, they cannot be efficient managers given their vast
fields of action. Finally, the various lobbies will compete to obtain
ever larger rents and will thus impede the search for efficient policies.

All in all, public choice literature concludes that chronic political
malfunctioning is the rule. The states' internal growth would generally
deteriorate the collective welfare. And the private interests that it involves always take the upper hand against general interest.

But, once again, the debate was recently revived by developments
in the analysis of public choices reversing the perspective. According
to this new current of thought, the democratic system or the competition among pressure groups would make political interventions
efficient. There would not be more "political failures" than "market
failures."[36] Then, the growth of the state could no longer be explained
by the virtuous correction of market imperfections or by the imperfections of political life itself, which encourages each individual to ask
for more state interventions to his own advantage.

Other explanations have been put forward suggesting that the

35. Harold Demsetz, "Information and Efficiency: Another Viewpoint," *Journal of Law and Economics*, 1969.

36. Gary S. Becker, "Competition Among Pressure Groups for Political Influence," *Quarterly Journal of Economics*, 1983. Donald Wittman, *The Myth of Democratic Failure: Why Political Institutions Are Efficient*, University of Chicago Press, 1995.

state's growth resulted from a succession of accidents that occurred over the years, such as the great wars, and required an immediate and sharp increase in public spending. Once the financial efforts were made and the new civil servants and habits introduced, there would be a kind of ratchet mechanism preventing from turning back. But where would that "ratchet effect" come from? Why would it be impossible to cut taxes and public planning once peace is restored?

According to some economists, it is because of the rise of bureaucracy, which had already started at the very end of the nineteenth century. As they have a monopoly in the supply of some services, bureaucrats can impose their own views and interests on policymakers and obtain in particular steady increases in their budgets, as Niskanen suggested. But why do taxpayers not protest against those growing expenditures if they are useless or simply inefficient? In other terms, why would they let the state rob them of their purchasing power to the benefit of the civil servants?

We can thus conclude to the existence of a "fiscal illusion" saying that taxes that are widely distributed among the whole population are relatively painless and can thus go relatively unnoticed, while the lobbies—which are highly aware of the precise amount of aid they receive—campaign efficiently against political authorities to obtain ever more public aid. In those conditions, the taxpayer would structurally be the victim of the lobbies. But that illusion must have its limits, otherwise the triumphant bureaucracy would already have monopolized the whole national income to redistribute it to the various organized groups that live on public income transfers.

Other authors, like Richard and Meltzer or Peltzman, suggested that in a democracy the skewed distribution of wealth would encourage a majority of voters with incomes lower than the median to always increase the fiscal burden weighing on a minority of high incomes. But, in that case, we would have to suppose that there is a widening gap between the median and average incomes—that is a growing asymmetry in the distribution of wealth—that explains this continu-

ous move toward more state growth rather than just a stable equilibrium level at which the proportion of the state in the economy would
settle lastingly. Has there really been a steady trend toward a more
asymmetrical statistical distribution of income in all the countries over
the century? Did it indeed reverse in the mid-century? No. On the
contrary, all the available data show that the range of wages and incomes tended to narrow from World War I to the 1960s and then
widened again during the recent decades. Thus, the explanation based
on the disparity between incomes and the demand for a redistribution
seems faulty too.

So, we are left with the ideological hypothesis. According to this
theory, the contemporary decline in state control (which was made
obvious by the general privatization wave) can be explained by the
return of the Liberal ideology, notably the free-trade and lower state
protectionism policies adopted and supported by the International
Monetary Fund and the World Bank in the form of the so-called
"Washington Consensus." But explaining the recent and relative slowdown in the state's growth by the revival of the liberal conceptions
only shifts the problem, as the factors explaining the revival of liberalism remain unexplained.

And must we admit that ideological changes determine political
changes? Are political ideas totally impervious to the supposedly discretionary social realities?

The Perspective of Optimal Organization

This explanation becomes much simpler and less arbitrary if we consider that any organization must have an optimal size. As a state is a
firm producing public services, its size depends on the same general
factors as any other hierarchy. In the geographical framework of a
given nation, it is the optimal dimension of the hierarchy that determines the size of the state firm within the economy.

The larger the optimal size of the state or private hierarchy (both depending on the cost of information, assumed to be the same for private and public bureaucracies alike) for a national economy of a given size, the more the state-firm will be eager to take control of numerous activities to reach its optimum. Just like expanding private firms and conglomerates, an expanding public hierarchy will tend to absorb all types of activities that are private by nature (for instance, car makers, chemical factories, mines and shipyards). It is the greater efficiency of centralized administrative management that drives the expanding state, just like any private firm, to take over other companies, including those whose activities could as well be managed by private centralized hierarchies. It should be clear that states are efficient because they are submitted to competition, both internal and external, but in a different way from private enterprises. They do not try to maximize profits. They maximize their political efficiency (maximization of votes or of survival prospect in power) by redistributing income, according to the demands on political markets, and relying on their comparative advantage in coercion which is their basic and original raison d'être. The state-firm does not absorb private companies simply to produce cars, chemicals or computers but rather to use their resources—their cash flow—to achieve its targets, that is, the production of services that redistribute wealth to various electoral clienteles. They do this as far as they value, for their own purpose, firms more than private investors do, as I showed in my theory of nationalization and privatization, that was confirmed empirically by the OECD countries' experiences.[37] It means that they develop the public sector as long as the state's cost of capital is lower than the private investor's cost of capital.

When the integration of various private activities into the state conglomerate becomes cheaper—either because the optimal size of the administrative pyramids increases or because the purchase cost of private pyramids falls—the state's field of action—the public sector—

---

37. Jean-Jacques Rosa, "Nationalization, Privatization, and the Allocation of Financial Property Rights," *Public Choice*, 1993.

grows. And conversely, it shrinks when large-sized pyramids become less efficient while the purchase cost of private companies increases.

This explains the development of vast public sectors which tended to operate as monopolies in various industries that are private by nature during the first twentieth century, and thus the trend toward privatization in the second twentieth century. That downsizing of the state resulted in a de-hierarchization, a reduction in the society's centralization rate.

Another consequence of the analysis concerns the choice of the internal political regime. There again, we are led to think that it is not the result of an absolute preference nor of an ideology, but of the costs involved or abundance of information since it depends on the size of the state pyramid.

This confirms the importance of information in a democracy, which has already been underlined by many classical authors. But they consider that, ideally, information is necessary for a democracy to run smoothly and to be effectively managed by the citizens. We just say in a positive and non-normative way, that in reality, the democracy will be all the less expensive and all the more efficient as information is abundant. Information is indeed more widely used when it is cheaper and more efficient.

After having developed these analyses, it is interesting to mention Shubik's intuition who, studying the functioning of the information economy, understood its impact on politics in general and the overall characteristics of the civilization of Enlightenment but without explaining it:

> The 18th and 19th centuries will probably be remembered as the brief interval during which the growth of communication means and knowledge compared with the population, the speed of social and political changes and the global amount of knowledge favored individualism and independence.[38]

---

38. Martin Shubik, "Information, Rationality and Free Choice in a Future Democratic Society," *Daedalus*, vol. 96, 1967.

Conclusion

In the analyses we have just developed, we implicitly suppose that the state is a nation-state with a given geographical size.

But the twentieth century also saw major geographical transformations in nation-states with imperialism and nationalism, colonialism, the concentration of the world's nations, then the reverse movement with the disintegration and collapse of all the empires. Can the theory of information and organization also explain these changes? Does the creative disintegration phenomenon also affect the external organization of the state-firm and the system of nation-states?

Does the analysis of organizations also explain the changes in the state's external dimensions? The answer is clearly yes because the state-firm is an organization which, like any other firm, has two ways to develop: either by selling more services to a given clientele (this is called "intensive" growth) or by broadening its clientele by itself (this is called "extensive" growth).

The state thus grows by offering more services, mostly redistributive ones which form a kind of retrospective insurance policy, a mutualization of risks after the accident has occurred. For example, the government will help people after oil slicks and droughts but also aid the people with no income, ill or maladjusted living on its territory. It finances that "internal growth" by increasing its fiscal and parafiscal revenues, and thus the "sales" corresponding to that clientele. But it can also use "external" and "extensive" growth, through the conquest and takeover of new territories, populations and "customers." In that case, it is the size of the nation-state that adjusts itself to the optimal size of the state's hierarchical apparatus and to its increasing capacity to produce services.

We will analyze this in the next chapter.

CHAPTER 7

The
System of
Nation-States

Just like firms, states are hierarchical organizations producing services and using scarce resources. They provide those services to populations gathered together in nations, this term designating both a group of people relatively homogeneous culturally and the territory on which they live. As for the other firms, the state's size is measured by its output volume and the number of its workforce. And again, like them, it can increase its output and size either by selling more services to a given clientele or by selling a given service to a broader clientele. The first strategy is that of internal growth, where its size increases within a given nation or territory. In this case, the state increases its scope in an even wider range of activities. This phenomenon, often referred to as *state growth*, largely characterized the first twentieth century. But the state can also choose an external growth strategy by providing services to larger populations through the conquest of other territories or by taking control of other nations. And that strategy is even older.

But these two growth strategies—or sometimes dis-growth strategies—are not fully discretionary. They are subjected to a number of constraints. Faced with the competition of other states and even other potential leaders within their own nation, rulers have to make efficient choices about the use of the resources they have collected, if they do not want to lose them. As a consequence, governments must optimize their allocation of public resources if they want to survive and reach their targets, whatever those may be. The state or government faced with competition must choose a more or less centralized production mode that will be the most efficient given the availability of goods and information, just like private producers do. The state pyramid will thus grow or shrink, depending of the relative scarcity of goods and information in that society, by combining internal and external growth in various proportions according to the circumstances and resilience of the population considered.

The internal dimensions of the state pyramid are measured by the share of the nation's resources that it absorbs, given the size of the population and territory of the considered economy, as explained in the previous chapter. But the state's strategy also concerns its external dimensions, the size of its territory and thus of the populations it controls.

Depending on how the various states define their geographical dimensions, the numerous political firms worldwide achieve a specific spatial balance in what is called the "system of states" or in other words "the society of nations," given by definition a state is supposed to be also a nation since the nineteenth century and the recognition of people's right to self-government. We have thus decided to continue to use the word "nation-state" in this book although the correspondence is not always exact.

The expansion of state hierarchies' territorial dimensions often results in geographical overlapping areas at their frontiers, zones that states fight over, and thus as many border conflicts result. The determinants of the external dimensions of state organizations thus shape their international political relations, the key to peace or war between countries, and the organizational structure of the society of nations, or in other words the world political system. Similarly, the internal politico-economic system depends on the expansion of public and private hierarchies within the nation's geographical boundaries.

In this chapter, we will first study the factors that determine a nation-state's optimal geographical size, that is the size of the clientele it serves. That size first depends on the government's target: productive efficiency or growth. It also depends on the production costs of collective goods when the size of the population supplied increases. The territorial growth of a state is limited by the fact that the quality of public goods deteriorates as the clientele grows, while the cost of administrative management rises with the size of the bureaucratic firm.

As each state tries to reach its optimal size, a spatial equilibrium emerges between the various states of different sizes within the "global state industry." Contrary to what many people think, this industry does not necessarily evolve towards a single global monopolistic state and has been in fact characterized during the second twentieth century by fragmentation and increased competition.

To conclude, we will examine how this geopolitical balance is obtained, through military actions, negotiations, conquests or secession, as the global state industry is mostly reshaped by wars and revolutions. The general conditions determining peace or war between states will as a consequence be clarified.

THE STATE'S ADDED VALUE

Peace, law and order are public goods. They are the necessary complement to private goods as without them the agricultural, industrial and service producers would not be able to devote themselves fully to wealth creation as they would constantly fear to be deprived of the fruit of their efforts and thus spend most of their time and energy defending themselves against robbers. In contemporary societies, it is the state that produces these public services. But things were different throughout most of human history when peace and order were preserved through spontaneous (or at least decentralized) cooperation between individuals.

To estimate the state's added value (its contribution to collective wealth creation), we must first be aware of the forces that prevent this creation when the state does not exist. In other words, we must understand how an anarchic society works.

Before Agriculture: Social Order without the State

Throughout most of human history, there were only small-sized and stateless societies, that is societies without a hierarchical organization specialized in violence and in the production of order and security. The whole world's population lived in such societies 40,000 years ago and this was still true of most of it only 10,000 years ago before the development of agriculture in the Fertile Crescent of the Middle East. Today, it is only the case of a few populations living in remote areas of New Guinea and Amazonia, and of the Pygmees, Bushmen, Australian Aborigines and Inuits—human groups which are in a way the fossil survivors of prehistoric societies.

Before the advent of agriculture, societies were few and far between. Because of the way their economy was built, prehistoric hunters-gatherers had to live in nomadic bands consisting of a few dozens of people belonging to the same family or of a few allied families that rarely totaled more than 100 to 150 people. And several hundred thousand years later, our mentalities are still influenced by this past experience which explains why it is still deemed as the ideal size for a group of people. According to E.O. Wilson, this is the maximum number of people that can know one another well, whether in Namibia or in Manhattan. This is also the traditional size that is chosen by the army for a company or section. Other authors, like Ken Murrell from West Florida University, suggest that the optimal group size is slightly higher. His management surveys and professional experience with firms have taught him that beyond 200 people it becomes hard to really know everybody and manage the complexity of human relations.[1]

In small societies of such sizes, conflicts were rather rare. When they occurred, they were settled without the intervention of a hierarchical authority, as customs codified the acceptable conditions for revenge. Indeed, small groups lend themselves to collective, decentralized and cooperative action that establishes spontaneous order much better than in large groups.[2] Many anthropologists have indeed confirmed that the most primitive tribes spontaneously managed to maintain relative peace within their group by mutual agreement, even if the number of lives wasted in the process was relatively high. And as Mancur Olson underlined, ancient observers like Tacitus and Caesar had already noted the same process in Germanic tribes, which was in sharp contrast with their Roman experience of life in society. In traditional societies, a universal form of human organizations which according to J. R. Hicks appeared before the command society and the market society, decisions are often made unanimously and without the help of a chief:

> Traditional economies . . . are known from historians and more especially anthropologists. The economy of a neolithic or early Middle-Age village or of the tribal communities who survived until recently in many areas of the world, was not organized around a ruler (if there were any) but rather a set of traditions. These traditions gave specific functions to individuals (and still do). It is important to underline that the "leader" of the organization (be it a King, a Chief, a Great Priest or the village elders) is itself part of the traditional structure. He too is given functions and related rights.[3]

1. Tom Brown, "How Big Is Too Big," *Across the Board*, July–August 1999.
2. Mancur Olson, *The Logic of Collective Action*, Harvard University Press, 1965.
3. J. R. Hicks, *A Theory of Economic History*, Oxford University Press, 1969, pp. 13–14.

Factors of Customary Order

In these small traditional societies, the production of social order is cooperative and decentralized. It consists of successive bilateral or multilateral negotiations that are governed by the elementary rules of kinship. That is why the members of these societies pay so much attention to their kinship and genealogy. It is on that knowledge that the survival of the social group depends.

Cooperation is made easier by genetic and cultural factors. The members of these small groups, which have been at the heart of human experience for over a million years, have a lot of genes in common. And because of the reproductive selection that occurred generations after generations, they are encouraged to show rational or selective altruism to the other members of their family who share the same genes. Some authors also call this "egoistic altruism" or "reciprocal altruism," as the "altruist" in this case will do whatever is good for him.[4]

But cultural factors are also at play. In nomadic bands of 20 to 25 people or groups of families of less than a hundred people, there is no private life. Everybody knows what the others have done, given information is extremely available.[5] That makes it easier to use the "tit-for-tat" strategy, a symmetrical behavior examplified by the traditional "an eye for an eye" type rule for instance, an incentive for each stakeholder to adopt a more cautiously cooperative behavior.[6]

Finally, in these small societies, the state of the social relations within the group depends directly and evidently on the responsibility of each of its members. Each individual automatically enjoys a sub-

4. R. L. Trivers, "The Evolution of Reciprocal Altruism," *Quarterly Review of Biology*, 1971; Richard Dawkins, *The Selfish Gene*, Oxford University Press, 1989; and Gary Becker, "Altruism, Egoism, and Genetic Fitness: Economics and Sociobiology," *Journal of Economic Literature*, September 1976.

5. Richard Posner, "A Theory of Primitive Society," *Journal of Law and Economics*, 1980.

6. Robert Axelrod, *The Evolution of Cooperation*, Basic Books, 1984.

stantial share of the benefits resulting from the peaceful attitude of all the others and consequently from its own.

There are thus many good reasons why a voluntary and spontaneous order should emerge, at a low personal and social cost, given little time and effort is required to make decisions in small groups. Thanks to the spontaneous biological hierarchy, which governs the deep psychology and instinctive behaviors of all animal societies and traditional patriarchal families, and the objective conditions for interpersonal relations in small groups, it is sufficient to establish rules to resolve conflicts through the simple arbitration of the chiefs and elders. In other words, customs and family relations are enough to maintain social order.

However, there are no widely-accepted rules regulating interaction between these simple societies because the aforementioned factors are not at play at this level. When two of them are in contact because of geographical proximity, conflicts arise mainly after murders and acts of revenge, most often because of rivalries concerning hunting areas or the women of rival bands, which are the main reproductive resource in these economies where the only type of capital is human capital, given equipment and financial capital do not exist. Anarchy prevails in the interactions between these societies and can cause high mortality rates among adult males.

Visiting anthropologists formerly idealized small band and tribal societies as gentle and nonviolent, because they observed no murder in a band of 25 people during a three-year study. Of course, they didn't: it is easy to calculate that a band of a dozen adults and a dozen children, faced with the inevitable deaths occurring for the usual reasons other than murder, could not perpetuate itself if one of the adults killed another in the band every three years. Indeed, much more extensive studies about tribal societies carried out over long periods reveal that murder is a leading cause of death.

As Jared Diamond underlines, when asked directly, the members of these societies speak of endemic violence often following incursions of neighboring bands.[7] When asked about their life histories and the name of their husband, New Guinea's Iyau women named several sequential husbands, all of whom had died violent deaths. A typical answer went like this: "My first husband was killed by Elopi raiders. My second husband was killed by a man who wanted me, and who became my third husband. That husband was killed by the brother of my second husband, seeking to avenge his murder."

Against this background of intertribal anarchy and of conflicts due to growing proximity, the general rule of behavior when two individuals meet is very simple: if the other person is an acquaintance, he is almost certainly a relative or an ally. He is thus part of the same group and should be spared. On the contrary, if he is not already known, he is probably a stranger belonging to another society, competing for the resources available and especially the hunting areas, and he must die.[8]

This probably explains why spontaneous xenophoby has survived until now in the minds of many individuals and populations.[9]

And yet, collective and even endemic conflicts between societies of hunters-gatherers are limited given there are only few reasons to justify them. It is not worth fighting for a territory or slaves, as the latter would not improve the production per capita nor the living

7. Jared Diamond, *Guns, Germs and Steel: The Fates of Human Societies*, Norton, 1999, p. 277.

8. "Those ties of relationships binding all tribal members make police, laws, and other conflict-resolving institutions of larger societies unnecessary, since any two villagers getting into an argument will share many kin, who apply pressure on them to keep it from becoming violent. In traditional New Guinea society, if a New Guinean happened to encounter an unfamiliar New Guinean while both were away from their respective villages, the two engaged in a long discussion of their relatives, in an attempt to establish some relationship and hence some reason why the two should not attempt to kill each other." (Ibid., pp. 271–272.)

9. In primitive societies, the stories of strangers being spontaneously adopted by tribes are often only local myths about the return of lost gods or the necessarily divine nature of unfamiliar creatures. They can also simply be due to the surprise and curiosity to discover totally different people like the Europeans, who could not be rival neighbor societies given their unfamiliarity.

standards of the group, given they would not be able to generate an excess production above the subsistence level. It is thus no use capturing them if they cannot be put to a productive use. In a society that does not accumulate wealth and where the existing productivity is just enough to survive, each individual attends to his own business. There are few opportunities to rob the others or to have them work as slaves. There is neither slavery nor predation as the specialization in predation is a self-defeating proposition.

However, as the pre-agricultural populations grew slowly over several millenia, proximity conflicts between small groups of hunters-gatherers became more common and they eventually had to fight for a hunting or gathering area. And as Carneiro underlined, one of the two groups had to emigrate to try and find free land a little farther where he would not have to battle with rivals.[10] If one of these societies became too large, the factors limiting conflicts would wane and transaction costs would increase, threatening the production of social order. The resulting schism would force the break-away group to settle elsewhere, thus recovering its smaller initial size where collective agreement is easier to reach. All in all, spontaneous social order requires small density populations and freely available space.

The State and the Agricultural Revolution

During most of human history, people have lived in nomadic groups with stable living standards.[11] The boom in food production is a recent innovation that has enabled demographic growth. E.O. Wilson notes that the agricultural revolution occurred almost simultaneously in the Middle East, China and Central America around 10,000 years

10. Robert L. Carneiro, "A Theory of the Origin of the State," *Science*, August 21, 1970.
11. Vernon L. Smith, "Economic Principles in the Emergence of Humankind," *Economic Inquiry*, January 1992.

ago, increasing greatly the density of hunter-gatherer societies.[12] According to the Malthus model, and to what we have learnt from all the animal species, the demographic growth rate increases when food becomes more abundant.

The invention of agriculture saw the advent of richer societies where the population was geographically concentrated in the most fertile areas. As wealth could now be accumulated and concentrated on a given territory, violence and predation became more widespread. And this violence had to be stopped if wealth creation was to continue. But the long-established institutions of biological families and customs are no longer enough to guarantee spontaneous social order when wealth can be accumulated in big quantities by large groups where individuals are not relatives anymore. Anarchy is no longer a practical alternative.

According to the constant rule of the biological kingdom, when preys become more numerous, so do predators. Thus, the growing number of shark attacks on people is due to an increase in the population of their favorite prey—seals—which is now protected by human laws[13] and thus more numerous.

The Emergence of Political Authority

As the society turns richer, internal and external predators become fully specialized in robbery, just like producers become more specialized when a market grows.[14] In turn, this leads to a growing demand within the group for the help of violence specialists to organize the military defense against internal and external aggressors.[15] It is often

12. E.O. Wilson, *Consilience: The Unity of Knowledge*, Knopf, 1998, p. 253.

13. Even the dimension of the predators depends on the number of preys available; see Paul Colinvaux, *Why Big Fierce Animals Are Rare: An Ecologist's Perspective*, Princeton University Press, 1978.

14. George Stigler, "The Division of Labor Is Limited by the Extent of the Market," *Journal of Political Economy*, June 1951.

15. Michelle R. Garfinkel and Stergios Skaperdas (eds), *The Political Economy of*

difficult to tell the difference between both since external predators who conquer agricultural societies and settle there automatically turn into internal predators. And this is often how state dynasties took power in the past.

Many authors consider that the state was born from the will to protect oneself against external aggressions and wars between neighbor societies. But, although it is true that small pre-agricultural societies are often in constant conflict with their neighbors, that assumption is no more necessary nowadays: we can show that states also appeared in remote societies that were not faced with external threats, as is the case of the Andean valleys in Peru where the Inca imposed themselves. The invention of the state despite the absence of external predators tends to prove that the main problem of any agricultural society is internal predation for the use of the existing resources which become increasingly scarce—especially land—when the society has a large population confined to a small area because they are surrounded by natural obstacles: an alluvial basin or the proximity of desertic or un-farmable land.[16]

But the state is the organization that succeeded in monopolizing violence, thus curbing it. Without the state, it would tend to increase rapidly in large and densely-populated societies. Thus, the history of the birth of state results from the specialization of a few very well-trained individuals in violence in densely-populated areas which increase the return of predation.

While the traditional social order was mainly based on the family and customs in the pre-agrarian societies, in the agricultural societies where the concentration of resources increases, the predatory state will replace customs with a monopoly of violence reinforced by religion used for the maintaining of social order. Religion appeared and im-

---

Conflict and Appropriation, Cambridge University Press, 1996; and Jack Hirshleifer, "Anarchy and Its Breakdown," *Journal of Political Economy*, 1995.

16. As R. L. Carneiro claims in "A Theory of the Origin of the State," *Science*, August 21, 1970.

posed itself in the intermediate societies which saw the first settlements and the development of agriculture. It is a more solemn and authoritarian form of customs. It both exaggerates and emphasizes the role of the traditional chief in the group. This is how the first cities in Mesopotamia organized themselves around their gods' temples. But these city-temples were gradually replaced by city-states when the demand for order and security increased as McNeill showed.[17] And the security that the state provides in turn stimulated the production, the specialization and trade, which finally results, beyond a stronger activity and more developed information technologies, in the rise of markets.

Indeed, the agricultural prosperity encouraged several villages to merge to trade together. It thus gave birth to societies of a few hundred or thousand people consisting of tribes, themselves composed of distinct groups, clans, always organized according to kinship. The former spontaneous social order, where all the people in a group shared the same genes, remains the cornerstone of the society's social order and the collective organization principle.

In societies of a few hundred people, task specialization is very limited as the production is very small. There is not enough demand for any non-farm good for a producer to specialize in and devote all its time to another task, and consequently no specialized institutions such as bureaucracy, the police, justice or taxes. The conflicts between individuals are arbitrated by an elder or a "chief" who rarely interferes, as each producer remains able to use its own physical strength to defend rights. Any member of the society is both a hunter/breeder and his own part-time security guard (or "policeman"). But in view of the growing population, and thus the increased interactions which are as many opportunities of conflict, it becomes obvious quickly that large-scale production of arbitration and order will be required.

17. William McNeill, *The Rise of the West: A History of the Human Community*, University of Chicago Press, 1963.

Thereby, some people have to become full-time specialists in these fields of justice and police.

Archeological studies show that, in these larger societies, new ways of organizing social order were invented: chiefdoms arose by around 5500 BC in the Fertile Crescent of the Middle East and around 1000 BC in Mesoamerica and the Andes. Precisely with the advent of agriculture and the densification of agricultural populations in fertile valleys.[18] The abundance of resources and the density of the population are factors determining the centralization of authority. And indeed, several times in history, rather large populations organized in chiefdoms—even those who had not yet developed agriculture—when the natural hunting and fishing resources were very abundant. It was the case with the North Pacific Indians, the Kwakiutl, Nootka and Tlingit, who had neither farming land nor domestic animals but who gathered together to form rather large societies because of the local abundance of salmon and cod.

In such societies headed by a priest, an elder or a warrior, the chief's monopoly of legitimate force also enables him to monopolize the luxury goods acquired through long-distance trade. In a way, he is rewarded for his high social productivity, his great usefulness for the community. As the population grows, it becomes harder to maintain the production of social order. More supervisors are required. From one or two initially, the number of hierarchical levels increases substantially in chiefdoms. And obviously, so does the taxation of field workers in order to pay the administrative workforce which does not directly produce food resources.

Then, as the density of population rose further with the agricultural revolution, the production of social order became centralized and hierarchical. As Finer notes, it is likely that the state was born

---

18. See Vernon L. Smith (op. cit.) and Allen W. Johnson and Timothy Earle, *The Evolution of Human Societies: From Foraging Groups to Agrarian States*, Stanford University Press, 1987.

before writing.[19] It is indeed already mentioned in the first written documents found in Mesopotamia and Egypt. It thus exists since the beginning of human history, given the latter is conventionally marked by the invention of writing, which is itself functionally linked to the introduction of hierarchical societies ruled by centralized bureaucracies.[20]

The Arithmetic of Conflicts

As the growing wealth and population creates a potential for chaos, an increased production of security is required. Conflict opportunities increase more than proportionally to the number of individuals in the group.

Jared Diamond estimated these possibilities just like we calculated the number of possible market transactions in Chapter 3. Relationships within a band of 20 people involve only 190 two-person interactions, and consequently 190 conflict opportunities (20 people times 19 divided by 2), but a band of 2,000 would have 1,999,000 dyads. In other words, while the population grew 100-fold, the risks of conflict were multiplied by more than 10,000. And collective decision making becomes harder and more costly to implement just like market transactions when the number of participants increases.

According to Carneiro, the rise in the conflict opportunities is enough to explain the birth of a state. But one should also take into account the new possibilities to specialize in predation. There is now

---

19. S. E. Finer, *A History of Government*, Oxford University Press, 1997.

20. The larger the population, the more hierarchical grades a centralized administration must have. As each superior can only supervise a small number of subordinates, an increasingly stratified superstructure of controllers will be required. Two supervisors are enough for 10 field workers if each of them can control five. These supervisors will also have to be supervised by someone. So, there will be three administrative employees. As such, 100 field workers will require twenty grade-1 supervisors, four grade-2 supervisors and a hierarchical superior (i.e., a total of 25 administrative employees).

wealth tempting everybody such as food surplus, jewelry, livestock, while the hunter-gatherers could only store a few perishable and hardly transportable goods. In such a society where there are a little more resources than it is necessary for the immediate, daily consumption, it becomes possible to obtain more goods without working productively, by specializing in theft and extortion. Agrarian societies benefit from a new alternative to production that the pre-agricultural societies did not have: interhuman predation.

Moreover, all the factors at the origin of customary order lose their influence in the larger agrarian societies. Agricultural advances determine the growth of a population and its concentration in fertile areas. Because of large population numbers—several tens of thousands of people instead of a few dozens—the individuals only benefit from their contribution to maintaining order at a rate of 1/10,000 instead of 1/100. Thus, each of them more or less renounces to contribute to the production of social order.

Besides, in larger populations, people are dramatically less informed about the others' individual behaviors. Monitoring individuals becomes harder, especially as the hereditary factor favoring altruism is no longer at play. As anonymity increases, it encourages people to break ethical rules, just as it becomes much more unlikely to identify, arrest and condemn delinquents in large anonymous metropolises than in small towns in the countryside where everybody knows each other.[21] Nobody is encouraged anymore to contribute to the produc-

21. There are plenty of articles comparing criminality in big cities with criminality in small towns and villages in the countryside. Most of them are based on the observations made over the centuries and especially by Emile Durkheim, Georges Simmel, and Max Weber.

According to Edward L. Glaeser and Bruce Sacerdote who use the very complete statistical data of the *National Longitudinal Survey of Youth* for the United States, the size of the town explains 12 percent of the crimes. But for murder, the influence is much stronger. The probability of being the victim of a crime exceeds 21 percent in towns of over 1,000,000 inhabitants while it is lower than 10 percent in cities of 1,000 to 10,000 inhabitants. Higher pecuniary benefits for crime in larger cities can explain approximately 27 percent of the effect for overall crime, while the lower arrest prob-

tion of collective goods requiring more complicated negotiations between larger numbers of individuals. Collective action becomes more costly and thus harder to obtain. It follows that the number of offences increases and the compliance to ethical principles declines, since delinquents can act with almost complete impunity in this new urban environment. It becomes impractical to achieve decentralized order.

Maintaining peace and order requires a lot of efforts that can only be obtained through a total specialization of some individuals in these tasks. Arbitration and policing work become full-time jobs. Like all the other activities, it is more productive if it is regularly performed by a specialist than if it is performed occasionally by a common individual—each producer of goods and services protecting itself against all the other members of the society.

At the same time, as the risks and the values at risk grow with wealth and the concentration of population, the demand for security also surges. Producers ask for better protection of their goods and themselves. The market demand for security now has a positive price. Being more specialized and productive, farmers produce more than they need to survive and can sell the surplus to others. Thanks to higher income and higher risks, they are now able to hire professional order-maintaining forces.

To fight efficiently the other predators, the order-maintaining professionals must be specialists of violence. In other words, predators. In small traditional societies, amicable settlements of disputes between people who know each other and are under the authority of the same traditional chief make it unnecessary to use such specialists.

---

abilities, and lower probability of recognition, explain at most 20 percent of the urban crime effect. The remaining 45–60 percent of the effect cannot be explained by these two variables but probably by the social influences and family structure ("Why Is There More Crime in Cities?" *NBER Working Paper*, January 1996).

Studying the L.A. riots of 1992, the same authors show that the rioters' opportunity costs of time and the potential costs of punishment influenced the incidence and intensity of the riots ("The L.A. Riots and the Economics of Urban Unrest," *NBER Working Paper*, February1996).

But when the society grows, there are more predators that become professionals because the resources available are large enough to let them specialize. Against them, the traditional chief's moral authority is not enough to maintain order. And he is powerless against external predators that are by no means related to his society. More of these full-time professionals are required to defend the producers. They are selected among those who have the physical capacity to exert pressure and this can lead them to also exercise moral authority, insofar as justice and police cannot be dissociated under a certain size of population and production and below a given number of conflicts.

This is why, although the benefits of law and order, deriving from a social pact or "social contract" are particularly important in large groups, no one has ever seen vast societies organize voluntarily according to such a fundamental social contract.

THE STATE AS A PREDATOR AND A PRODUCER

The role of the state has given rise to controversy between the dirigistes and socialists who consider it as the source of all morality and prosperity and the Liberals who view it only as a Leviathan exploiting the credulity and wealth of its citizens. This seemingly endless debate reminds one of the story of the Big-Endians and Little-Endians in Swift's *Gulliver's Travels*. While the former could only eat a boiled egg by the big end, the latter could not imagine eating it otherwise than by the small end. With the state, the debate is more a question of degree: to what extent should it be developed and does it have an optimal size? Our aforementioned analysis of organizational economics shows that there is no absolute ideal and timeless standard. A minimal state is not any more likely to have an optimal size than a "minimal company" would. And the same is true of both the maximal state of the Socialists, Communists and other totalitarians, and a giant private conglomerate that would produce all the goods and services that the consumers would long for.

This debate is Swiftian in the sense that the protagonists are intellectually too lazy to consider anything else other than their preferred solution, while both could be "right." This is due to the fact that the choice of market or hierarchy is, at the level of the individual, antagonistic: in a market, the relation between two people cannot be hierarchical, and conversely in a hierarchy. But when it comes to understanding and explaining the role of the state in all the contemporary societies, our limited individual experience can only cause misunderstanding.

It is true that the existence of the state is paradoxical, as its very nature seems ambiguous. Admittedly, as it guarantees security, its usefulness is universally acknowledged nowadays even if the most liberal, or libertarian, share the nineteenth-century analysis of Gustave de Molinari who advocated competition of private suppliers of security services in lieu of the state monopoly.[22] Here, however, the Buchanan remark that the monopoly of a "bad" (extortion) is superior to competition because monopoly typically undersupplies, applies. Nevertheless it is equally justified to consider that the state acts like a predator when it pumps tax revenues that are quite often not used to finance essential public goods. How can a producer of public goods pursue at the same time his personal interests given they can be very different from those of its principals? While some say that public productions are always in the interest of the public at large by definition, others believe that the citizens' means to control politically the state are pretty inefficient and biased. Both theories seem easy to criticize.

Starting implicitly with societies before the birth of a state, Mancur Olson solves the contradiction by presenting a convincing analysis of the origins of the state and its great superiority in the production of social order. Rather than making a precise and detailed historical

---

22. Gustave de Molinari, "De la production de la sécurité," *Journal des Economistes*, février 1849.

description, Olson has preferred to present a stylized economic analysis that summarizes the issue. According to him, it is the predators that are the key to the development of the structure of authority, guided by the invisible hand of their own interests, and that will involuntarily contribute to the well-being of the producers they rob by imposing a new social order aiming at their own advantage.

In a society of anarchical violence, the predators' victims lose not only what is destroyed and stolen but also all incentive to start producing again. Indeed, the fruit of their further work might be destroyed and robbed again by people stronger than them. And if they decide to fight against them, they will have to devote as much time and efforts to defending themselves as the predators spend attacking them, which will prevent them from focusing on their production of goods. There will thus be a few or no productions, except those required for survival. In the absence of law and order, the production falls back to the subsistence level, in a society where, according to Hobbes, life is "poor, solitary, nasty, brutish and short."

The establishment of law and order thus has a huge positive impact on the individuals' wealth and well-being. Those gains can, possibly, be shared between all the members of the society, so that each of them will benefit from them. But can such an order arise spontaneously or, more precisely, in a decentralized way?

It is likely in small groups but very unlikely (if not impossible) in large human groups. The rationale of collective action indeed shows that in a decentralized order each individual bears the full costs and makes all the necessary efforts to maintain order, while individually he would only obtain a fraction of the extra wealth production that the whole society enjoys. The larger the society, the smaller the part of total wealth thus created each individual will receive, and the more efforts he will have to do to help and maintain peace and order. All the individual incentives make us lose interest in the functioning of the whole society when it is large and this leads to anarchy. It can thus seem impossible to maintain social order.

But the answer lies in the self-interested behavior of the war chiefs and other armed looters that rob the farmers. Roving predators of that kind are extremely destructive since they rob the people as much as possible to leave nothing to the other bandits: they carry out the scorched-earth policy, which had the advantage of deterring and warding off potential rivals. On the contrary, a "stationary" bandit, settled and sedentary, having decided to permanently exploit a given population would be well advised to leave them at least enough seeds for the next crop if he wants to have something to eat next year. From a social point of view, the sedentary exploiter is thus preferable to the nomadic exploiter. He allows the development of farm production and leaves to the exploited farmers a few incentives to pursue their efforts. He then renames his extortion "tax" or "tribute" and claims that he collects it for the protection of the "general interest," which is not totally wrong.

The huge increase in production resulting from the law and order established by a sedentary bandit—and especially having the monopoly of violence—will benefit him very largely. This will encourage him to broaden as much as possible his "clientele" of "protégés" by extending his "offer" of violence to new populations and territories. The extortion specialists will thus extend their exclusive field of control to a population of farmers as large as they can deal with. This means suppressing any uprising of the "constituents" but also warding off all the other potential predators and rivals, whether internal or external.[23]

Thus, the formation of a well-established government within vast social groups will not result from a voluntary social contract concluded between the farmers following a consensual negotiation, but from the initiative of the individuals the most competent to use force who try to obtain the monopoly of extortion in imposing their own will on these vast groups.

23. Regarding the internal competitors, see Gordon Tullock's analyses of the calculations of the dictator who at first does not trust his civilian and military people, *Autocracy*, op. cit.

In that case, there is no social contract but rather a "social quasi-contract," which merely consists in accepting fiscal extraction in exchange for relative security. It is a quasi-contract, first because it is implicit, but above all because the exchange will not result solely in benefits for both parties in various proportions, but includes also violence and extortion. It will be less profitable to the farmers than to the sedentary bandits but their life will be much better than when they were victims of nomadic and competitive bandits.

Admittedly, farmers could decide to voluntarily hire violence specialists like in *The Magnificent Seven* but the transaction costs would be too high if the farmers were too many.[24] And the price to pay should be close to the amount already extorted by another sedentary looter.

As a result, it will be less expensive to accept willy-nilly the domination of the most efficient monopolist, the one who will beat all the others in the competition for domination and will be the most capable to defend his subjects against other predators afterwards. This is by the way how things happened in a few African tribes which only chose their leader after a fight to the death between the pretenders. And the same process took place in most Western states during the wars for succession, in Rome but also in most monarchies until the Renaissance.

The acceptance of a hierarchical and predatory state or the "consent of the governed" can be explained by the greater efficiency of the hierarchical solution over the decentralized anarchic situation[25] in which a great number of bilateral contracts—or quasi-contracts—are

24. That scenario was used in an endless number of westerns in which a population robbed by local predators willing to hire a tough sheriff or traveling mercenaries launches a competition. In fact, they are likely to be better off with sedentary predators than itinerant mercenaries.

25. According to Hirshleifer, op. cit., anarchy is defined as follows: "A structure of society in which participants can seize and defend lasting resources without regulation from above or from social pressure."

concluded between individuals whose relations are governed both by trade and violence.

The level of collective services provided by the single exploiter will be all the greater that he will possess wide-ranging interests covering all the society's production activities. This is exactly the same situation as when a business manager can use the wealth of the shareholders to serve his own interests (the "agency problem" analyzed in business and financial literature) but will be much less tempted to do so if he holds a significant part of the capital, that is when he is himself one of the firm's owners. Being a shareholder himself, he is better off defending the interests of all the shareholders. Thus, when a monarch appropriates all the land in his kingdom (or almost) and when he hopes to remain for long on the throne or to bequeath that land to his heirs, he is more willing to make the investment necessary to develop it and is more concerned about the well-being of the farmers, simply to maximize the tax revenues in the long run. Temporary exploiters are more dangerous than long-lasting ones. Their horizon is indeed shorter. They do not mind leaving the country in ruins behind them. With regards to this, the hereditary monarchy is a good political system and we understand better the traditional "Long Live the King" which was for that reason probably sincere.

As Olson wrote:

> History teaches us that it was the system where an autocrat takes most of the resources of a given population through taxes that enabled the development of the civilization. Indeed, from after the first agricultural innovations to say the French Revolution, most people were submitted to autocracy and tax exploitation. Until recently, history has mostly seen the civilization develop mostly and gradually under the rule of stationary bandits from time to time briefly interrupted by nomadic looters. From when Sargon created by conquest the empire of Akkad to the time of Louis XVI and Voltaire, the civilization developed significantly, and mostly under the reign of sedentary bandits.[26]

26. Mancur Olson, op. cit., p. 538.

That is why the debate opposing the view of a Leviathan state—an exploiter—to Rousseau's social contract remains caricatural and excessive, and allows no solution. First, it only considers the two extremes of the existing range of possibilities but, above all, it does not take into account the fact that an exploiter can also be useful to the people exploited. In reality, the state is always a producer and a predator but in varying proportions which depend on its rulers' personal goals—on the agency and control relation that links them to the subjects or citizens.

THE PARADOX OF VIOLENCE

The cause of the paradox is to be found in the nature of the service provided by the state and in the monopoly it appropriates. While the monopoly of a good thing is generally bad for the consumer, the monopoly of a bad thing can be something good.

Obviously, the predators who maintain order by means of force in an agricultural society have an interest in the monopoly of violence on the territory they exploit as it makes their task easier and their predation more profitable. Consequently, they forbid all the populations they control to resort to violence and above all to possess weapons. The other members of the society give up their right to use force, either voluntarily or by the coercion of the predator and its soldiers, and especially in trade. Thus, the free, non-forced, voluntary trade that develops involves the mutually advantageous market transaction which is analyzed in economics. Since both parties agree to do so, it must contribute to the enrichment of both, even if in unequal proportions. On the contrary, an exchange imposed by one of the parties can be absolutely unfavorable to the other.

But progress requires mutually advantageous transactions. Unlike predation, it is a filter for the socially productive operations, a guarantee of the net enrichment of the community. It also increases everybody's incentive to produce and thus stimulates collective wealth creation. It is thus essential for the individuals to choose—if they can—to live and work in communities where violence is restrained and where collective wealth can thus increase.

Although this can also seem paradoxical, this is advantageous both to the extortion specialists and to those who have a comparative advantage in wealth creation. Indeed, extortion will be all the more lucrative for the predators that there are few of them and it will be easier and more worth it in terms of efforts agreed and risks taken if they do not have to put up with other predators likely to challenge, wound or even kill them, and who have already taken their share of the resources left to the producers.

The reduction in violence thus benefits all, whether producers or predators. That is why violence can be defined as a social "evil," the opposite of a "good." It reduces the utility and the living standards of all the individuals. On the contrary, peace and order are a good, a "filter" of human interactions which only lets through the wealth-creating operations and exchanges.

It is indeed remarkable that the conclusions of the classical analysis of monopoly are perfectly applicable to the monopoly of violence. Indeed, it shows that the main difference between this market structure and competition is that the quantities produced are voluntarily reduced. For instance, an oil cartel will diminish the quantities in circulation on the world market to maximize its profits. And the same is true of all the monopolies and cartels in the industry or the services.

But the process is exactly the same for the monopolies of "an evil" or "nuisance" as for the monopolies of "a good." The monopoly of violence will thus reduce the total amount of violence "produced" in a given society, which makes violence more profitable for the monopolist. That is why the public authorities and the police generally prefer to deal with organized crime—or cartelized crime—than with the unorganized crime, which is competitive crime. The latter maximizes violence in the society, as is the case in gang wars, and makes it closer to a situation of anarchy, while the former minimizes it.

While competition is better for the production of "good things," the monopoly is preferable for the production of "bad things."[27]

It is thus better for the legitimate authorities to hold a real monopoly of violence rather than take part in a cartel and this is why they try to remove as far as possible their rivals, such as the Mafia for instance, as this involves a situation of duopoly and thus of (partial) competition on the market of protection and extortion. The state and the Mafia are in that sense rivals.[28]

That paradox about the state's monopoly of legitimate violence explains the divergence between the political conceptions of a predatory state, the Leviathan whose only goal is to exploit the producers of goods and services and extort from them a maximum of resources, and that of the producer state, who defines and implements the social rules that make profitable private activities possible and thus increases the collective prosperity.[29]

It is true that the state is both a predator and a producer. But it is a producer because it is a predator. As Mancur Olson very clearly showed, the state is a self-interested predator but, by this very fact, it is also useful to all the members of the society. To obtain the greatest possible amount of resources from a given population, it is in its interest that each member of the community thrives. It must thus make sure that nothing slows the production and prevents individuals from growing richer by ensuring the safety of people and goods and supplying the public services necessary to the private productions.[30]

27. James Buchanan made this assumption in "A Defense of Organized Crime?" in Simon Rottenberg (ed.), *The Economics of Crime and Punishment*, American Enterprise Institute, 1973.

28. Hershel I. Grossman, "Rival Kleptocrats: The Mafia versus the State," in Gianluca Fiorentini and Sam Peltzman (eds.), *The Economics of Organized Crime*, Cambridge University Press, 1995.

29. A dual approach underlined by Douglass North in the introduction of the chapter "A Neoclassical Theory of the State," in *Structure and Change in Economic History*.

30. Mancur Olson, "Dictatorship, Democracy, and Development," *American Political Science Review*, September 1993.

Just like Adam Smith's butcher or grocer must serve his customers kindly to grow richer, the state must give the people it controls and taxes the means to improve their own prosperity to obtain abundant tax revenues. Rulers do not do that by pure altruism but rather in rationally pursuing their well-understood interest.

Adam Smith's invisible hand thus also works in politics, which is not surprising given we explained earlier that politics is only a sector of the economy. Thus, when Smith tells us that "it is not from the benevolence of the butcher, the brewer, or the baker, that we expect our dinner, but from their regard to their own interest,"[31] we can add similarly that "it is not from the benevolence and the good intents of those who govern us that we expect protection, safety, law and order but from their exclusive regard to their own interest."

Thus, there is a kind of invisible hand guiding the competition between the predators which works in the opposite way than the invisible hand guiding the competition between the producers: the competition between the producers is desirable because it increases the quantity of "goods" and the monopoly of the predators is desirable because it reduces the quantity of "bads."

As a result, there is an implicit exchange of mutual advantages between the state and the people it controls, even though the state uses coercion: the safety the population benefits from is paid by the taxes to which it is bound. That exchange, which includes both a mutual agreement and the use of force, has all the characteristics of a quasi-contract.

However, a universal monopoly of violence does not exist. The predatory states' areas of geographical control do not stretch over the whole planet as there is more than one state in the world. The constant competition between the predators and the producers of monopolistic order can lead to war and thus destroy most of the advantages provided by the state to the population it controls.

31. *The Wealth of Nations*, p. 14.

But war is not inevitable. It has determining factors that we will study below. When these factors favor the peaceful coexistence of states because the use of violence has been ruled out, competition regains its virtues just like on the other economic markets and becomes advantageous for the safety consumers, that is the residents and citizens. The peaceful competition between the states to control populations encourages them to offer greater safety and better public services at a lower tax cost. The international and domestic social order thus results from the ever-changing balance between the rulers' taxation capacity and the mobility on which depends the governeds' acceptance of the ruler's authority and taxation system.

That leads us to examine the conditions of the violent or nonviolent competition between the states and the balance that is reached between the security-providing predators in the world industry of nation-states. There is another, no less interesting, paradox: the predatory state which produces social order and encourages the development of a market within its area of control, finds itself in a situation of anarchy when faced with the other states in the world, that is, a situation where everyone can use violence to conquer resources, without having a higher-ranked authority or social pressure to prevent him from doing so.[32]

32. Jack Hirshleifer, "Anarchy and Its Breakdown," *Journal of Political Economy*, 1995.

CHAPTER 8

The Industry of States and the Society of Nations

The state, which is both a predator and producer of collective goods, has imposed itself in the large (by historical standards) and wealthy modern societies as the universal organizational structure. Nation-states are thus an essential component of the social and political life on both a national and international level. There is no space left on this planet that escapes their control.

However, they have appeared in space and time in many forms and sizes, ranging from the small city-states of ancient Greece or the Renaissance to the ancient and modern empires. Their size often changes over time, as periods of expansion and conquest eventually give way to periods of decline and fragmentation. This process was seen throughout the twentieth century with the rise and fall of European empires or more recently of the Soviet Empire.

Far from being some sort of intangible reality, the geography of states and the geopolitical balance are the contingent result of transformations which need to be explained. We must therefore examine the factors which determine the size of each of these states and the resulting structure within the states' population, that is, within the society of nations.

The external growth of a state and its optimum geographical size, is a matter of choice. It is thus an economic problem, since economics is the science of choice. The effective decision will depend not only on the decision maker's goals (more specifically, on his preference for large- or small-sized firms) but also on the constraints which prevent a manager's capacity from getting all he wants.

THE STATE'S GOALS

The state is a firm, it is not a person. In this respect, it makes no decisions and has no personal preferences. The leaders of the firm or the state make the decisions in the name, and under the more or less strict control, of their constituents and they are therefore more or less in a position to pursue their own goals. The decision makers are the CEO or the board of directors in a business firm and the president or the prime minister or its government in the state.

However, we will continue to use that rather convenient expression "the state's objectives" to designate those which result from a compromise fashioned by the relations of power and of the law between the leaders and their constituencies, that is, between the government and its citizens or subjects.

Whatever his deep-seated motives, the leader of the state-firm needs resources, just like any other individual. Firstly, for his own consumption, and secondly to maintain or increase his power over the inhabitants of his territory as well as over his external competitors and rivals. He needs to be able to repel his rivals' attacks.

In the recent years, a whole range of economic theorists have tried to explain the states' behavior just like they would with the other organizations subject to economic analysis, for instance private firms.[1]

1. Frederic C. Lane, "Economic Consequences of Organized Violence," *Journal of Economic History*, December 1958; Douglass C. North and Robert Paul Thomas, *The Rise of the Western World: A New Economic History*, Cambridge University Press, 1973; Douglass C. North, "A Neoclassical Theory of the State" in *Structure and Change in Economic History*, Norton, 1981; Mancur Olson, "Toward a More General Theory of Government Structure," *American Economic Review*, May 1986; Richard D. Auster

For Auster and Silver, the traditional analysis of the firm easily explains the behavior of the states fighting in a monopolistic competition for geographical control.[2] According to them, the production of a state is measured by the degree of order it produces on a given territory for a given population.

But all forms of production require resources. The financial needs of modern states engaged in cut-throat competition are considerable and directly influence all their policies.[3] Applying Schumpeter's analysis, political scientist Margaret Levi stated that "the history of State revenue production is the history of the evolution of the State."[4] Starting from the hypothesis that leaders are predators seeking to extract from the population as much income as possible, she emphasizes that these rulers' goals do not influence their behavior in any way. They can use fiscal resources for their own consumption, to increase their power, to finance social policies or even to follow their ideological preferences. They can be altruistic or egocentric, peaceful or aggressive. But anyway, they will need resources to achieve their goals. And leaders reach their personal and social goals through the state policies and with tax revenues. As a result, they try to maximize the latter, which we consider as a form of predatory behavior.

However, the behavior of firm managers varies greatly depending on whether they seek to maximize sales or profits. A company which tries to optimize its revenue (its sales) will probably not maximize its profits. By accepting a decrease in its profits, it can lower prices and, depending on the elasticity of demand, sell more and achieve higher overall sales.

and Morris Silver, *The State as a Firm: Economic Forces in Polical Development*, Martinus Nijhoff, 1979; Albert Breton, *The Economic Theory of Representative Government*, Aldine, 1974; and Norman Frohlich, Joe A. Oppenheimer and Oran R. Young, *Political Leadership and Collective Goods*, Princeton University Press, 1971.

2. Richard D. Auster and Morris Silver, op. cit.

3. Gabriel Ardant, *Histoire de l'impôt*, 2 volumes, Fayard, 1971 and 1972; Joseph Schumpeter, *The Crisis of the Tax State*, 1918; and Margaret Levi, *Of Rule and Revenue*, University of California Press, 1988.

4. Margaret Levi, op. cit., p. 1.

The strategy chosen depends on the way the firm is controlled. If shareholders have their say, they will prefer to maximize profits. On the contrary, if the leaders are independent of their shareholders, they can choose a growth strategy where they play a greater social role which enables them to support higher personal expenses because they can be spread on larger production volumes, which allows them to increase their own wages, since the leaders are generally better paid in large corporations than in small firms. And it is on these conflicts of interest (better known as the "agency problem" in the management literature) that the firm's strategy in terms of size and growth depends.

The state and the political production suffer from the same "agency problem." A state can decide to maximize either its tax revenues or the added value of the service it provides to the people it governs.

MANAGERIAL STATE, PATRIMONIAL STATE

The state's turnover is measured by its tax revenues. Quite clearly, it is in the leaders' interest to increase taxation whenever possible, regardless of their own ultimate goals. The equivalent to the shareholders' profits is the state's added value, that is the services provided to the citizens and residents minus their public production cost. Generally, the maximum added value does not correspond to the maximum level of taxation that a state can levy from its population because higher taxation rates may encourage private producers to reduce their output. So that excessively high tax rates result in lower wealth creation.

But in a sense, citizens are the state's shareholders or financial backers. If the existing political constitution gives them some control over the government, their own interests and profit strategy would definitely win over. If, on the contrary, the government is not controlled by the citizens-taxpayers, it tends to pursue a strategy maximizing the turnover, which implies, among other things, geographical expansion.

Thus, a managerial (dictatorial) state tends to be expansionist. A democratic state does not seek territorial growth for its own sake. Instead, it prefers to limit its spending for a given level of services and give priority to wealth creation and profits.[5]

However, it must not be forgotten that the state can be to a large extent the property of the leader, as was the case of bygone monarchies. As in commercial firms, the owner-manager prefers to follow a profit strategy that will increase his assets rather than a growth strategy that will reduce them. This is the meaning of Olson's distinction between a ruler with an "all-encompassing interest" in the company he runs and one whose only narrow interest is to collect taxes. The first

---

5. This is the managerial conception of international relations. According to international relations specialists and to the practitioners (state rulers), the state's objectives boil down to the quest for power and size. It results from the simple need to survive against the other nations which are more or less rivals. This is the fundamental law of international politics, already expressed in 321–296 BC by Kautilya, minister of the first Indian emperor, Chandragupta, in his political and diplomatic treaty.

He suggests that rulers should follow these principles:
1. Strengthen your own country so that it becomes more powerful than the other states.
2. All the states which are your immediate neighbors are potential enemies. They must be defeated and conquered as often as possible, i.e. when they are weak and lack trustworthy allies.
3. Do everything you can to weaken your potential enemies.
4. Your enemies' neighbors are potential allies for you, if they are not also your neighbors. Try and convince them to help you resist or defeat your (potential) enemies.
5. As soon as your former allies become your neighbors, they turn into potential enemies.
(Peter Bernholz, *The International Game of Power*, Mouton, 1985, pp. 17–18.)

The immediate target of a state or nation is then to preserve its independence and protects its territory or expand it by means of diplomatic alliances or by declaring war, if need be. Each state will try and extend its geographical area as a firm would try to broaden its clientele. In both cases, these strategies are a way to increase the resources available.

is a manager-owner while the second is only a temporary manager whose assets will not suffer from the cumulated consequences of his strategies. He is closer to being a "roving bandit" than to a sedentary predator.

The managerial state is thereby strategically distinct from the two varieties of "patrimonial" state: the dictatorial patrimonial state and the democratic state.

Political rulers always pretend to work for the "public good." In other words, they attempt to deny the existence of a conflict of interest between themselves and the governed. Obviously, such a justification is given because it has a more noble and reassuring ring for the tax-payers than the simple pursuit of the ruler's personal interests. It is however partially true, as, in pursuing his own advantage, the sovereign must provide public goods to maximize his tax revenues. For his own sake, he must care for the interests of his subjects, who are, in a certain sense, his financial backers. History has shown that when the sovereign was in urgent need of resources, often because wars against neighbors and rivals, he did not hesitate from time to time to expropriate wealthy individuals. But he cannot do this too often or too extensively, for fear of discouraging producers and innovators as well as reducing production, and therefore future tax revenues. Expropriation cannot be a permanent financing means.

Frederic C. Lane, who was probably the first to develop an economic analysis of the equilibrium size of the state as a firm specialized in violence and providing protection to a given population, believes that throughout history most states have been managed in the leader's interests rather than their subjects' or citizens'. Thus, the state is usually a company which economists would define as "managerial," that is, where the manager is not the owner and pursues his own self-interest even to the detriment of the legitimate owners who have appointed him.

Indeed, over the course of history, most of the firms offering protection have been controlled by the upper echelons of the army and

police, that, is by their managers. In those conditions, the main objective of the rulers was to keep the firm running, and maximizing its
size was more important than optimizing profits. Occasionally, members of the lower echelons in the army or in the other administrative
departments of these firms were able to take control or at least limit
the discretionary power of the rulers by using force. But when the
workers gained control, they were absolutely not interested in mini-
mizing the taxes used to ensure the protection of the population or
reducing the cost that their wages represented for the firm. They too
were eager to make the state-firm bigger, not unlike some modern
labor unions.

A different policy characterized the governments controlled by a
prince or emperor with a sufficient degree of absolute power to consider himself legitimately the owner of the firm offering protection.
In that case, it was in the state's owner-leader's interest to give priority
to the profits rather than the turnover and this encouraged him to try
and reduce production costs while maintaining the price of his services (taxation) unchanged. Like Henry VII in England or Louis XI in
France, they sought to use the least expensive methods to assert their
legitimacy, maintain internal order and dissuade neighboring princes
from attacking them to be able to lower their own military expenses.
By reducing their costs and/or increasing taxation thanks to a stable
territorial monopoly, they were able to show a surplus, a sort of monopoly income.[6]

That analysis is exactly the same as for a firm controlled by its
manager, its workers or its owner. But the latter can also be the manager. As Olson explained, in that case, state policies can directly serve
the population's interests. However, they would be even better served
by a state which sought to maximize profits, as underlined earlier.
Lane explains that, according to the democratic conception, the firm

---

6. Frederic C. Lane, "Economic Consequences of Organized Violence," *The Journal of Economic History*, December 1958, p. 406.

with a monopoly of violence should cut the tax cost of its services to the level of its production and protection costs. However, a government will only behave this way if it is controlled by its customers, the service users. That is the basic postulate of the theory of representative government: the control over the leader arises from the competition between would-be managers for the leadership of the firm, which is arbitrated by the "shareholders" (the voters and the taxpayers). The government is responsible for its policies before the general assembly of owners at the time of elections.

There is, however, another alternative or at least a complementary solution: the control over the leaders can also arise from the mobility of voters who decide to renounce ownership and go into exile to become citizens of a competing state. In that case, each government faced with competition from the other states will have to provide the best public service at the lowest price possible to avoid losing an increasingly large percentage of its tax base. External control, which is like shareholders selling their shares to purchase others, also helps to align the government's policy with the population's true interests.

Given the competition between states and the more or less democratic nature of the political regimes, each government will continue to seek the optimal geographical size that will provide the highest revenues, paying more or less attention to the costs incurred depending on the population's control over its strategies.

BENEFITS AND COSTS OF THE EXTERNAL DIMENSION

A pure public good has an average cost that tends to zero when the number of users increases, as the fixed production costs are spread over a growing number of consumers-taxpayers. National defense is the best example of that, but in practice it is almost never the case. States' production costs increase with the volumes produced and the size of the territory. If it were not so, there would only be one state in the world, while in reality there is a multitude of states and the number is currently rising.

This is because, in fact, public goods such as the national defense, the legal system and the development of infrastructures are not "pure": more money per taxpayer must be spent to ensure the protection of a large territory than a small one, and police and legal systems cost even more per inhabitant in large urban concentrations than in small rural towns. The cost of security is all the higher that it is complete. Increased security or additional infrastructures end up costing more and more.

In addition, administrative control declines when the bureaucracies grow. In this respect, states are no different from any other firm. Finally, a heterogeneous population—and the diverse demands for public services that it involves—also contributes to increasing the complexity and production costs of state services. It is harder to amortize the production of a single universal public service when regions are separated by natural, linguistic or cultural barriers.

When a state seeks to extend its area of control to gain additional resources, it compares the costs and benefits of increasing its production even further. It is in the interest of the ruler or possibly of the owner of the state to take as many resources as possible from the territory he controls, and to increase its geographical area as long as additional revenues are larger than additional costs. The population he controls prefers to pay as little as possible for his protection.

Thus, the state's ideal size is determined by the additional revenue coming from an increase in the geographical area of control compared to the cost of that increased dimension. A large state may be tempted not to expand its territory as it may cost it more than it will gain. Thus, imperialism is self-limiting. For each concrete state there exists an optimal size. But all the optimal sizes of all states may not be be compatible. Thus, competitive conflicts may arise for the control of a given territory.

A state's basic geographical calculation consists in comparing the new sources of revenue available and the military and administrative cost of control. This is the calculus of the optimal external dimension.

Several factors contribute to limiting this size. First of all, the rising cost of the public services that are not "pure" but whose quality decreases when the number of users rises, as for instance defense, police, justice or any other collective good which involves the development of an administrative pyramid. Second, the geographical distribution of economic activity and wealth which explains that territorial expansion does not always provide the same amount of revenues. Finally, the type of management of each state and their rulers' goals do not always allow pursuit of the maximization of size.

The geographical equilibrium size will thus depend on the government's precise goals (full taxation or net revenues minus costs), the concentration of the resources and populations within a given geographical area and the rising cost of providing public services, and of the administrative control of territories and populations.

The Geography of Tax Resources

People and wealth are not distributed uniformly in space.

It follows that the frontiers of a state will be defined by the geography of wealth, by the concentration of economic activity in certain regions. A rational predator will prioritarily try to control the wealthiest and most easily exploitable areas and only then acquire the less profitable ones.

Foreign trade has long been states' main source of revenue because it is easier to tax than land or domestic trade. Changes in trade routes and trade flows could therefore be considered as the key to higher revenues.[7]

7. An hypothesis proposed by Brooks Adam, quoted by Gilpin: "Historically, trade taxation has always been a major source of revenue for the State. That is why trade is so important for the distribution of economic surpluses and consequently of power. Unlike the other sources of revenue (e.g., land taxes or foreign trade), inter-

This conception has been more specifically developed by David Friedman.[8] He shows how, in the fourteenth-century Italian city-states, trade taxation led to the inclusion of all the trade routes within a single nation, as it would not have been efficient to levy a multitude of taxes set by independent political authorities on a given route. A contrary example would be the existence of several successive road and river tolls during the Middle Ages, especially on the Rhine, the one and only trade route between the Mediterranean and the North Sea.

Generally, a labor tax is harder to levy if the population is mobile. It can only be maximized if the workers cannot emigrate or are immobilized. Language is a factor that limits mobility of its speakers to the areas where it is spoken. As a consequence, when a labor tax represents an important part of a state's revenue, nations will not organize themselves according to the trade routes but will rather try to control the area where the people speak the same language, to reduce as much as possible the external mobility of the population taxed. Friedman thus explains the regular increase in the rate of linguistic homogeneity in the main European nations since the twelfth century.

Various authors have underlined the historical relation between the urbanization rate and the development of the state which also corresponds to the thesis according to which the origins of the state can be found in the higher population density. When the population is dense, it is easier to amortize the fixed costs of public goods and to control individuals than when they are dispersed over vast areas. The decline of the Roman Empire can be explained by de-urbaniza-

---

national trade is rather easy to control and impose.

. . . And Brooks Adam, in his provocative study, *The Law of Civilization and Decay* (1943), rightly considered shifts in trade routes and their control to be the key to human history" (Robert Gilpin, *War and Change in World Politics*, Cambridge University Press, 1981, p. 113.)

8. "A Theory of the Size and Shape of Nations," *Journal of Political Economy*, 1977, no. 1.

tion, as the trend towards feudalism resulted from a contraction of the Empire's urban and trade tax base. And the same was true of other civilizations. According to Auster and Silver, the barbarian raids that led to the contraction and subsequent depopulation of the Mycenean cities also caused the fragmentation of the Mycenean state into many small states with rural economies. Similarly, it was the changes in the trade routes that led to the extreme rural de-concentration of the industry of states in the Dniepr basin in the twelfth century and in Prussia in the fifteenth century.[9]

In Sumer, urbanization is said to have apparently preceded the emergence of numerous city-states and then facilitated the centralization of the entire region under the authority of the Akkadian military leader, Sargon, in 2340 BC. Despite short-lived pauses because of invasions, the entire southern part of Mesopotamia remained organized after the time of Akkad, in centralized and highly urbanized empires which promoted a policy of forced settling and urbanization of the populations.

In the same way, the rapid urban growth in ancient Greece from 800 BC and in Western Europe during the eleventh and twelfth centuries, also contributed to a re-concentration of political authority. Continued urbanization was accompanied by the rise of national monarchies, as several thousands of small principalities or "states" were gradually replaced by large security firms which, at the beginning of the twentieth century, numbered only 30.[10] The first Russian state was formed when peasants evicted from the steppes by Tartars came together and reached a sufficient degree of demographic density to found a state.

These various historical examples illustrate the influence of the population density, and thus of the concentration of resources, on the profitability of the security firms. Dense resources make taxation easier

9. Auster and Silver, op. cit., p. 33.
10. Ibid., p. 35.

but also reduce the cost of public services for taxpayers, shorten the distances and increase the homogeneity of the population. In their study, Ulrich Blum and Leonard Dudley demonstrate how public services provided to more distant and heterogeneous populations lose their effectiveness, whilst the cost of military control of the territory and population increases with distance and heterogeneity.[11]

The economies of scale that characterize the production of public goods and always encourage states to try and expand their population and territory are offset by the increased administrative costs of large security firms: top-down transmission of information loses efficiency when a certain size is reached and so does the control of the enforcement of management directives when the number of hierarchical grades increases. Beyond a certain geographical size, production costs of public goods inevitably increase, as do the military costs to protect the territory against secessionists, separatists and foreign powers.

Local Public Goods

In real life, public goods are never "pure." When the number of users increases, the quality of the service provided tends to deteriorate. As a consequence, the users are increasingly reluctant to pay taxes when the demographic and geographical size of the state increases because this generally results in a deterioration of public services and an increase in the effective price of the services, for a given quality.

In addition, the taxation process requires an administrative and fiscal organization whose operating costs rise with the geographical size and demographic dispersion. It follows that, beyond a certain point, a state seeking to grow will find it increasingly difficult to extract from the population it wants to control the resources it needs to run. Even without a rival neighbor. This explains why states cannot

---

11. Ulrich Blum and Leonard Dudley, "A Spatial Approach to Structural Change: The Making of the French Hexagon," *Journal of Economic History*, 1989, and "A Spatial Model of the State," *Journal of Institutional and Theoretical Economics*, 1991.

increase their resources beyond a certain level. At some point, their geographical size reaches its optimum.[12]

There are costs inherent in state expansion: acquisition costs (wars with rival states) but also higher managerial costs (larger administrative structures). The quality of public services also deteriorates as the number of users rises. For example, in the field of law and order. It is harder to provide this service to the very large population of a major metropolis, where delinquents are more difficult to identify than in a village with a population of a few hundreds where everyone knows everybody else and what they do.

Moreover, law and order are more difficult to implement in the distant, peripheral areas of a nation or empire than in its capital city. This implies that this collective service is "impure" or "local": its quantity and quality vary according to the number of users and their geographical remoteness.

It is the same control problem as in a firm where the manager, or the "manager's higher level of information," is a "public good" which loses part of its value when the firm grows, for instance during mergers and acquisitions as we explained in Chapter 4.

In practice, public goods are almost never "pure" in the sense that when the consumption of some people increases, the others' consumption capacity decreases, and it is more or less possible to prevent consumers from gaining access to them. Thus, in the areas of education or justice, the necessarily limited number of schools and courts implies that these services be scarce. Thus, an additional student or trial deteriorates the quality of the service available to everyone else. In the area of security (police and justice), everyone does not have access to exactly the same service. This depends on their place of residence or their knowledge of laws and regulations. Some will be better protected than the others.

12. Leonard Dudley develops these issues in *The Word and the Sword*, Blackwell, 1991.

Another good example is the radio and television broadcasts. In theory, when a program is broadcast, all the users can receive it and the broadcaster will spend the same amount of money to reach 100,000 or 500,000 additional people. However, in practice, if these additional users are dispersed over a vast area, they will receive poor quality broadcasts or nothing at all. The reception quality will decrease or drop to nothing due to the increased distance and the natural obstacles such as mountains and valleys. It follows that a television program, which is a "pure" collective good in a limited geographical area, requires additional investment (for instance relay stations, cables) to reach remote and dispersed populations. The cost of such equipment can be very high depending on the size and geographical dispersion of the additional or marginal populations to be served. If they are too few or dispersed, the fixed costs of the additional equipment will not be covered by a sufficient number of users. The average costs will remain high. It may be too expensive to serve remote populations. The provider of public goods (the state, in this case) can thus determine the economic limits of its geographical expansion.

The national defense may also benefit unequally the most remote areas of the territory that are more exposed than others to rival military attacks. Border regions, for example, are often the first to be sacrificed and invaded in the event of a conflict. They are thus not as well protected as the center of the country.

Beyond a certain size of clientele, public goods begin to resemble private goods in that the quantity offered decreases while users compete to access them. Public goods are often only public on a local level. For instance, the French national defense system cannot protect all the inhabitants in the world. The greater the distance between these populations and France, the less this defense can technically benefit them. In other words, public goods are not "international" but rather national, regional or communal depending on the situation.

Rising Administrative Costs

As all public goods are managed in a centralized way, they require a hierarchy and thus a bureaucracy. The competition of suppliers then arises between hierarchies of different sizes, from an empire to a village. The winning size, the most efficient, will depend on the abundance of information.

In recent years, the internal administrative organization of the firm has become a major topic of industrial economics. The effectiveness of bureaucratic management indeed contributes to determining the firm's optimal size. The larger the firm, the more difficult it becomes to control the entire production process and each employee. Inefficiency tends to increase and the firm's costs tend to rise. While the technology of production of goods and services determines the output volume that minimizes the average cost, it is the cost of the firm's internal management that determines the overall optimal firm size.

These analyses can also be applied to the firms involved in several production processes and thus in different sectors. They are called "conglomeral firms" when they have several, possibly unrelated, production activities, for example cars and televisions. These firms are vertically integrated when they are active in several activities representing successive production stages, for instance the manufacture of clothes and their retail sale via chain stores.

For such firms, it is essentially the degree of efficiency of the internal administration that determines the overall dimension of the various production processes and the total number of employees.

For an optimal level of production (when the average production cost is at a minimum), the managerial cost may be minimal or not. The minimum production costs and the minimum administrative costs do not necessarily coincide.

Thus, if a firm manufacturing cars cannot reach the optimal bureaucratic size that such a production requires, it will have to create a joint venture with another small firm. Both firms will keep their own brand and remain independent but cooperate to produce the same model of car which they will then market separately. Conversely, if the optimal size of a firm's administration is bigger than the optimal size of its production, it can have several sites, for example, in different countries.

The same is true of state-firms. If the size of the administration is larger than the size of the production of public services, the latter will be decentralized as was the case for instance at the time of feudalism. With that system, security was produced locally by the lord of the castle who nevertheless submitted to his overlord who could decide on peace or war in the name of all his vassals. It is the same today with the trend towards decentralization and regional autonomy, where the effective production of public goods such as education or police is relegated to a lower level of authority.

Conversely, when the optimal size of the administration is smaller than the size of the production of public goods and services, there can be military alliances, the payment of a tribute from one nation to another or a participation of independent nation-states in international organizations in specific areas such as the production of a world legal or commercial order.

The cost of the public services provided by the state tend to rise beyond a certain territorial dimension. No army can grow to the point its optimal size is the whole world. Moreover, the state must develop an administrative system to levy taxes in the territories it runs directly. The military system will not be sufficient to accomplish this task: it can seize goods through pillage but not regularly levy taxes on all types of productions as this requires a specialized, permanent and sedentary organization. On the contrary, an army must remain mobile. Here again, costs first decrease but then pick up. Altogether, a state's optimal territorial size is defined by the minimum combined average cost of these two functions. But as for firms, the state's various functions may be dissociated or grouped together under a single authority, depending on the importance of what economists call "economies of scope." For example, a firm manufacturing automobiles can also produce trucks or two-wheeled vehicles if the combined average cost of these different productions managed by a single central department is lower than the average cost of each production carried out separately by two different firms. A state can thus subcontract certain functions to independent organizations and change the range of services it produces by itself. Some small states do not produce their own national defense but place themselves under the protection of larger states. Within a nation, some produce education, while others entrust this task to the private sector. However, these operations destructuring or restructuring the usual range of public services do not necessarily impact on nation-states' geographical size.

When the size of hierarchies increases or decreases, so does the state's optimal size. However, the state hierarchy can change its dimension in two ways: internal growth (it levies more resources from a given population on a given territory) or external growth (it extends its control over larger populations on larger territories).

Both types of optimization can be performed simultaneously. But they can be considered separately for the purposes of analysis, as we have done. Internal growth reaches its limits when the marginal cost of taxation is higher than the marginal revenue it produces, as I indicated in my theory of nationalization and privatization.[13] When tax rates rise, individuals are less willing to produce. Ultimately, production will stagnate, which means that the social cost of taxation, measured by the decrease in wealth creation, rises. The state can then consider abandoning certain activities to reduce its social costs and thus allow the private production to resume and its tax revenues to pick up thanks to a larger production while at the same time reducing

---

13. "Théorie économique de la nationalisation de la privatisation," *Finance*, December 1988, and "Public Choice Aspects of Privatization Policies: Driving Forces and Obstacles," in Herbert Giersch (ed.), *Privatization at the End of the Century*, Springer, 1997.

its expenses. It will thus regain budget flexibility and be able to reach its chosen objectives. Conversely, when the conditions necessary for the development of a hierarchical pyramid are met, the state absorbs numerous private activities one after the other. This is nationalization and interventionism. But that internal growth will be limited by the rising social cost of the taxes that the state must levy to finance these new activities. So, it comes back to the preceding problem.

There is an alternative for a state that has not reached its maximum capacities of administrative management: external growth. It provides new opportunities for taxation but also requires that the state grows to the detriment of another state and gains a higher capacity to control a given region. Military superiority is useful but not sufficient. It is also necessary to have an administrative and managerial superiority and a complementarity with state activities in its initial dimensions.

Once a hierarchy has reached its optimal size, the neighboring populations find themselves closer to other public production "centers," other nation-states. These individuals will have to choose between the two nation-states which are "equidistant" as far as the cost and quality of their collective services is concerned. Their decision will depend on particular circumstances and technological advances. This is true of border areas often disputed in history, the "threshold" of an empire or realm. Neighboring states compete for these areas to define more precisely the scope of their territorial jurisdiction.

When a group of states all try to reach their optimal geographical size, there can only be peace if the frontiers they respectively chose are compatible with those selected by their neighboring states. This compatibility, this simultaneous definition of acceptable frontiers, is the essence of diplomacy and war. Attaining this balance is the goal of geopolitics. But it ultimately depends on the respective optimal dimensions of the neighboring nations.

GEOPOLITICAL EQUILIBRIUM

In the finite world of the twentieth century, the whole planet consists of contiguous states. There are no more white areas on the world map, no *terra incognita* still to be discovered by explorers and conquerors. So what happens when the geographical optimization decided by some states are incompatible with those of the others? And how will the mosaic of states be structured? Will there be a large number of small states or a few large empires? Will a single world state arise, as the single gigantic firm that Lenin wanted to build to organize the entire Russian production? And will the frontiers coveted by each state be compatible with the other's aspirations? Will the geographical balance of the "industry of states" be stable or unstable, consensual or confrontational?

The balance within a given population of states depends on their individual behavior. Each state and its neighbors, trying to reach their optimal size, make reciprocal adjustments to draw a particular patchwork of the population of states. Depending on the economic conditions that determine the evolution of the organizations' optimal size, a society of nations tends either towards a competitive structure (or, in economic jargon, an "atomistic" structure) consisting of a large number of small individual competitive states, or toward an "oligopolistic" or "monopolistically competitive" structure composed of a few large states.

The concentration rate of the world industry of nations can be explained the same way as in any industrial or service sector. When the average size of firms in a given sector rises and the market's demand is stable, there is only enough space for a smaller number of firms. Thus, the population of firms concentrates. Inversely, if the average size of a firm decreases, the number of firms in the industry increases and the population of firms de-concentrates.

Economic theory shows that the optimal size of a firm, its output volume, depends on its costs. The lower the production costs of a given volume, the more the firm is encouraged to increase its production. But the costs of a given production vary according to the technologies used. Consequently, it is the production technology that determines the optimal size of each firm and thus the organizational structure of the sectors of activity, a standard conclusion in industrial economics.

The same is true of the states. Their optimal size will depend on the production costs of collective services, and especially security services, which means that it depends on their military effectiveness, as well as on the cost of administrative management of the populations and territories.

Given that the size of the states depends, for a given geographical distribution of the population and wealth, and for a given level of military technology, on the relative size of the administrative hierarchies, the states' world concentration will thus directly depend on the factors that determine the optimal size of the hierarchies, and more especially the scarcity or abundance of information in a society. When the hierarchical mechanism is more efficient than the market mechanism, the number of states decreases and their size increases. And conversely when the market mechanism is more efficient than the hierarchical mechanism. This also determines the distribution of the decision-making power between a variable number of nations and consequently between a variable number of state rulers worldwide.[14]

14. As Auster and Silver wrote: "Let's consider the level of concentration in an ordinary sector as the possible result of an effort to reduce the cost of the intermediate service that is decision-making. . . . Generally, we can conceive two polar forms of the decision-making mechanisms: totally centralized planning and totally free markets. In every sector, the decision-making mechanism stands somewhere between these two extremes within the range of possibilities. The more concentrated the sector, the more often the decisions will be taken as part of a centralized planning process and conversely. The comparative statics of concentration levels can be determined the usual way, provided the agents try to reduce their costs, which seems to be the case in real life. In that case, the factors which increase the cost of one of the polar forms of decision-making will reduce its relative weight in the decision-making process which will turn directly affect the level of concentration" (Auster and Silver, op. cit., pp. 41–42).

314 The Fundamental Question

During the "second twentieth century," the structure of the population of states undeniably tended towards de-concentration and they became increasingly numerous. However, the optimal size of each state may have remained unchanged, as this burgeoning could be due to the demographic boom that started in the early century. As the demand for state services grew because of the rising number of "consumers," new firms (states) had to be created to meet these needs if the average optimal size of such firms remained unchanged. Thus, the increase in the number of states could result from a combined stability of these state-firms' optimal size and a higher number of consumers, which would explain the higher number of state-firms and the deconcentration of the industry of states.

However, there are several signs that the absolute optimal size of a state is diminishing. Thus, we can observe a burgeoning of states even in areas where the population has not risen (for instance, in Europe). Or even separatist and secessionist trends in areas where the population is stagnating or falling (for instance in the USSR or some Eastern European nations). At first sight the evolution of the European Union, from the initial common market institution towards a burgeoning super-bureaucracy in Brussels, with the clear ambition to create a federal Europe, the first step being the creation of the Euro in 1999, totally contradicts the above analysis. But precisely, this enterprise should be forecast to be doomed given the economic and organizational fundamentals delineated in this book.[15] Recent negative political reactions to the project of a "European constitution" in several countries, including the Netherlands and France, a growing disillusionment with the Euro and doubts about its future, as well as continuing economic difficulties and stagnation in the "Old Europe" which basically coincides with the eurozone, all point to the practical impossibility of transforming, today, a free trade area into a single,

15. This is the argument of my 1998 book, *L'erreur européenne*, Grasset, translated as *Euro Error*, Algora, 1999.

even if federal, nation-state. The current trend, at the time of writing,[16] is one of rapidly spreading euro-skepticism and of the return of nationalist policies in France, Germany and Italy, not to mention the always reluctant United Kingdom.

The above remark about this general de-concentration or "institutional atomization" trend is very important to understand peace and war between nations, as the changes in the structure of the industry of states, the transformation of the structure of the society of nations, is the main determinant of the type of inter-state relationships.

Since the end of the nineteenth century, "nationalistic" conflicts have multiplied between expanding states that gradually grew into rival empires. The dispute reached its height at the end of World War II with the worldwide conflict between the two remaining superpowers, the United States and the Soviet Union, who were locked in a cold war for a half-century. At the same time, other large European empires dissolved and were replaced by a multitude of smaller-sized nation-states. Then, with the triumph of the United States and the implosion of the Soviet Union, a plethora of small independent states arose from the ruins of communism.

The global nation-state system, the "society of nations," has thus undergone profound structural changes during that century.[17] Taken together, these nation-states represent a world sector of specific activities, a planetary industry producing collective services, or in other words, a collection of state-firms more or less in competition with

16. This revised version, fall 2005.
17. We might as well use the expression of "industry of the states" to refer to the nations of the planet, as a whole. But it could easily be mistaken with the state industries, the industrial sectors owned by the states, the companies whose economic and trade activities have been integrated in the political sectors through nationalization. The industry of the nations experienced in the first part of the twentieth century a concentration wave that led to the virtual duopoly of the cold war and then an "atomization" of its structure that made it closer to the pure and perfect competition model mentioned in economics textbooks. This is what happens today with the persistent separatist and secessionist movements in all the regions of the globe and, specifically, in Quebec, Kosovo, Scotland, the Basque Country, Corsica or Nigeria.

each other via trade, diplomacy and sometimes war, depending on the period.

The optimal structure of the sector can change over time, especially with technological advances as they can modify the optimal size of state-firms. As the state's new frontiers are established in a finite space (a space completely occupied by neighboring and rival firms), the expansion of any of them will necessarily imply the contraction of another.

So, how can the size of a nation-state change when the territory coveted is disputed, necessarily the case as the entire planet already consists of contiguous nation-states since the end of the nineteenth century.

The frontiers can be redefined by mutual agreement, with or without a compensation and payment. That was the case of a state buying another's territory, for instance when France sold Louisiana or when Corsica was purchased by France from Genoa, or also when states exchange territories. In a second case, an independent population or even a population already a member in another state joins democratically the state of its choice, as was the case of the referendum annexing the Savoie region to France in the nineteenth century or the recent amicable separation of the Czech Republic from the Slovak Republic.

However, the use of force cannot be totally ruled out because the world society of nations is anarchical. There is no higher authority in a position to impose an order on the society of nations. No single producer has the monopoly of violence over the whole planet. Nor is there an accepted hierarchy that can impose the domination of one state over all the others or the domination of an organization other than a state, be it the UN or other international organizations. In such a context, as in a society composed of individuals, a mutually agreed exchange may be advantageous, but it could also be that predation is preferred to production and voluntary exchange. It all depends on the comparative superiority of each nation (or individual) in terms of production and predation.

The Confrontation of Interests

The rational goal of every state-firm is to reach its optimal geographical size, the one that will, depending on the respective power of the rulers and the governed, either maximize the tax revenues net of the production costs of public services or the maximal territorial size at which the taxpayers can still accept the tax rate without rebelling.

Thus, it is from the simultaneous optimization of state's respective territories that conflicts can arise. If each nation is at its optimal dimension and their behavior is rational, no conflicts should occur.

But there are other scenarios that we may simplify by considering two states: (1) if both need to shrink to reach their optimal dimension there must then be secessionist or separatist movements within each of them, (2) if one of them must grow to reach its optimal dimension and the other must shrink, (3) if both must grow or, alternatively, if one must stay unchanged while the other grows. In the first two cases, there is no risk of conflict as each state can restructure independently of the other. But in the third case, there is a conflict of interest.

Indeed, if a given territory can enable both neighboring states to optimize their surface through integration, then the state that will lose it or be unable to control it will be deeply negatively affected. In this case, competition is a "zero-sum-game" situation: what one wins, the other will necessarily lose.

This implies that in a finite world, a universal increase in states' optimal size will necessarily generate widespread border conflicts, as two neighboring nations cannot both extend their territory simultaneously.

If, on the contrary, there is a universal decrease in the optimal size of nation-states, there will be a general proliferation of secessionist and separatist movements and the states will fall apart at the end of internal conflicts, as it was the case in Yugoslavia and in the USSR.

If several regions of a given state want to become independent nations, they can do so by common consent with no conflict of interest, provided they do not seek control of the same territories. The dismantling of the USSR and Czechoslovakia, as opposed to the situation in Yugoslavia, is quite telling. The first two were achieved peacefully while the latter plunged the country into a bloody conflict. This contrast can be explained by the existence or absence of territorial and demographic disputes. In the first two cases, homogeneous populations wanted to constitute new, clearly independent, states. There was no territorial overlap. On the contrary, in Yugoslavia, the inextricable mix of populations obviously made the process controversial and logically resulted in deep conflicts and confusion. It is those overlapping interests of opposed parties that triggered the conflict.

But, in general, a reduction in the optimum size of state-firms will not raise that kind of problem as the populations of a same region have been able to homogenize over their history. In that case, the fragmentation of a large state composed of distinct but separate regions can be achieved peacefully. Conversely, the expansion of two neighboring states necessarily leads to territorial claims—each state wanting the territories that belong to the other—and thus inevitably to a conflict.

However, the geographical optimum of each state changes over time as its determining factors evolve. For example, a change in the political regime following internal transformations in the economic or demographic structure, or a modification of the trade routes or of the location of some activities, or also as a result of transformations in organizational technologies and, more especially, in storage and information transmission techniques.

To predict how the global society's overall organization will develop, we must ask ourselves how the optimal size of the most basic organization will evolve. That is, what populations and what territories can a government or a state control economically? And as a consequence, how many independent governments (governments that do not share a hierarchical relation with others) can coexist in the world at a given moment?

The answers to these questions give an indication of the competition, trade rivalry, that will exist between these governments, and to what extent the inter-governmental coordination will be handled by a higher authority. It is in short, the problem of secessionism and federalism analyzed by Donald Wittman.[18]

His analysis takes into account all the general factors that simultaneously influence all states. It is highly probable that, faced with similar tasks, such as the production of order, security, and other collective goods, the various states will share very similar conditions of production. In a given sector, firms can be of very varied sizes but nevertheless all of them tend to evolve simultaneously in the same direction when the production technologies improve. Thus, all car makers will try almost simultaneously to grow or shrink, as will all bankers and pharmaceutical firms.

As we saw in Part 1, these general trends developed both in private companies and state-firms during the twentieth century. There can also be special factors that result in the isolated growth of a firm while the optimal size of all the others remains unchanged. But, by definition, these exceptions cannot explain the general trends observed during the great organizational cycle.

The Contractual Solution

Like Donald Wittman, David Friedman suggests a contractual solution to territorial rivalry between states: the conflict could be resolved through sale or purchase.[19] The territory becomes the property of the

18. Donald Wittman, "Nations and States: Mergers and Acquisitions, Dissolution and Divorce," *American Economic Review*, May 1991.

19. David Friedman, "A Theory of the Size and Shape of Nations," *Journal of Political Economy*, 1977, n. 1.

state that considers it the most valuable, as for goods and services in general. In an auction, the buyer of a painting is not always the richest bidder but rather the collector who places the highest subjective value on the piece. In the case of full employment, the firm that will attract the best workers will be the one in which the worker will be the most useful, the most productive. It will indeed be able to pay him a higher salary than its less productive competitors.

Similarly, one can assume that the nation that successfully wins control over a disputed border area will be the one that considers it the most useful for its economy or military strategy, as for instance the Golan heights for Israel and Syria, or Alsace-Lorraine for France and Germany.

In a world where anarchy reigns between nations, one could believe that the most powerful country would necessarily win through force, since it can destroy its competitor in the last resort if necessary. But in a world with many nations, such a strategy seems dangerous and hardly plausible. Indeed, if the most powerful state devotes a lot of its resources to crushing a competitor to win a given territory, it will weaken against all its other competitors because it must consume rare resources to be victorious. Moreover, by increasing its size, the conqueror will become less efficient. Thus, it is a losing strategy in the medium term, unless the value of the coveted territory significantly strengthens the competitive potential of the victorious country.

We can thus assume that when nations compete it is not necessarily the most powerful that manages to expand its territory, but rather the nation for whom the disputed territory is the most valuable, which brings us back to the case of market transactions. The value also depends on the competitors capacity to levy taxes from the population coveted, a capacity that in turn depends on the efficient use of violence as well as administrative management. Two predators with different degrees of efficacy will not give the same value to the same territory, and the most efficient predator should win the competition for its control.

However, in these conditions, why can all territorial disputes not be solved peacefully or with a financial compensation, the country that considers the disputed region as the most valuable paying the other country to renounce its claim? Despite that additional cost, the purchasing country would still be able to reap the benefits of its acquisition, just as a collector can enjoy the painting he has purchased at a higher price than any other potential purchaser.

It thus seems that war should not exist. Admittedly, we could believe that war is a way to avoid to pay a compensation to the country that renounces the territory. But, in fact, this is not the case given a war will be at least as costly as a peaceful transaction. So how can we explain war?

Why War?

Several conditions are required for a war to begin. First, there must be a conflict of interest. Second, the situation must be anarchic in that the use of force is viewed as a possible strategy, instead of consensual exchange. Third, there must be doubts about the value of each opposing party's stakes, net of costs.

The first two conditions are obvious. If there is no conflict of interest or if a higher authority can effectively forbid the use of violence between subordinate political entities, there will be no war. But anarchy prevails in today's world industry of states. In the absence of a sufficiently powerful state whose optimal size would be the whole world and with the ability to monopolize violence worldwide, violent competition will prevail between some states. As in a society of individuals, anarchy allows both predation and production to collect resources, depending on the optimization of each player's calculations and relative capacity to handle both types of activity. Both means (violence or consensual negotiation) are substitutes, and this is why many believe that war is only the continuation of politics in another form.

Nevertheless, a situation of anarchy will force all the states to consider the strategy of violence as a possibility. The potential purchaser of a territory may pay a compensation for it, or exchange it for another territory, or even agree to military expenses that will enable him to annex the territory without giving a financial compensation or any other kind of payment. Against such a competitor, the current owner of the territory has no other choice than to use violence. If he did not, he would lose a competitive weapon. He would surely be defeated, as would any country that in a war would refuse to use a certain type of weapon, such as the navy or air force.

Thus, in general, there will be no purely contractual negotiation without the use of violence (or at least the threat of) between the states that each seek their geographical optimum.

However, the threat of violence does not automatically imply that it will be used. To explain war, we must understand how a state decides to switch to effective violence.

It is thus the third condition which determines why a contractual solution can be ruled out, leading to war.

If each state competing for a same territory knew everything about the other (how valuable it considers that land and its available resources), a peaceful solution would automatically be found without negotiation. The optimal division of space would necessarily favor the state with the greatest need for the territory given the military or financial costs required to convince the other potential purchaser or current owner to renounce it.

And this solution would prevail even if the territorial division favored only one of the two as the winner could use its increased productivity to compensate at least partially the loser whose productivity would decrease. By definition, the winner will be the state that considers the land the most valuable and thus has the ability to compensate the loser for his income loss and still benefit from a net gain.

This assumes, first of all, that one of the states has a clear managerial advantage over the other and that both protagonists are also completely aware of that. But in fact, there is always a degree of in-certitude. And in this case, each must prove that he is prepared to better develop the conquered land than the other. To do so, he must make the highest bid as in an auction, that means that he has effec-tively to pay the purchase price to really show how valuable he con-siders the coveted territory.

During an auction, the bidder promises to pay the bid price if no one makes a higher offer. Thus, he truly devotes his resources to the competition with no possibility of backing out. Between states, there is no auctioneer to force them to meet their commitments. But on the contrary, war requires to pay progressively an increasingly high price until one of the belligerents finds the cost excessive compared to the value at stake and decides to cut their losses by proposing an armistice and negotiating peace.

In a situation of anarchy, only the use of force can reveal which of the competing firms is (or believes it is) the most efficient, that is, which firm is able to levy the most taxes from the population and the disputed territory. War is a high-risk spending designed to convince the adversary of one's higher capacity to develop a territory.

If it is in the interest of all nations to simultaneously increase their size (for example, because military or administrative technologies have evolved), only a military victory will enable the victorious nation to approach its new optimal size. The other nation(s) will have to retain their sub-optimal size, which implies a higher operating cost and a loss of well-being. Consequently, there can be no mutually advanta-geous negotiation, no purely consensual transaction. Each party tries to win through violence. As Georges Sorel said (although for different reasons), violence plays a useful social role especially when anarchy prevails. It reveals who places the highest value on a given resource, who is ready to pay the highest price or even who makes the most of the available resources.

The industrial organization—or systemic—economic approach to the society of nations explains that wars result from an increase in the nations' optimal size. This is apparently the most significant common factor of all the past conflicts, as we will see below. But the political regime may also be a determinant whose influence has not yet been properly demonstrated, because the observers did not take into account both the structural and dimensional aspects analyzed above.

It follows that the periods of general expansion of the size of states, implying a concentration in the population of states, are also periods of war. And even more so when the state's internal political system is managerial rather than patrimonial. A hypothesis we can now test by looking at the past.

THE TERRITORIAL HYPOTHESIS VINDICATED

The traditional approach to war seeks responsibilities in the behavior of one or several states, especially those connected by treaties and alliances. It is true that a single state may happen to be a warmonger responsible for war. War may also occur as a local conflict circumscribed to only two states while other states remain at peace. But in these cases, the causes of war are specific, particular, and there is no general trend toward conflicts.

In the same way, although each firm's strategy is unique, there are key factors which affect all the individual strategies in a given industry at the same time. The equilibrium of the sector indeed depends on a multitude of individual decisions, but they are all affected, to varying degrees, by these common factors.

It is all the more important to take into account these universal factors in the case of twentieth-century conflicts between nation-states shown earlier, that such conflicts arise from territorial disputes and, precisely, it is no longer possible for a state to "freely" expand its frontiers since the end of the nineteenth century.[20] Finally, the decisive

20. See William H. McNeill, *The Global Condition, Conquerors, Catastrophes & Community*, Princeton University Press, 1992, and more especially the first part entitled "The Great Frontier: Freedom and Hierarchy in Modern Times."

importance of these common factors is attested by the fact that the optimal sizes of all the state pyramids have decreased simultaneously with the advent of new information technologies.

All these arguments support a "systemic" rather than anecdotal approach to the origins of war as recommended by many authors such as Mansfield and Gilpin.[21]

Centennial Experience

Our vision of war has been deeply influenced by the European nation building since the fifteenth century, a period of constant conflicts for territorial expansion, especially in the case of France. Throughout this period, nations' optimal size increased. This doubtless explains the widespread belief according to which the largest and most powerful country must win the war, barring major management mistakes, a lack of courage and resolve or internal dissent. Hence, the obsession that size matters and that bigger is better, the fear of big countries that haunts the whole geopolitical debate.

According to Jared Diamond, history and archeology prove that through the centuries war has been a means to an ever-increasing concentration of nations. And where it is not war itself, it is the threat of war that determines the mergers and acquisitions of states.[22]

21. Edward D. Mansfield, *Power, Trade, and War*, Princeton University Press, 1994, and Robert Gilpin, *War and Change in World Politics*, Cambridge University Press, 1981.

22. "The amalgamation of smaller units into larger ones has often been documented historically or archaeologically. Contrary to Rousseau, such amalgamations never occur by a process of unthreatened little societies freely deciding to merge, in order to promote the happiness of their citizens. Leaders of little societies, as of big ones, are jealous of their independence and prerogatives. Amalgamation occurs instead in either of two ways: by merger under the threat of external force, or by actual conquest. Innumerable examples are available to illustrate each mode of amalgamation" (Jared Diamond, p. 289).

"All these examples illustrate that wars, or threats of war, have played a key role in most, if not all, amalgamations of societies. But wars, even between mere bands, have been a constant fact of human history. Why is it, then, that they evidently began causing amalgamations of societies only within the past 13,000 years?" (ibid., p. 291).

Like Carneiro, he suggests that population density explains the concentration of states. In a low-density geographical space, conquered populations can flee elsewhere. In a moderately populated space, they cannot flee but are of no use to the conqueror and everyone is exterminated except the women. In a densely-populated area, the conquered cannot flee but are used as slaves or taxpayers. This happened in history as a big step toward the use of slavery as an alternative to extermination.[23]

More systematic studies have been conducted by specialists in international relations to explain under what circumstances wars occur. Many studies on that subject have been published since the 1930s.[24] However, most of this literature is empirical and the conclusions remain rather unconvincing and somewhat incomplete.

These studies are based on *ad hoc* intuitive factors, such as the proximity of belligerents, the political regime, the balance of powers and the psychology or pathology of the leaders. Under such conditions, these attempts at empirical verification often give contradictory results and are difficult to interpret.

Geller and Singer review the main studies seeking to identify the determining factors of wars, and especially those written by authors who participated in the "Correlates of War" project sponsored by the University of Michigan in 1963–1964. It is clear for social scientists that we need to amass a vast amount of information on the factors associated with war before attempting to explain its causes.

Accordingly they surveyed more than 600 articles published since the end of the 1960s, all of which use data collected about wars and their associated variables. In addition to these studies, all published

---

23. "Thus, food production, and competition and diffusion between societies, led as ultimate causes, via chains of causation that differed in detail but that all involved large dense populations and sedentary living, to the proximate agents of conquest: germs, writing, technology, and centralized political organization" (ibid., p. 292).

24. Daniel S. Geller and J. David Singer, *Nations at War*, Cambridge University Press, 1998.

in the five major journals in that field, they also examined two dozen books providing a rigorous and systematic analysis of the international political problems and more especially armed conflicts.

Their main conclusions are as follows. They observe that the status of "major power" is a decisive factor and as, by definition, great powers are usually large-sized, we can assume that they benefited from the start of some specific advantage in looking for growth.

For the whole population of states, they conclude that the factors determining the probability and gravity of a conflict are the number of frontiers separating the nations, the polarization of the system of states and the instability of the inter-state hierarchy. Obviously, the more common frontiers there are between these states, the more likely they are to seek control of the same territory, a factor that we present as the first cause of war. The polarization of the system of states, the asymmetry between them, illustrates the concentration of resources between states, which necessarily has a geographical dimension, and thus logically increases the risk of border conflicts. For this reason, incomplete but continuing polarization (that Geller and Singer call the "instability of the hierarchy of states") must result in increased competition for control areas and a more frequent use of war to allocate the disputed territories and their resources.

It follows that the most contemporary studies on wars between nations tend to confirm that the general and ultimate cause of war in the world society of nations is the increase in nations' average size. However, the latter depends partly on the nature of the political regimes, as managerial (dictatorial) regimes tend to pursue growth for itself as opposed to patrimonial regimes (monarchic or democratic). This strongly supports the mostly negative relationship between war and democracy, or war and trade, that was observed in many econometric studies but remains only partially explained. Indeed, democracy particularly develops in areas where organizations are not too centralized and consequently where managerial political regimes are weaker. Moreover, all things being equal, democracy requires leaders to provide public services and to limit tax increases, which is incompatible with the pursuit of growth and the discretionary building of empires.

War and the World Concentration of Nations

Two other analyses of different nations and periods support the territorial explanation of the origins of war: Bergesen and Schoenberg's analysis of waves of expansion and contraction of colonial empires,[25] and Mansfield's study, which is more precise as it only concerns the relations between the major powers during a shorter period, from 1820 to 1965.[26]

Bergesen and Schoenberg start by noting the importance of colonialism in the modern world system. From its beginning in the sixteenth century to the 1960s, it concerned at one time or another, most of the surface of the globe. In 1800, about 35 percent of the planet was or had been controlled by Europeans. In 1878, this figure rose to 67 percent to reach 84 percent in 1914.

The authors collected a historical series of the number of colonies created by the European nations over these centuries. It revealed two periods of intensive colonization: first, the sixteenth century, and second, from the end of the nineteenth century to the beginning of the twentieth. But it also shows two periods of intensive de-colonization (which is a decentralization of the world system of nation-states): the eighteenth century, the Age of Enlightenment, and the end of the twentieth.

It is particularly interesting to note that the periods of colonization are also periods of mercantilist trade policies and decline in free international trade and that, conversely, the periods of de-colonization

---

25. Albert Bergesen and Ronald Schoenberg, "Long Waves of Colonial Expansion and Contraction, 1415–1969," Chapter 10 of Bergesen, ed., *Studies of the Modern World-System*, Academic Press, 1980.

26. *Power, Trade, and War*, Princeton University Press, 1994.

are characterized by a liberalization of world trade, first between 1820 and 1879, and later on with the GATT agreement in the 1950s.

However, the most interesting observation about the origins of war is the overlap between periods of strong colonization and major wars between European powers at the end of the seventeenth century and then during the twentieth.[27] The periods of geographical expansion of the European nations thus coincided with an intensification of the wars between those nations. More precisely, wars were more frequent when the states tried to build empires, that is when the optimal size of all the European nations was growing quickly. This supports our view that war results from border conflicts between expansionist nations and expanding state hierarchies.

In the other study, Edward Mansfield reached similar conclusions. In a systematic and statistical analysis of the 1820 to 1965 period, he tried to determine the factors governing the declarations of war between major powers. But the question he asked himself was slightly different from ours: how can the distribution of forces or powers between nations influence the structure of international trade and explain the wars between them?

For that, he first measured the concentration of the "capacities" of the five major world states among the twelve largest, at different dates during the 1820–1965 period. These capacities were measured by the economic, demographic and military dimensions of the nations concerned. The identity of some of these nations changes over time, as it was not always the same five nations that were the most powerful during the nineteenth and twentieth centuries. But what is interesting is that this measurement of the concentration of the "capacities" of the major powers is a direct equivalent to our conception of the optimal economic, demographic, and thus geographical concentration of nations. Because a nation with many economic, demographic and military resources is also necessarily a "great" nation geographically-speaking.

27. See chart 105 in Bergesen and Schoenberg.

Mansfield then examined the relation between his indicator of the concentration of nation's size and the degree of hegemony exercised by the then most powerful nation together with the number of conflicts between states and the importance of international trade.

He thus observes[28] that a size conentration of major nations reduces the volume of international trade but also increases the frequency of conflicts between nations in a statistically very significant way.[29] What is even more interesting is that an increase in the concentration of nations, which we interpret as a general increase in the size of nations, also contributes very significantly to an increase in the probability of war between these nations. This corresponds exactly to our analysis of the probability of military conflicts between nations pursuing an expansionist policy and that confront each other in border conflicts about territories coveted by both.

Going back to the historical description, Mansfield notes that the periods of low concentration of the nations' "capacities" (which means for us, "of their sizes") were the very periods of cooperation between the European nations in the early nineteenth century, while concentration reached its maximum level in 1946 at the beginning of the cold war between the two remaining empires, the two world cartels of nations.

This cycle of state concentration and de-concentration during the twentieth century also appears in the more cursory indicator of the concentration of domestic products.

The proportion of the highest domestic product in the world product rose from 6 percent in 1820 to 11 percent in 1900, then 29 percent in 1950 before falling back to 22 percent in 1992.

The proportion of the five highest domestic products in the world

28. Mansfield, op. cit., p. 187, table 5.4.

29. Mansfield thus explains 50 percent of the conflicts that occurred between the great nations during the 1820–1965 period, which is—in the field of social sciences in general and in the knowledge of geopolitical in its infancy in particular—an extremely high score.

product surged from 19 percent in 1820 to 41 percent in 1900, 47 percent in 1950 and then came back to 41 percent in 1992.

For the fifteen highest domestic products, the figures are 22 percent, 57 percent, 60 percent and 51 percent at the same dates.

Thus, at the end of the century, the structure of the world industry of states almost returned to what it looked like in 1900, after a phase of maximum concentration in the middle of the period.

THE REASONS FOR THE GREAT CYCLE: MONOPOLIZATION AND DEMONOPOLIZATION

The chaos and extreme clashes of this totalitarian century are simply the expression of a growing concentration of power within the system of nations and in the nations' internal systems. The first twentieth century was marked by a transition from state competition to an oligopoly and then a duopoly or, more precisely, a bipolar cartel. Within the states, it was first marked by a shift from economic and political decentralization to the concentration of large firms, large parties and mass unions, and then by a transition towards totalitarianism and the single party system with a single party line.

This transition led to instability and increasingly radical confrontations based on the all-or-nothing approach. Whereas atomistic competition means that each producer can live and let the other producers live, with the rise of monopoly there can only be one and all the other competitors must die. That is full-blown war.

Globally, the system of nation-states evolves according to the decisions made by each state on the optimal size of its geographical area of control. When the optimal size of the state pyramids grows, states use both external and internal growth. The world population of nation-states becomes more concentrated. This concentration results in rivalry for the control of territorial, demographic and economic resources. Given the uncertainty about the value each protagonist places on the coveted resources and in the absence of a higher authority likely to impose by force a peacefully negotiated solution on the competitors, war is the only way to reveal which competitor will be the most efficient in using these additional resources. It follows that wars occur more frequently at times when the average size of hierarchies, and thus of states, is on the rise.

The size of the hierarchical organization is thus the key factor determining the structure of the society of nations and the conditions of war and peace between them. The current period, characterized by the atomization and dismantling of the major hierarchies and states, is thus a period where the probability of war is low. As long as this technologically-based trend towards a decrease in the size of hierarchies and an expansion of markets continues, we will experience a relatively peaceful period where conflicts will be limited to internal wars: civil wars and secession wars.

We are also moving away from the periods of hegemony where a large country imposed its will on smaller states.

The major impact of the size of the hierarchies on the organization of the society of nations also explains the differences of organization between small and large states. If the absolute size of the hierarchy is big but that, for several reasons, the country cannot increase its geographical size (for example, because of the natural characteristics of the environment along its borders, such as mountains, seas or oceans), the state will view internal growth as a better way to optimize its organizational capacity than external growth.

The smallest states, all things being equal, will thus be characterized by a higher taxes-to-GNP ratio than the larger ones. This explains Alberto Alesina's observation whereby the states the most open to international trade are also those with the highest public spending. Alesina explains this by the higher risk of instability in the most open economies. But there is no obvious relation between actual public spending (mostly on health insurance and pensions) and the risk of economic instability due to international trade.

We would rather base our explanation on the fact that small states are necessarily more open to international trade than larger states. The observed relation between external trade and the state's influence on the economy thus merely reflects the relation between the optimal size of a state, defined in the absolute by the number of subordinates in the hierarchy, and the size of the economy, which is small in small countries by definition. When the size of the hierarchies grows, the states of the smallest countries find, more than any others, new activities to invest in in their economies. This may explain the strong tradition of interventionism and socialism in Nordic countries.

Finally, the periods of hierarchical concentration explain the change of tone in the relations between nations and the intensity of the conflicts between societies. The number of organizations that can survive within a given sector or society depends on their size. And the number of organizations within a given sector or society defines the type of relations that will arise among them. Atomistic competition does not imply the same relationships between firms as an oligopoly or a duopoly. And the perspective of an evolution of the latter towards a monopoly will determine the full-blown conflict between the last two producers in a given sector, the survival of one implying the disappearance of the other.

In atomistic competition, each producer decides individually and develops his own business independently of the others. The decision-making process is decentralized. Each consumer or user can choose his supplier. In a monopoly, a single individual decides. He imposes his choices on all others within the firm and outside the firm. There is only one centralized source of orders, imposed on all. Hence, the intense conflicts for the control of the organization which decides everyone's fate.

This gives us a very different vision of the ongoing developments. The second twentieth century is not, contrary to what is feared by those who still have in mind the first part of the century, a time of hegemonic domination by a single power, a single organization, thanks to the elimination of its main rivals. It is no longer time for the globalization of a single empire that Napoleon, Hitler and Stalin sought. On the contrary, it is time for renewed diversity, atomistic competition and decentralization. To a live and let live philosophy.

Thus, good understanding of the past sheds new light on the present and near future.

CONCLUSION

The
Rationale
of History

The twentieth-century enigma challenges us to find a rationale of history, to discover a guiding thread and more importantly to understand the causes of its apparently chaotic course. The need for an explanation—a coherent simplification—is all the greater that the trends were complex and puzzling, contradictory and obscure. To understand the transformations that all the societies underwent over that period, their conflicts and their internal economic, political and cultural restructuring, it is necessary to look at the broad picture, to take into account all the contributions of the various social sciences as these transformations have affected both the political and economic conditions of individual lives and altered their temporal course, that is, their history. But literature has fallen short of the task despite the vast historical panoramas, from Toynbee to Kennedy and more recently Landes, as they are more descriptive than explanatory.[1]

According to Mancur Olson, these shortcomings explain the persistent interest for Marx's analyses—although his economic concep-

---

1. Arnold J. Toynbee, *A Study of History*, Oxford University Press, 1972; Paul Kennedy, *The Rise and Fall of the Great Powers*, Random House, 1987; and David Landes, *The Wealth and Poverty of Nations: Why Some Are So Rich and Some Are So Poor*, Norton, 1998.

tions and forecasts have been proved totally false by the subsequent course of history—which is due to that fact that he gives an economic overview of the political and social institutions and their evolution in time.[2]

That can also explain the past success of Rostow's analyses collected in *Stages of Economic Growth: a Non-Communist Manifesto*.[3] Similarly, Nobel Prize and economic historian Douglass North, who substantially contributed to explaining the emergence of the European states and their political constitutions from the particular, fiscal and financial constraints they were faced with, encourages his colleagues to take more into account the "institutions, property rights, the state and ideology."

Naturally, we need to discover the reason why, to analyze the causes, in order to understand what is going on in the world and find our bearings. People often oppose instinct to reason but the latter is itself part of human instinct. What is restrictively called instinct—a

---

2. Marx's fatally weak point is undeniably its historically dated economic analysis based on the erroneous conception of the labor theory of value and on the excessively rigid idea of homogeneous class behaviors that left no room for individual optimization. It is only around the end of his life that the marginal value theory emerged and the theory of collective decision making, sketched out by Wicksell in the late nineteenth century only made a big leap forward with Mancur Olson during the second half of the twentieth century. And so did the economic theory of public choice first with Downs and then with Buchanan and Tullock in the 1960s. Obviously, Marx lacked all these elements to develop his economic analysis of political and social changes.

As he believed that a class was a sort of standard unit, an indivisible element of the analysis, he did not explain how the individuals could take unanimous decisions simply because of their position in the production process. Thanks to the works of Mancur Olson, Buchanan and Tullock, the economists can now analyze how the social groups form by analyzing if an individual will want to join it or not. As such, the group (or organization) becomes a variable that can be explained by economic analysis rather than an artificial unit whose existence is supposed to be constant for the needs of the cause.

3. Mancur Olson, Review of Charles P. Kindleberger and Guido di Tella's book (eds), *Economics in the Long View: Essays in Honor of W.W. Rostow*, Columbia University Press, 1982.

form of automatic reaction—is not enough to guide people's actions and decisions in new and complex circumstances. As a consequence, reasoning—the ability to calculate and simulate the real world in one's mind—is an advantageous complement and has become essential. This explains the pursuit of knowledge and the development of sciences—not only biology but also the sciences of human interactions.

History thus gives rise to a need for scientific theories. In science, a theory is an explanation based on a corpus of established facts. The whole point of the theoretical approach is to discover the common factors that explain many phenomena of different kinds. And a theory is all the more powerful, useful and deep-impacting, that it explains with as few hypotheses as possible an even greater number of varied phenomena. For example, the Darwinian genetic theory of evolution that was developed by a whole school of researchers, ranging from Mendel to Crick and Watson, the DNA pioneers, explains both the diversity and universality of the living world.

But obviously simplification has its limits. Although all the sciences must simplify and reduce complex phenomena to a handful of explanatory factors, it must also respect Albert Einstein's humoristic advice: "Simplify things as much as possible—but no more."

Polybius's Question

The need to understand the evolution of the twentieth century takes us back to the source of the discipline, to the question asked by Polybius, one of the founders of history and political science, second century BC. According to him, historians' essential task should be to discover the causes of the events they study. Rather than just recounting a story, they must explain it, using one logical and plausible principle at a time, to show "the general and global economy of events," and only make assumptions in last resort. He thus stands in the continuity of Thucydides, who distinguished between the apparent causes and the true reasons, the eternal laws of history, and Aristotle, according to whom "wisdom is knowledge of the causes."[4]

But how can events be explained? With what tools, concepts, logic and science? As history is itself closer to narration, it must rely on other social sciences such as psychology, sociology and economy to find the causes. But Polybius already resolved the problem of methodology in his study of the second Punic War as he distinguished between the beginning, the excuse, and the true cause. The cause (*aitia*) is the intentions, the reasoning and the feelings at the origin of that decision or project.[5]

Economists will have recognized their own methodology which consists in analyzing the individuals' calculations as a function of their personal goals. This approach is the one used in the theory of decision-making, the theory of choices. And if history is considered as the science studying the evolution of human societies—which is the case today—the explanation of history relies ultimately on economic analysis, the analysis of human decisions, given a society is an organization of human relations and that this organization results from a multitude of individual choices made in isolation or combined within a collective framework.

This assertion can seem surprising to those who take a restrictive view of economic analysis limited to material self interest and monetized transactions. But over the last decades, its specialists have substantially enlarged its field of application to neighboring disciplines such as law, politics, sociology and demography. An endeavor that Gary Becker perfectly summarized in his Nobel lecture in Stockholm.[6]

The economic methodology takes as granted the personal preferences whether they be selfish or altruistic, loyal or spiteful, hedon

4. Guy Bourdé and Hervé Martin, *Les Ecoles historiques*, Points Histoire, Le Seuil, 1983, 1997.
5. Ibid., p. 35.
6. Gary Becker, "Nobel Lecture: The Economic Way of Looking at Behaviour," *Journal of Political Economy*, 1993.

istic or masochistic. It then consists of showing how the decisions are made according to those preferences, under the constraint of relative scarcities, including income, time, imperfect memory and limited calculating and knowledge capacities. And those individual choices are also largely determined by the private and collective actions of the other individuals and organizations in the society. This very general behavioral model applies equally to monetary and non-monetary decisions: there is thus an economic analysis of families, demography, crime, elections and politics, arts and religion.

But this approach of human behavior which was notably used to rationally explain the constitution and the development of European states[7] or the mercantilist policies[8] has not been applied to the political and economic transformations of the twentieth century, except by the many authors who try to determine the causes of the state's growth, especially in western democracies.[9]

On the contrary, many believe that an inexplicable drift into irrationality is the only plausible cause to the mishaps of the past century, of its excesses, its conflicts and its frequent episodes of barbarism.

The Surrender of Reason

As a consequence, although the history of the twentieth century seems to be a challenge to reason, the main explanations that have been

7. Douglass C. North and Robert Paul Thomas, *The Rise of the Western World: A New Economic History*, Cambridge University Press, 1973.

8. Robert B. Ekelund Jr. and Robert D. Tollison, *Mercantilism as a Rent-Seeking Society: Economic Regulation in Historical Perspective*, Texas A&M University Press, 1981.

9. For an overview of this literature, see Dennis C. Mueller, *Public Choice*, Cambridge University Press, 1989, and Norman Gemmel (ed.), *The Growth of the Public Sector: Theories and International Evidence*, Elgar, 1993.

We would also mention Ronald Wintrobe's book, *The Political Economy of Dictatorship*, Cambridge University Press, 1998.

given relied on irrationality and were thus themselves a sign that reason had caved in.

Blinded by the intense conflicts between big rival nations and the idealized images of themselves that these nations propagated through ideologies, both the observers and actors only saw in the past century a conflict between political and economic systems: liberal capitalism, national-socialism, fascism or corporatism and communism.

As they were committed to their personal preferences, they believed in the absolute superiority of one of these systems, so that when another one prevailed, they concluded that it was just a mistake or an illusion. Others, more opportunistic, concluded that only the best could survive and that consequently all the previous systems were necessarily past errors. All supposed that the people and individuals had been ideologically infected by dangerous ideas. All believed that there was one good system, the best being the same for always and under any circumstances.

But that conception of an absolute truth is in total contradiction to history, that is, to the evolution of societies, and leads to the surrender of reason given all the realities which do not fit in with the favored model cannot be explained and are thus viewed as the consequence of human errors.

All the developments that drive the society in other directions or "unpleasant" ways, are viewed as mere evidence of utopianism, madness, pathology or self-interest of leaders. But these disturbances are not explained any better and seem to emerge haphazardly. They can affect the psychology of the rulers and that is how many authors often analyze fascism and nazism. But, because of their personal preferences, they rarely do so with the other more murderous and barbarian forms of communism that existed in Russia and China. Unlike for Hitler, the psychopathology of Stalin or Mao Zedong has seldom been analyzed (not to mention Pol Pot and Kim Il Sung). And few specialists would accept to justify the emergence of the communist systems by the sole pathology of their leaders. Anyway, that approach raises the issue of the rather conscious and active consent of the governed but cannot provide an answer.

Some other authors consider that the source of irrationality lies in mass behavior, and develop the ancient works of Gustave Le Bon concerning the behavior of crowds. But it is difficult to prove that it is the masses that determine the characteristics of a regime and effectively manage it.

One is then left to believe in the irrationality of the entire mankind. All people would be victims at a time or another of harmful ideologies or deleterious ideas. As Lugwig von Mises wrote, developing a topic that Keynes tackled latter on:

> The history of mankind is the history of ideas. For it is ideas, theories, and doctrines that guide human action, determine the ultimate ends men aim at, and the choice of the means employed for the attainment of these ends. The sensational events which stir the emotions and catch the interest of superficial observers are merely the consummation of ideological changes."[10]

This is how various authors explain the totalitarianisms of the first twentieth century by the loss of their taste for freedom, the racist doctrines, the ultra-nationalism and the "Lebensraum." According to them, people simply became mad. But why? Where do these absurd ideologies come from? By what mystery are they massively adopted? Nobody knows. Most often, people mention the pernicious influence of the (wrong) ideas and intellectuals, whose thoughts have been amplified by powerful interest groups. It is worth again to quote the famous passage of Keynes, who himself expressed a conception found again and again among intellectuals:[11]

10. Ludwig Von Mises, *Planned Chaos*, Foundation for Economic Education, 1947, p. 62.

11. For instance Heinrich Heine (1797–1856) who writes: "mark this, ye proud men of action: ye are nothing but unconscious hodmen of the men of thought who, often in the humblest stillness, have appointed you your inevitable work," *Religion and Philosophy in Germany*, J. Snodgrass tr. Boston: Beacon Press, 1959. Cited by Joseph Stiglitz. A "hodman" carries brick or mortar for a mason.

The ideas of economists and political philosophers both when they are right and when they are wrong, are more powerful than is commonly understood. Indeed, the world is ruled by little else. Practical men, who believe themselves to be quite exempt from any intellectual influences, are usually the slaves of some defunct economist. Madmen in authority, who hear voices in the air, are distilling their frenzy from some academic scribbler of a few years back. I am sure that the power of vested interest is vastly exaggerated compared with the gradual encroachment of ideas."[12]

It is just a half truth, a half of the complete picture. In such a conception ideas could well be completely arbitrary and social evolution the random result of the war of intellectuals. In that case, all that we know is that we must teach the opposite ideology to the one we dislike and think wrong, one of moral improvement and unconditional defense of human rights, to protect ourselves against a possible new fit of madness. Ideologies, good or bad, are thus the very foundation of social order. This is the Platonic view of the cavemen who only distinguish the distorted shadows of reality and grope their way along from one mistake to another. A more realistic view would accept that men of actions are often, or even always, the prisoners of "academic scribblers" of all persuasions, but that intellectuals derive their ideas from the evolution of the real world constraints and opportunities.

Another approach of the issue, more to the point, explains the collapse and replacement of the existing politico-economic regimes by their opposites, by the experience of their shortcomings and failures. Thus, socialists like Karl Polanyi justified the decline of nineteenth-century liberal capitalism by the fact that autoregulated markets could not work, while the free-marketeers generally believe that communism could not survive lastingly. And yet, the market system reconquered the world half a century after its nadir during World War II. And

12. *The General Theory of Employment, Interest and Money*, 1936, New York: Harcourt, Brace & World, ch. 24, p. 383.

communism "survived" 70 years despite its alleged incoherence. Which is long enough for a reputedly unviable system!

Paul Krugman tries to avoid this contradiction, saying that the USSR, which was far from being as inefficient as some pretend today, did not defeat the German army on its territory thanks to the superior intelligence of its generals, decimated by Stalin's purges, nor simply to western support, but rather thanks to the power and efficiency of its economic and military productions: its industries ran at full capacity and manufactured high-technology tanks, planes, guns capable of thwarting the German despite the latter's excellence.[13] And during the postwar period, the Soviet economic performance was not limited to some occasional technical exploits such as the launch of the Sputniks and other satellites, achieved by the concentration of massive resources to the detriment of the rest of the economy. Overall, the economy enjoyed strong growth from 1930 to 1965.[14] Admittedly, Stalin transformed Russia, a mostly backward agricultural economy, into a big industrial power supported by an extremely competent pool of scientists and engineers.

The same is true of the other totalitarian systems: Nazi Germany and the militaristic Japanese empire were dreadfully efficient. They threatened the very existence of the few democracies that remained in the world at the beginning of World War II and enjoyed the unconditional support of their respective peoples.

But the fundamental question remains unanswered: just like liberal capitalism almost disappeared in the early twentieth century after a period of remarkable success in the late nineteenth century, why did the communist system collapse in the 1980s while it managed to compete with the strongest western powers in the '40s, '50s and '60s?

Krugman notes, in passing and to reject it, the possibility that

13. Paul Krugman, "Capitalism's Mysterious Triumph," *Nihon Keizai Shimbun*, 1998, and "The Trouble with History," *Washington Monthly*, March 1998.

14. R. W. Davies, *Soviet Economic Development from Lenin to Khrushchev*, Cambridge University Press, 1998.

technological advances may have changed the economic rules of the game: the mid-century was a time of heavy industries perfectly adapted to central planning, of the big private corporations and of the Gosplan. But the same is not true of the new microelectronic technologies who can only develop in a decentralized and competitive context. This would explain the Soviet Union's collapse and the current difficulties of Japan, a bureaucratic and centralized country.

This concurs with the hypothesis that we have put forward and explained in this book, but Krugman finally prefers a moral explanation where the ideologies play a major role. According to him, communism failed because people no longer believed in it, and not the opposite. However, this thesis is untenable as it does not explain how people gained and then lost confidence in the system, nor why the constituent ideas of a regime impose themselves at a given moment and in a given country. It is more likely that the Russians stopped believing in communism because it could no longer generate as many advances as it had during its first decades.

Although it is true that ideas are essential to guide action, it does not mean that arbitrary ideas can drive the world one day toward the market production mode and decentralization and the other toward central planning. That conception of the discretionary power of ideas reminds us of the theories of the critics of advertising who pretended a while that advertising could manipulate at will the consumer to make him buy anything. Obviously, this is wrong for a simple reason: if advertising had such an influence on business expenditures, 99 percent of the firms' expenses would be devoted to communication and only 1 percent to production. But advertising costs do not exceed a few percentage points of the national products. This is a proof that their efficiency is in fact limited.

Similarly, if ideas had such power and were totally malleable, the intellectuals (the producers and sellers of ideas) would be the most powerful and richest people in the private and public sphere. But as it does not seem to be so, we believe that the ultimate source of historical transformations cannot be arbitrary, contagious and changing ideas.

Profound Coherence

If we put aside the vision of the world that immediately reflects the conflicts between the superpowers and the opposition between their respective ideological propaganda, to observe the common factors of the economic and political organization of societies in the twentieth century, we see again profound coherence in the century's developments. It comes from the great cycle, with first a centralization wave and then a decentralization wave. It implies, if these developments are rational, the superiority of a certain organizational mode, at a given moment in the history of technologies, which then loses its advantages to the benefit of a different social organization at another moment and in another environment.

And in that view, the century finally proves to be remarkably coherent. Whatever the organization (firms, states, the economy, politics, social and cultural relations) and existing regime (liberal capitalism, fascism or communism) we consider, the first twentieth century saw the same evolutions, the same anti-market, self-centered, anti-individualist, collectivist and authoritarian ideologies, and the second saw the exact opposite.

Thus, we can witness what the biologist Edward O. Wilson coined the "Ionian Enchantment," borrowing this expression from the physicist and historian Gerald Holton. It means a belief in the unity of sciences—a very deep conviction that the world is orderly and can be explained by a small number of natural laws. Its roots go back to Thales of Miletus, in Ionia, in the sixth century B.C., who believed that all matter consisted ultimately of water, thus justifying its materialist vision of the world and the unity of nature. Although that precise view was far-fetched, Wilson considers that the perspective can nevertheless be applied in a different context to modern sciences including social sciences and literary disciplines.

Einstein experienced this enchantment as he wrote to his friend Marcel Grossman in a letter:

> It is a wonderful feeling to recognize the unity of a complex of phenomena that to direct observation appear to be quite separate things.[15]

The profound unity of the last century's economic and political transformations helps us find a common and rational explanation to the various and complex phenomena that are often put down to human irrationality and to the supernatural power of ideas, in last resort. But in fact, that unity results from the economic calculus.

The Economic Hypothesis

If we only look at how efficiently their societies were organized, liberal capitalism, communism, corporatisms and all the other fascisms have made no mistake.

Although that assertion will surprise some readers and certainly shock them, we would like to underline that it is in no way a moral judgment, an approval of the systems of the first twentieth century, but simply an acknowledgement of the existence of objective determinants of the past transformations of the political systems.

The political and economic organization has changed everywhere with technological advances. There has thus been successive phases during which the market first had the advantage, then lost it to the hierarchy and finally regained it. And this is true of all the public and private production sectors given technology is universal.

Organizational choices depend on the comparative costs and ben-

---

15. Mentioned by Gerald Holton in *Einstein, History, and Other Passions*, American Institute of Physics Press, 1995 and quoted by E. O. Wilson, *Consilience*, p. 5.

efits of the two basic modes: consensual market transactions or hierarchical subordination.

Indeed, the political and social selection of the institutions, the organizations, depends, just like monetary or non-monetary consumption or investment choices, on the theory of choices, the theory of decisions, that is, on economic analysis. As we underlined previously, the economic theory is not limited to monetized market transactions. It explains all the human behavior which were until then considered as non-economic: votes, governments' redistributive policies, crime, the family and its structures, demography, educational choices, health standards and living habits. It can also explain the evolution according to time and various other conditions of these behaviors which are still currently viewed as the objects of distinct disciplines.

The choices that have influenced the past century were made according to the individual costs and benefits of the various organizational modes. And the resulting politico-economic regimes were thus the unexpected consequences of all these individual choices. The hierarchization of the American production apparatus in the first twentieth century was not a deliberate and preconceived plan. It was only the consequence of the choices made by Henry Ford, the management of the main railway lines, General Motors, and IBM and by the millions of people who preferred to work in corporations rather than as independent craftsmen, each reacting to the new technological and economic conditions and pursuing their personal preferences and those of their associates, in accordance with all the users and consumers who ratified those decisions about the production by making purchases.

Those costs and benefits evolved with technological advances, especially in the fields of information production, storage and transmission. These technologies changed the way large-scale hierarchies were managed. By determining a growing size of public and private bureaucratic pyramids, they transformed the internal and external structure of all the organizations.

Marx already deemed essential the impact of production technologies on the whole society in *Capital*:

> Technology reveals the relation between man and Nature, the production process through which it subsists, and thus also the development of social relations and the resulting mental conceptions.

It follows that, in the well-known Marxian analysis, just as the manorial mill makes the feudal society, the steam engine makes the factory and defines the structure of the capitalist society of the Industrial Revolution.

So, is it all simply a question of technological determinism? Not really, as technology is itself "filtered" by individual economic choices. It only gives the range of possibilities and it is actually the organizational economics that drives the actual choices specifically toward one of those possibilities. And technology is not the only factor influencing individual decisions: there is also the personal preferences and the availability of resources. Other variables more especially account for the differences of organization that exist between several countries at the same date and with the same information technologies. For instance, in states, the geographical concentration of people and production activities determines the location of tax resources and thus the direction in which the state will grow preferably. As for individuals, it is their education, social incentives and personal experience together with their subjective preferences and their income, that determines how they choose their activities, consumption and investments.

Is it a purely materialistic explanation? Does morality play no role in the choice of the economic, political and social organization? Can the worst systems be adopted unscrupulously?

It would be too simplistic to support such a view. Morality defines the socially acceptable human behaviors in a given organization. It includes some universal precepts fixed in our minds by several million years of a life as small itinerant groups of hunters-gatherers. But it also includes more recent and rather flexible rules which depend on the needs of the societies in which we live today. These kinds of rules vary according to the societies. According to the moral principles of Stalin's USSR or Hitler's Germany, denunciation, submission, the negation of the individual and dying for one's country were regarded as superior values. Ethnography and history provide us with plenty of examples of moral values peculiar to a given population at a certain time. We just have to go back to the Middle Ages to find striking examples of that moral variability.[16]

And yet we must admit that the technologies of the nineteenth and twentieth centuries generated worldwide a politically and morally regressive organization compared to some of the universal standards and to the individualistic morality of the nineteenth century. Admittedly, the search for productive efficiency has become more important than the respect of that humanist and individualistic morality. Indeed, moral pressure plays a role but cannot determine alone all human behaviors as there may also be a trade-off with efficiency. The rationale of history is not always the morality of history.

Consequences: The Competitive State and Global Civilization

The economic hypothesis helps us better understand the present transformations and speculate about the future, with an approach totally opposed to the current interpretations. Nowadays, it is considered that globalization is the ultimate cause of everything, the *deus ex machina* of economic, political and social developments. But the development of world markets is only a symptom of the underlying technological and organizational advances, of the economic hypothesis at work.

16. See for instance A. R. Bridbury, "Markets and Freedom in the Middle Ages," in B. L. Anderson and A. J. H. Latham (eds), *Markets in History*, Croom Helm, 1986.

What are the factors determining a state's external growth? The competition for resources and the relative costs of the hierarchy and the market. Which social variables govern the choice of politico-economic systems? The competition between states and private hierarchies and the relative costs of the hierarchy and the market which depend on information technologies.

Must we fear an irresistible rise toward corporate gigantism and must we hope for the creation of a giant world state or even for the intermediate or temporary solution of a very large continental state in Europe? These omnipresent concerns result from a deep misunderstanding of the ongoing transformations. The growth of global markets does not necessarily imply a globalization of the organizations and more especially firms. On the contrary, it replaces that globalization. The immediate consequence of markets' big size is an atomization of the hierarchical organizations as both mechanisms compete and are substitutable. That substitutability appears as a kind of organizational paradox but a paradox that is nevertheless economically rational.

The Paradox of Size

The economic and social revolution of the second twentieth century has given rise to a lot of misunderstanding and misinterpretations, especially concerning the size of firms in the global economy, the standardization of culture and consumption, the end of the nation-state, the Americanization of the world and the growing economic instability.

Are we heading toward globalization and gigantism of the corporation? Not at all.

The globalization of the markets is accompanied by an atomization of the firms. That process is well illustrated by the difficulties the biggest corporations are faced with. Many of the leading companies among the 500 largest global firms have steadily cut their workforce over the past twenty years. A few of them, like IBM, have had to split into several units to regain their dynamism. The recent troubles of Coca-Cola and McDonald's show that it is not necessarily profitable to be a global firm, a world corporation

Behind the headlines announcing ever larger M&As, a broad disintegration of the big corporations can be seen.[17] Twenty-five years ago, one out of five American wage-earners was employed by one of the 500 leading U.S. companies ranked by the magazine *Fortune*. Today, that proportion has fallen to one out of ten. The largest employer is no longer General Motors nor IBM, but Manpower, a company specialized in part-time work.

Besides, the idea that the development of open markets in most world countries necessarily involves that all companies must establish themselves everywhere is false. For instance, the large pharmaceutical companies tend to close their units in quite a few countries to concentrate their activities in a few major poles. And business strategies can show that it is more profitable to export than to set up subsidiaries abroad. Furthermore, all the products are not universal. Some of them are better adapted to the specific preferences of local consumers. The small Italian cars will never be a big hit in the United States. French cheese is most successful around its production sites. Indian movies do not fascinate the British and the German. In short, the globalization imperative is only a myth. It is only true of a few economic activities and even there it has many substitutes, like franchises, business alliances or subcontracting.

Are we heading toward the globalization and the standardization of consumption and culture? Not at all.

With the end of Fordism began an era of diversification and per-

___

17. Thomas W. Malone and Robert J. Laubacher, "Are Big Companies Becoming Obsolete? The Dawn of the E-Lance Economy," *Harvard Business Review*, September–October 1998; and Lynda Applegate, James Cash and D. Quinn Mills, "Information Technology and Tomorrow's Manager," *Harvard Business Review*, November–December 1988.

sonalization of the products, which are by the way manufactured on request. Today, your car is not manufactured until your order has been recorded. You can choose between dozens of options and various colors, the number of doors that suits you best, the model you prefer (a station wagon, a sedan or a convertible), diesel or gas and so on. This is in total contrast to the Ford T which only existed in black.

In work also, the individual tasks became more diversified and elaborate. Assembly-line work disappears or is only performed by electromechanical robots. Finally, the dominant individualism favors the differentiation of cultural consumptions. The variety of books, magazines, TV programs and websites has never been so large as today. All the major cities offer a complete range of restaurants serving every type of cooking in the world. There is an endless number of musical styles and art schools. The increase in wealth is by itself enough to justify that demand for diversity. But the rise in the international supply sustains it even further.

It is an era of diversity rather than uniformity. And the fact that the same brands and the same clothes, luggage and camera shops can be found in the shopping streets around the world does not mean that the range of goods that can be consumed by people is decreasing but rather that the variety of products in most of the countries is increasing.

Are we heading toward the collapse of the nation-state? Not at all.

Like the famous announcement of Mark Twain's death, that death notice seems very premature. On the contrary, the nation-state structure has proved hugely successful all around the world. The number of small states is increasing and they are thriving. Admittedly, the largest and most heterogeneous states have disintegrated or are faced with centrifugal forces. But when they disappear they are replaced by several smaller states. We can thus conclude that we are witnessing a change in their optimal size rather than their extinction.

Unlike what a few doctrinaire economists hastily maintain, these smaller states are totally capable of running independent policies. They are not subjected to the domination of the financial markets. Just like larger states, they must simply put up with the same constraints of obtaining resources. And the same is true of all the firms, big or small. Everyone who wants to borrow funds or set the exchange rate of his currency must inspire confidence in his potential creditors. But that's nothing new. The only change regards the identity of the lender. A few years ago, the main lenders were the International Monetary Fund, other states or major banks. Today, they would most likely be the private savers from any country in the world. But that does not alter the fundamental laws of economics or finance.

At the same time, the people hoping for the setting up of a world state to regain the "room for maneuver" that has been lost with the globalization of markets should ponder over the growing difficulties of the large global public structures such as the United Nations, the IMF or the WTO. The present time is that of independence and competition between small states together with the disintegration of all the giant administrative structures.

Those large bureaucratic organizations, which in fact help to manage cartels of nations, have the same drawbacks as any cartel and bureaucracy, public or private: they are all faced nowadays with the same disintegrating forces whether they be the United Nations, the IMF, the World Bank, the WTO or the European Union.

Also note that the so-called anarchy on global markets is just an illusion. All the exchanges take place within national areas and are governed by national or international laws under the control of the state since the whole planet has been split into nation-states. Hence, areas of no-law do not really exist. The dominance of the law of the jungle, or the international economic chaos are no realities, but fantasies. There is on the planet a diversified system maintaining order and working as well as the nineteenth-century alliance of nations and free trade.

The idea according to which there can be no order without a

world state was instilled during the totalitarian era. It is the invention of people who have never worked with a decentralized cybernetic order nor understood what it is. And on the purely political level, it is worth thinking of the implications of such a single state. Bertrand de Jouvenel underlined he had been favorable to a world state until the day when, during World War II, he was compelled to take refuge in Switzerland, hunted by the German police. Plurality and the competition between states are the best guarantors of fundamental liberties.

Are we heading toward an all-American planet? Not at all.

The U.S. economy will not grow at such a stunning pace forever. It cannot reverse the fast development of new economies around the world. The United States and Europe are bound to gradually lose their role of leading producers, but that does not necessarily mean that the living standards will no longer improve in our countries. It is the catch-up in the production levels and living standards of the more numerous and poorer countries that will alter the relative weights of the economies, not the long-announced decline of the wealthiest countries, even though such a decline is always possible in some cases such as Great Britain before the conservative revolution, or France today.

In military matters, it is true that the collapse of the USSR radically changed the balance of power, but the European countries do not seem more dependent on the United States today than before. In fact, it looks as if it was the contrary, now that the threat has vanished.

As for cultural imperialism, it should be noted that this very concept is unfounded. The American government does not try deliberately to impose Coca-Cola or the Hollywood movies in Europe or Asia. It is just that these companies look for markets and find them where their products are competitive. As far as this is concerned, the consumer is no doubt the sovereign. Nobody can compel you to eat a Big Mac or drink a Coke. On the contrary, Mao Zedong forced all the Chinese to wear the same unisex tunic. Looking at the competition on private markets from a military point of view would be totally distorting the reality of the market economy.

Also note that these are two-way exchanges of tangible and cultural goods and not a one-way flow. The export of French fashion goods or German cars is not the expression of French or Germanic cultural imperialism whatsoever. These propaganda campaigns denouncing cultural imperialism confuse the narrow interests of the cultural producers faced with competition, with the broader and totally different interests of the national consumers who are fascinated by the new diversity of supply. In fact, the critics of "cultural imperialism" try to subordinate the latter to the former.

Finally, if Americanization is understood as the development of markets, of the price mechanism and of business productivity, then that process should be renamed "Anglicization" or "Frenchification" in honor of Adam Smith or Jean-Baptiste Say. Indeed, in the late eighteenth century, long before the United States, Great Britain, and France were already developing free markets, technical advances and firms seeking higher productivity and wealth creation.

And finally, should we fear that globalization increases the economic instability? Not at all.

As large markets are more stable, the economic cycle became much less volatile during the second twentieth century as the economies became much more open and as the international trade regained its major role of before 1913.

In terms of finance, the fluctuations on national stock markets and those on national foreign exchange markets tend to offset each other to a certain extent as those markets and assets are not perfectly in phase. The international diversification of portfolios is thus the guarantee of a certain stability compared with the exclusive concentration of capital into a single country.

As a result, the fears about globalization, that is, of the opening of national economies, are mostly illusory or explained by the defense of specific interests. On the contrary, the advantages of the global civilization are very much real and general, starting with those resulting from the new peaceful competition between states.

Competitive Civilization

Technological advances disrupt our civilizations, that is, "all the relations between people."[18] Indeed, these relations rely on behaviors which change when they take place within different organizations, under the influence of particular incentives and specific constraints.

Thus, the changes in the organizational structures, in the ecology of organizations, affect the whole life in society, the economy, politics and culture. While large hierarchies favor monopolization, submission and collectivism, small hierarchies boost competition, consensual market transactions and individualism.

During the second twentieth century, the states were faced with fierce but generally peaceful competition as all tended to reduce their external dimensions and their areas of geographic control. The citizens could then choose to join another state that was competing to keep its economic resources. It is a buying market for mobile private individuals. The tax price of a given level of public service thus tends to decrease. And the same is true of firms, which move toward structures of atomistic competition, even though there is a concentration in a few sectors that have reached their maturity and must switch to new types of production. It is a godsend for both the consumers and the citizens.

Like the other firms, a competitive state provides more services at a smaller cost. It is better controlled by its customers, who are in this case both citizens and taxpayers. It is thus democratic and must meet the expectations of its voters.

That recipe was already successful on three occasions in the past. First, in Athens, with the competition of the Greek city-states during

---

18. According to the French dictionary "Robert."

the fifth-century B.C. cultural and informational revolution. Then, when the competition between the European states open to foreign trade and maintaining law and order within their frontiers, during the Renaissance in Europe, and then even more during the Enlightenment age, a period of stunning scientific and information advances. Finally, during the second twentieth century, for all the reasons that have been mentioned in this book.

Does this give us an idea of what will happen next? Nobody knows for sure. Evolution, in economics as in biology, depends on the capacity of adaptation to the conditions of scarcity and abundance of the environment. If the environment changes, the course of evolution is altered. But we cannot foresee the endless number of conditions that define the natural environment, not to mention the social and cultural environment.

Yet, the totalitarianism that so deeply characterized the first twentieth century represented a kind of exception in the history of societies. It was due to the exceptional progress of the production of material goods compared with the slower development of information technologies. That informational backwardness caused the bureaucratic and hierarchical reaction of the early period. It seems today that such a situation is quite unlikely to happen again, given the current pace at which information technologies evolve. The abundance of information determines its diffusion. Information diffusion decentralizes power and weakens hierarchies. It frees the individuals. Our best hope can thus only be that the second twentieth century tendencies will be vindicated and extended as far as possible, well into the coming decades of the twenty-first century.

The Future of
Terrorism, or
The Dark Side
of Freedom

Terrorism, the war of small groups against states, is on the rise since the end of the cold war and the collapse of communism. The new war is not anymore mostly between states, but mostly against states. This is not surprising at a time when the role and power of nation-states is challenged on all fronts by privatization, tax-cutting, decentralization and devolution, secession and fragmentation. And the changing fortunes of states is part of a general trend toward the weakening of all hierarchies, public and private, as market transactions replace hierarchical organizations, whether business firms or public bureaucracies.

Because the wave of terrorism is worldwide, it must have common causes. The current rise of competitive violence is a consequence of the erosion of the monopoly of violence, the main business and the "raison d'être" of states. The retreat of the state leaves room for the growth of competitive markets and more freedom but also allows for a larger supply of competitive violence which partly jeopardizes the newly gained individual liberties. The cold war combination of civil

A shorter version of this paper entitled "Why Globalization Breeds Terrorism" appeared in the *Wall Street Journal*, January 30, 2003.

peace—whether democratic or totalitarian—and external conflict is thus replaced by external peace and civil insecurity.

To understand how to win the war on terrorism we must first understand what makes terrorists tick. Unfortunately, since 9/11, but also before, most explanations have had to do with specific acts of terrorism. Commentators have tried to explain each terrorist campaign in terms of past wrongs, present errors, alleged injustices or abject poverty generating desperate rebellions. In this psychological approach, terrorism is seen as revenge.

The trouble is, these same motives were also present in the past, at a time when terrorism was less prevalent than today. So what is needed is a wide scheme that generally explains a current revival of predominantly non-state—that is decentralized—violence, variously motivated by regional and secessionist, ethnic or religious, and ordinary urban crime objectives, often mixed in changing combinations.

The plain fact is that small organizations specialized in violence seek to impose their will on more or less homogeneous populations by force and blackmail. The goal is to accelerate the retreat of the state and take control of some part of the population for extracting revenues. They wage new forms of guerilla warfare on larger states, demanding ransom in exchange for sparing the lives of civilians and soldiers in these states. What has made this offensive so daunting is that the competitive advantage of these small organizations has recently been increasing. The general retreat of state power since the 1970s, an otherwise healthy development, has enabled these organizations to prosper and challenge governments and their armed forces.

Large states reached their zenith in the middle decades of the past century, but have been declining since the mid-'70s. The basic reason for this is that large hierarchies, firms as well as states, thrive on economizing information while smaller production units have to transact mainly through markets where the use of information is intensive. Thus large hierarchies are more efficient when information is costly but smaller hierarchies and larger markets are more efficient when information is cheap.

With the revolution of information in the '60s and '70s, the cost of storing, processing, and communicating information has plummeted. It followed that large hierarchies such as conglomerate firms and huge, heterogeneous states, lost their comparative advantage and disintegrated everywhere in the world, trying to downsize or being replaced by smaller units, while markets expanded rapidly.

This revolution of organization is also at work in the "war business." Contracting states, both in terms of reduced share of taxes as a percentage of GDP and receding borders (through secession and fragmentation, devolution being a less extreme form of disintegration), are not looking for new territories to control, especially with curtailed military budgets. Thus traditional wars of conquest between rival and often adjacent states, tend to disappear. At the same time, this retreat has left the field open at the margins for rival organizations that produce violence, whether organized crime, regional political groups trying to establish their own state to control resources on a smaller territory, or whatever group can carve out a clientele in the old state population.

This helps explain why smaller interest groups and communitarism is the new rage in the politics of wealthy countries. Today, unlike previously, smaller is more efficient in matters of political pressure and military action, as larger monopolizers of violence—the traditional states—contract their activity and presence.

Terrorism is the form of violence that is best adapted to the small-group advantage. A small group willing to seize power from the state cannot finance a regular army with an airforce, a navy and large ground forces. It has to resort to guerrilla tactics and violence against isolated buildings, a few military targets and, preferably, civilians. Weakened traditional states have been proved vulnerable to guerrilla tactics in several postcolonial wars, and more recently in Vietnam as well as in Afghanistan. Terrorism amounts to going one step further in that direction. The diversity of the small, competitive, and violent groups and their nonterritoriality make them difficult to identify and to control. As a consequence, terrorism is here to stay for as long as the disintegration of large state hierarchies continues to be determined by the information revolution.

In this new form of war, which replaces the world duopoly of the cold war, the position of the United States, however more powerful than that of other states, is nevertheless weakened. Far from being a "hyperpower" able to control the whole world, as French diplomacy pretends, it has to rely on allies and alliances to fight even a smaller contender such as Iraq. But the call of many Europeans for world governance and an international rule of law administered by the UN is fundamentally mistaken. The international rule of law is breaking down precisely because of the atomization of the world population of states and the weakening of the power of each one of them. Absent such a superpower as the United States was during the cold war, there is no conceivable international rule of law, UN or no UN. The increasingly decentralized terrorist violence has to be faced by decentralized forces and by occasional, and changing, alliances between a few most concerned states. The decentralized terrorist challenge has replaced the monopolistic Soviet challenge. And it is here to stay.

BIBLIOGRAPHY

Acs, Zoltan J., and David B. Audretsch, *Small Firms and Entrepreneurship: An East-West Perspective*, Cambridge University Press, 1993.

Adam, Brooks, *The Law of Civilization and Decay*, University Press of the Pacific, 1943, 2002.

Alchian, Armen A., and Harold Demsetz, "Production, Information Costs, and Economic Organization," *American Economic Review*, December 1972.

Allais, Maurice, "Le Problème de la Planification Economique dans une Economie Collectiviste," *Kyklos*, July and October 1947.

Allen, G. C., *The Industrial Development of Birmingham and the Black Country, 1860–1927*, London, 1929.

Ansliger, Patricia L., Steven J. Keppler, and Somu Subramaniam, "Après les fusions, les scissions," *Expansion Management Review*, September 1999.

Applegate, Lynda, James Cash, and D. Quinn Mills, "Information Technology and Tomorrow's Manager," *Harvard Business Review*, November–December 1988.

Ardant, Gabriel, *Histoire de l'impôt*, 2 volumes, Fayard, 1971, 1972.

Arendt, Hannah, *The Origins of Totalitarianism*, Harvest Books, 1973.

Aron, Raymond, *The Elusive Revolution: Anatomy of the Student Revolt*, Praeger Publishers, 1969.

Audretsch, David B., *Innovation and Industry Evolution*, MIT Press, 1995.

Auster, Richard D., and Morris Silver, *The State as a Firm: Economic Forces in Political Development*, Martinus Nijhoff, 1979.

Axelrod, Robert, *The Evolution of Cooperation*, Basic Books, 1984.

Barro, Robert J., *Determinants of Economic Growth. A Cross-Country Empirical Study*, MIT Press, 1997.

Bauman, Zygmunt, *Modernity and the Holocaust*, Cornell University Press, 1989.

Becker, Gary S., "A Theory of the Allocation of Time," *Economic Journal*, September 1965.

———, "Crime and Punishment: An Economic Approach," *The Journal of Political Economy*, March–April 1968.

———, "Altruism, Egoism, and Genetic Fitness: Economics and Sociobiology," *Journal of Economic Literature*, September 1976.

———, "Competition among Pressure Groups for Political Influence," *Quarterly Journal of Economics*, August 1983.

———, "Nobel Lecture: The Economic Way of Looking at Behaviour," *Journal of Political Economy*, June 1993.

Beckmann, Martin J., *Tinbergen Lectures on Organization Theory*, Springer-Verlag, 1988.

Bell, Daniel, *The Coming of Post-Industrial Society: A Venture in Social Forecasting*, Basic Books, 1973.

Beniger, James R., *The Control Revolution*, Harvard University Press, 1986.

Bergesen, Albert and Ronald Schoenberg, "Long Waves of Colonial Expansion and Contraction, 1415–1969," in Albert Bergesen (ed.), *Studies of the Modern World-System*, Academic Press, 1980.

Berle, Adolf A., and Gardiner C. Means, *The Modern Corporation and Private Property*, Macmillan, 1932.

Berlin, Ira, *Many Thousands Gone*, Belknap, Harvard University Press, 1998.

Bernholz, Peter, *The International Game of Power*, Mouton, 1985.

Blanqui, Jérôme Adolphe, *Histoire de l'économie politique*, Guillaumin, 1837, 1842.

Blum, Ulrich and Leonard Dudley, "A Spatial Approach to Structural Change: The Making of the French Hexagon," *Journal of Economic History*, June 1989.

———, "A Spatial Model of the State," *Journal of Institutional and Theoretical Economics*, March–April 1991.

Boulding, Kenneth E., "Economics as a Not Very Biological Science," in Thomas Wiegele (ed.), *Biology and the Social Sciences. An Emerging Revolution*, Westview Press, 1982.

Bourdé, Guy, and Hervé Martin, *Les Ecoles historiques*, Points Histoire, Le Seuil, 1983, 1997.

Braudel, Fernand, *The Perspective of the World: Civilization and Capitalism 15th–18th century*, Harper & Row, 1979.

———, *Civilization and Capitalism, 15th–18th Century*, part 2: *The Wheels of Commerce*, Harper Collins, 1981–1984.

Breton, Albert, *The Economic Theory of Representative Government*, Aldine, 1974.

Breton, Albert, and Ronald Wintrobe, "Organizational Structure and Productivity," *American Economic Review*, June 1986.

Breton, Albert, and Ronald Wintrobe, "The Bureaucracy of Murder Revisited," *Journal of Political Economy*, October 1986.

Bridbury, A. R., "Markets and Freedom in the Middle Ages" in B. L. Anderson and A.J.H. Latham (eds.), *Markets in History*, Croom Helm, 1986.

Brown, Tom, "How Big Is Too Big," *Across the Board*, July–August 1999.

Brynjölfsson, Erik, Thomas W. Malone, Vijay Gurbaxani, and Ajit Kambil, "Does Information Technology Lead to Smaller Firms?" *Management Science*, December 1994.

Buchanan, James M., "A Defense of Organized Crime?" in Simon Rottenberg (ed.), *The Economics of Crime and Punishment*, American Enterprise Institute, 1973.

———, "Socialism Is Dead; Leviathan Lives," *Wall Street Journal Europe*, July 19, 1990.

Burchfield, R. W. (ed.), *A Supplement to the Oxford English Dictionary*, Oxford University Press, 1972.

Burnham, James, *The Managerial Revolution*, Indiana University Press, 1941.

Carneiro, Robert L., "A Theory of the Origin of the State," *Science*, August 21, 1970.

Caron, François, *Les deux révolutions industrielles du xxe siècle*, Albin Michel, 1997.

Chamberlin, Edward H., *The Theory of Monopolistic Competition*, Harvard University Press, 1932.

Chandler, Alfred, *The Visible Hand: The Managerial Revolution in American Business*, Belknap, Harvard University Press, 1977.

——, "The Emergence of Managerial Capitalism," *Harvard Business School Case*, 1992.

Chao, Johny C. P., and Herbert Grubel, "Optimal Levels of Spending and Taxation in Canada," *The Independent Institute*, 1999.

Clark, Colin, *The Conditions of Economic Progress*, London, Macmillan, 1939.

Coase, Ronald, "The Nature of the Firm," *Economica*, 1937.

Cohen, Elie, *L'Etat brancardier : politiques du déclin industriel*, Calmann-Lévy, 1989.

——, *Le Colbertisme high-tech*, Pluriel, Hachette, 1992.

Cohen, Stephen, John Bradford de Long, and John Zysman, "An E-economy?" Bradford de Long homepage: www.j-bradford-delong-net, December 1999.

Colinvaux, Paul, *Why Big Fierce Animals Are Rare: An Ecologist's Perspective*, Princeton University Press, 1978.

Courtois, Stéphane, et al., *The Black Book of Communism: Crimes, Terror, Repression*, Harvard University Press, 1999.

Davies, R. W., *Soviet Economic Development from Lenin to Khrushchev*, Cambridge University Press, 1998.

Dawkins, Richard, *The Selfish Gene*, Oxford University Press, 1976.

Demsetz, Harold, "Information and Efficiency: Another Viewpoint," *Journal of Law and Economics*, October 1969.

——, *Economic, Legal, and Political Dimensions of Competition*, North-Holland, 1982.

Desai, Herman, and Prem C. Jain, "Firm Performance and Focus: Long-Run Stock Market Performance Following Spinoffs," *Journal of Financial Economics*, October 1999.

de Sola Pool, Ithiel, Hiroshi Inose, Nozomu Takasahi, and Roger Hurwitz, *Communications Flows: A Census in the United States and Japan*, North-Holland, 1984.

Dial, Jay, and Kevin J. Murphy, "Incentives, Downsizing, and Value Creation at General Dynamics," *Journal of Financial Economics*, October 1995.

Diamond, Jared, *Guns, Germs and Steel: The Fates of Human Societies*, Norton, 1999.

Downes, Larry, and Chumka Mui, *Unleashing the Killer App: Digital Strategies for Market Dominance*, Harvard Business School Press, 1998.

Dudley, Leonard, *The Word and the Sword*, Blackwell, 1991.

Dunning, John H., *Governments, Globalization, and International Business*, Oxford University Press, 1997.

Ekelund Jr., Robert B., and Robert D. Tollison, *Mercantilism as a Rent-Seeking Society: Economic Regulation in Historical Perspective*, Texas A&M University Press, 1981.

Evans, Christopher, *The Micro Millenium*, Pocket Books, 1979.

Ewald, François, "Des masses à l'individu," *Enjeux*, January 1999.

Fama, Eugene, and Michael Jensen, "Separation of Ownership and Control," *Journal of Law and Economics*, June 1983.

———, "Agency Problem and Residual Claims," *Journal of Law and Economics*, June 1983.

Farber, Henry S., and Alan B. Krueger, "Union Membership in the United States: The Decline Continues," *NBER Working Paper*, no. 4216, November 1992.

Feenstra, Robert C., "Integration of Trade and Disintegration of Production in the Global Economy," *Journal of Economic Perspectives*, Autumn 1998.

Finer, S. E., *A History of Government*, Oxford University Press, 1997.

Friedman, David, "A Theory of the Size and Shape of Nations," *Journal of Political Economy*, February 1977.

Frohlich, Norman, Joe A. Oppenheimer, and Oran R. Young, *Political Leadership and Collective Goods*, Princeton University Press, 1971.

Fukuyama, Francis, *The End of History and the Last Man*, Avon Books, 1992.

Garfinkel, Michelle R., and Stergios Skaperdas (eds.), *The Political Economy of Conflict and Appropriation*, Cambridge University Press, 1996.

Geller, Daniel S., and J. David Singer, *Nations at War*, Cambridge University Press, 1998.

Gemmel, Norman (ed.), *The Growth of the Public Sector, Theories and International Evidence*, London: Elgar, 1993.

Geneen, Harold, and Alvin Moscow, *Managing*, Doubleday, 1984.

Gerschenkron, Alexandre, *Europe in the Russian Mirror*, Cambridge University Press, 1970.

Gilpin, Robert, *War and Change in World Politics*, Cambridge University Press, 1981.

Glaeser, Edward L., and Bruce Sacerdote, "Why Is There More Crime in Cities?" *NBER Working Paper*, January 1996.

———, "The L.A. Riots and the Economics of Urban Unrest," *NBER Working Paper*, February 1996.

Goestchy, Janine, and Danièle Linhart, *La crise des syndicats en Europe occidentale*, La Documentation française, 1990.

Goody, Jack, *The Domestication of the Savage Mind*, Cambridge University Press, 1977.

Gregor, A. James, *The Ideology of Fascism*, The Free Press, 1969.

———, *Interpretations of Fascism*, Transaction Publishers, 1997.

Grossman, Hershel I., "Rival Kleptocrats: The Mafia versus the State," in Gianluca Fiorentini and Sam Peltzman (eds.), *The Economics of Organized Crime*, Cambridge University Press, 1995.

Groth, Lars, *Future Organizational Design: The Scope for IT-based Enterprise*, Wiley, 1999.

Hannah, Leslie, *The Rise of the Corporate Economy*, Methuen, 1976.

Hardin, Russell, *One for All: The Logic of Group Conflict*, Princeton University Press, 1995.

Hayek, Friedrich, *The Road to Serfdom*, Routledge, 1944.

Hicks, John R., *A Theory of Economic History*, Oxford University Press, 1969.

Hirshleifer, Jack, "The Technology of Conflict as an Economic Activity," *American Economic Review*, May 1991.

Hirshleifer, Jack, "Anarchy and Its Breakdown," *Journal of Political Economy*, February 1995.

Hobsbawm, E. J., *The Age of Empire, 1875–1914*, Weinfeld and Nicholson, 1987.

———, *The Age of Extremes*, Michael Joseph, 1994.

Holton, Gerald, *Einstein, History, and Other Passions*, American Institute of Physics Press, 1995.

Hubbard, Glenn, and Darius Palia, "A Reexamination of the Conglomerate Merger Wave in the 1960: An Internal Capital Market View," *Journal of Finance*, June 1999.

Idson, Todd L., and Walter Y. Oi, "Workers Are More Productive in Large Firms," *American Economic Review*, May 1999.

Innis, Harold A., *Empire and Communications*, Oxford: Clarendon, 1950.

INSEE, "Le poids des grandes entreprises dans l'emploi," *INSEE Première*, no. 683, November 1999.

Jefferson, Thomas, "No Patent on Ideas: Letter to Isaac Mcpherson," *Writings*, New York: Library of America, 1813.

Jensen, Michael C., "The Modern Industrial Revolution, Exit, and the Failure of Internal Control Systems," *Journal of Finance*, July 1993.

——, "A Revolution Only Markets Could Love," *Wall Street Journal Europe*, January 3, 1994.

Johnson, Allen W., and Timothy Earle, *The Evolution of Human Societies, From Foraging Groups to Agrarian States*, Stanford University Press, 1987.

Kaplan, Steven N., and Michael S. Weisbach, "The Success of Acquisitions: Evidence from Divestiture," *Journal of Finance*, March 1992.

Kay, John, "Globalisation, dimension et avantage compétitif," *Le Figaro*, June 26, 1998.

Kay, John, and Leslie Hannah, "Myth of Critical Mass," *Financial Times*, 1999.

Kennedy, Paul, *The Rise and Fall of the Great Powers*, Random House, 1987.

Keynes, John Maynard, *The General Theory of Employment, Interest and Money*, New York: Harcourt, Brace & World, 1936.

Khanna, Tarum, and Krishna G. Palepu, "Why Focused Strategies May Be Wrong for Emerging Markets," *Harvard Business Review*, July–August 1997.

Klein, Benjamin, Robert Crawford, and Armen A. Alchian, "Vertical Integration, Appropriable Rents, and the Competitive Contracting Process," *Journal of Law and Economics*, October 1978.

Krugman, Paul, "The Trouble with History," *Washington Monthly*, March 1998.

——, "Supply, Demand, and English Food," *Fortune*, July 20, 1998.

——, "Capitalism's Mysterious Triumph," *Nihon Keizai Shimbun*, 1998.

Lamberton, D. M. (ed.), *Economics of Information and Knowledge*, Penguin, 1971.

Lamoreaux, Naomi, *The Great Merger Movement in American Business, 1895–1904*, Cambridge University Press, 1985.

Landes, David, *The Wealth and Poverty of Nations: Why Some Are So Rich and Some Are So Poor*, Norton, 1998.

Lane, Frederic C., "Economic Consequences of Organized Violence," *Journal of Economic History*, December 1958.

La Porta, Rafael, Francisco Lopez-de-Silanes, Andrei Shleifer, and Robert W. Vishny, "Law and Finance," *NBER Working Paper*, July 1996.

Leijonhufvud, Axel, "Information Costs, and the Division of Labour," *International Social Science Journal*, May 1989.

Lenin, Vladimir Illyich, *The State and Revolution*, Penguin Classics, 1918, 1993.

Levi, Margaret, *Of Rule and Revenue*, University of California Press, 1988.

Lewis, W. Arthur, *The Principles of Economic Planning*, London: George Allan & Unwin Ltd, 1949.

Linder, Staffan Burenstam, *The Harried Leisure Class*, Columbia University Press, 1970.

Loveman, Gary, and Werner Sengenberger, "The Re-emergence of Small-Scale Production: An International Perspective," *Small Business Economics*, 1991.

Lucas, Robert Jr., "On the Size Distribution of Business Firms," *Bell Journal of Economics*, Autumn 1978.

Machlup, Fritz, *The Production and Distribution of Knowledge*, Princeton University Press, 1962.

Malone, Thomas W., Joanne Yates, and Robert I. Benjamin, "Electronic Markets and Electronic Hierarchies," *Communications of the ACM*, June 1987.

Malone, Thomas W., and Robert J. Laubacher, "Are Big Companies Becoming Obsolete? The Dawn of the E-Lance Economy," *Harvard Business Review*, September–October 1998.

Manoïlesco, Mihaïl, *The Century of Corporatism: The Doctrine of Total and Pure Capitalism*, Alcan, 1938.

Mansfield, Edward D., *Power, Trade, and War*, Princeton University Press, 1994.

Markides, Constantinos C., *Diversification, Refocusing, and Economic Performance*, MIT Press, 1995.

Marschak, Jacob, "Economics of Inquiring, Communicating, Deciding," *American Economic Review*, May 1968.

Mazover, Mark, *Dark Continent: Europe's Twentieth Century*, Penguin, 1998.

McLuhan, Marshall, *Understanding Media: The Extensions of Man*, McGraw-Hill, 1964.

McNeill, William, *The Rise of the West: A History of the Human Community*, University of Chicago Press, 1963.

McNeill, William H., *The Global Condition: Conquerors, Catastrophes, and Community*, Princeton University Press, 1992.

Mead, Margaret, *Culture and Commitment: A Study of the Generation Gap*, Doubleday, 1970.

Meade, James Edward, *Planning and the Price Mechanism: The Liberal Socialist Solution*, London: George Allen & Unwin Ltd, 1948.

Michael, Robert T., "Education in Non-market Production," *Journal of Political Economy*, March–April 1973.

Milgrom, Paul, and John Roberts, *Economics, Organization and Management*, Prentice-Hall, 1992.

Mokyr, Joel, "Are We Living in the Middle of an Industrial Revolution?" *Federal Reserve Bank of Kansas City, Economic Review*, Second Quarter, 1997.

Molinari, Gustave de (1849), "De la production de la sécurité," *Journal des Economistes*, February, translated by J. Huston McCulloch as "The Production of Security" (*Occasional Paper Series #2*, New York, Center for Libertarian Studies), 1977.

Moore, Gordon, "Cramming More Components onto Integrated Circuits," *Electronics*, 39 (8), 1965.

Mueller, Dennis C., *Public Choice*, Cambridge University Press, 1989.

Newhouse, John, "Europe's Rising Regionalism," *Foreign Affairs*, January–February 1997.

North, Douglass C., and Robert Paul Thomas, *The Rise of the Western World: A New Economic History*, Cambridge University Press, 1973.

North, Douglass C., "A Neoclassical Theory of the State," in *Structure and Change in Economic History*, Norton, 1981.

———, *Institutions, Institutional Change and Economic Performance*, Cambridge University Press, 1990.

O'Brien, Richard, *Global Financial Integration: The End of Geography*, R.i.i.a, 1992.

Olson, Mancur, *The Logic of Collective Action*, Harvard University Press, 1965.

———, "Review" of Charles P. Kindleberger and Guido di Tella (eds.), *Economics in the Long View: Essays in Honor of W. W. Rostow*, Columbia University Press, 1982.

———, "Toward a More General Theory of Government Structure," *American Economic Review*, May 1986.

———, "Dictatorship, Democracy, and Development," *American Political Science Review*, September 1993.

Phillips, Kevin, *Mediacracy: American Parties and Politics in the Communications Age*, Doubleday, 1975.

Piore, Michael J., and Charles Sabel, *The Second Industrial Divide: Possibilities for Prosperity*, Basic Books, 1984.

Posner, Richard A., "A Theory of Primitive Society," *Journal of Law and Economics*, 23 (1), 1980, 1–53.

Redlich, Fritz, *The Molding of American Banking: Men and Ideas*, Hafner, 1951.

Robinson, Joan, *The Economics of Imperfect Competition*, Macmillan, 1933.

Romer, Paul, "Ideas and Things," *The Economist*, 150 Economist Years Issue. September 1993.

Rosa, Jean-Jacques, "Théorie économique de la nationalisation et de la privatisation," *Finance*, December 1988.

———, "Nationalization, Privatization, and the Allocation of Financial Property Rights," *Public Choice*, January 1993.

———, "Public Choice Aspects of Privatization Policies: Driving Forces and Obstacles" in Herbert Giersch (ed.), *Privatization at the End of the Century*, Springer, 1997.

———, *L'erreur européenne*, Grasset, translated as *Euro Error*, Algora, 1999, 1998.

Rosen, Sherwin, "The Economics of Superstars," *American Economic Review*, December 1981.

———, "Authority, Control, and the Distribution of Earnings," *Rand Journal of Economics*, Autumn 1982.

Rottenberg, Simon (ed.), *The Economics of Crime and Punishment*, American Enterprise Institute, 1973.

Rummel, R. J., *Lethal Politics: Soviet Genocide and Mass Murder since 1917*, Transaction Publishers, 1990.

————, *China's Bloody Century: Genocide and Mass Murder since 1900*, Transaction Publishers, 1991.

————, *Democide: Nazi Genocide and Mass Murder*, Transaction Publishers, 1992.

Salsbury, Stephen, *The State, the Investor, and the Railroad: The Boston and Albany, 1825–1867*, Harvard University Press, 1867, 1967.

Samuelson, Paul, "The Pure Theory of Public Expenditure," *Review of Economics and Statistics*, November 1954.

Schumpeter, Joseph A., *The Crisis of the Tax State*, trans. in *International Economic Papers*, W. F. Stolper and R. A. Mugrave, London: Macmillan, 1918, 1953.

————, *Capitalism, Socialism and Democracy*, Harper and Row, 1942.

Scott Morton, Michael S. (ed), *The Corporation of the 1990s*, Oxford University Press, 1991.

Scully, Gerald W., *Constitutional Environments and Economic Growth*, Princeton University Press, 1992.

Shapiro, Carl, and Hal R. Varian, *Information Rules: A Strategic Guide to the Network Economy*, Harvard Business School Press, 1999.

Shleifer, Andrei, "State versus Private Ownership," *Journal of Economic Perspectives*, Autumn 1998.

Shubik, Martin, "Information, Rationality and Free Choice in a Future Democratic Society," *Daedalus*, 1967.

Simon, Herbert A., "Organizations and Markets," *Journal of Economic Perspectives*, Spring 1991.

Smith, Adam, *An Inquiry into the Nature and Causes of the Wealth of Nations*, Methuen and Co., 1776, 1904.

Smith, John Maynard, and Eörs Szathmáry, *The Origins of Life: From the Birth of Life to the Origin of Language*, Oxford University Press, 1999.

Smith, Vernon L., "Economic Principles in the Emergence of Humankind," *Economic Inquiry*, January 1992.

Sombart, Werner, *Der Modern Kapitalismus*, 3 volumes, Dunker & Humblot, 1902, 1922.

Steiman, Lionel B., *Zygmunt Bauman's Modernity and the Holocaust*, Cornell University Press, 1989.

————, *Paths to Genocide: Anti-Semitism in Western History*, Macmillan, 1998.

Stigler, George J., "The Division of Labor Is Limited by the Extent of the Market," *Journal of Political Economy*, June 1951.

———, "The Economics of Information," *Journal of Political Economy*, June 1961.

Subrahmanyam, Avanidhar, and Sheridan Titman, "The Going Public Decision and the Development of Financial Markets," *Journal of Finance*, June 1999.

Szostak, R., "The Organization of Work: The Emergence of the Factory Revisited," *Journal of Economic Behavior and Organization*, May 1989.

Tanzi, Vito, "The Demise of the Nation-State?" *IMF Working Paper*, August 1998.

Taylor, Frederick Winslow, *Principles of Scientific Management*, Norton, 1911, 1967.

Taylor, Robert, "Collective Responsibility," *Financial Times*, September 13, 1999.

Touchard, Patrice, Christine Bermond-Bousquet, Patrick Cabanel, and Maxime Lefebvre (1992), *Le siècle des excès. Le xxe siècle de 1870 à nos jours*, Presses Universitaires de France, 1992.

Touraine, Alain, *The Post-Industrial Society*, Random House, 1971.

Toynbee, Arnold Sr., *Lectures on the Industrial Revolution*, A. M. Kelley, 1884, 1969.

Toynbee, Arnold J., *A Study of History*, Oxford University Press, 1972.

Tracy, James D. (ed.), *The Political Economy of Merchant Empires: State Power and World Trade, 1350–1750*, Cambridge University Press, 1991.

Trivers, Robert L., "The Evolution of Reciprocal Altruism," *Quarterly Review of Biology*, 1971.

Tsutui, William M., *Manufacturing Ideology: Scientific Management in Twentieth-Century Japan*, Princeton University Press, 1998.

Tullock, Gordon, *The Social Dilemma: The Economics of War and Revolution*, University Publications, Center for the Study of Public Choice, 1974.

———, *Autocracy*, Kluwer, 1987.

———, *Economic Hierarchies, Organization and the Structure of Production*, Kluwer, 1992.

U.S. Government Printing Office, *Economic Report of the President*, 1997.

Visser, Jelle, "Survol européen," in Janine Goetschy and Danièle Linhart, *La crise des syndicats en Europe occidentale*, La Documentation française, 1990.

Von Mises, Ludwig, *Planned Chaos*, Foundation for Economic Education, 1947.

Weber, Max, *Wirtschaft und Gesellschaft*, translated in English as *Economy and Society* (1978), Berkeley: University of California Press, 1925.

Weede, Erich, *Economic Development, Social Order, and World Politics*, Lynne Rieder, 1996.

Welch, Finis, "Education in Production," *Journal of Political Economy*, January–February 1970.

Whyte, William H., *The Organization Man*, University of Pennsylvania Press, 1956.

Williamson, Oliver, "Hierarchical Control and Optimum Firm Size," *Journal of Political Economy*, April 1967.

Wilson, Edward O., *On Human Nature*, Harvard University Press, 1978.

———, *Consilience: The Unity of Knowledge*, Knopf, 1999.

Wintrobe, Ronald, *The Political Economy of Dictatorship*. Cambridge University Press, 1998.

Wittman, Donald, "Nations and States: Mergers and Acquisitions, Dissolution and Divorce," *American Economic Review*, May 1991.

———, *The Myth of Democratic Failure: Why Political Institutions Are Efficient*, University of Chicago Press, 1995.

Womack, James P., Daniel T. Jones, and Daniel Roos, *The Machine That Changed the World*, Maxwell Macmillan International, 1990.

WTO, *Annual Report 1998*, Geneva, 1998.

Yates, Joanne, and Robert I. Benjamin, "The Past and Present as a Window on the Future," in Michael S. Scott Morton (ed.), *The Corporation of the 1990s*, Oxford University Press, 1991.

INDEX